Next Generation Internet

Peter Hoffmann

Next Generation Internet

The Merging of Reality and Virtuality in the Metaverse

Springer

Peter Hoffmann
Rorschach, Switzerland

ISBN 978-3-658-46423-3 ISBN 978-3-658-46424-0 (eBook)
https://doi.org/10.1007/978-3-658-46424-0

This book is a translation of the original German edition "Next Generation Internet" by Peter Hoffmann, published by Springer Fachmedien Wiesbaden GmbH in 2024. The translation was done with the help of an artificial intelligence machine translation tool. A subsequent human revision was done primarily in terms of content, so that the book will read stylistically differently from a conventional translation. Springer Nature works continuously to further the development of tools for the production of books and on the related technologies to support the authors.

This Springer imprint is published by the registered company Springer Fachmedien Wiesbaden GmbH, part of Springer Nature.
The registered company address is: Abraham-Lincoln-Str. 46, 65189 Wiesbaden, Germany

Acknowledgments

At this point, I would like to extend a heartfelt thank you to all those who have been inspired by my enthusiasm for immersive worlds and the concept of the metaverse. These are particularly the many students of the FOM University of Applied Sciences for Economics and Management at the Munich study center, with whom I was able to discuss many of the aforementioned sub-aspects, sometimes very controversially, and who were not deterred by these discussions and went on to write term papers in the context of the metaverse. Even greater thanks go to the students who also wrote their theses in the extended context (and in some cases continue to work on the topic):

- Antje Bärmann
- Dustin Bos
- Jasmin Böhm
- Natascha Ilmberger
- Timon Linke
- Tobin Schneider-Pungs
- Elaine Yasargil

And last but not least, my two iTigers Oskar and Paul must, of course, not go unmentioned, who serve as the prototypes and models for real reality and who often brought me back from the sometimes highly immersive writing world into reality. And in doing so, they made me realize that cats, cat pictures, and cat videos will also play a significant role in the Next Generation Internet 😊

Contents

Abbreviations

AR	Augmented Reality
AV	Augmented Virtuality
BIM	Building Information Modeling
CAVE	Cave Automatic Virtual Involvement
DID	Decentralized Identifier Documents
EU	European Union
GAN	Generative Adversarial Network
GPT	Generative Pre-trained Transformer
GUI	Graphical User Interface
HCI	Human-Computer Interaction
HMD	Head-mounted display
KI/ AI	Artificial Intelligence/ Artificial Intelligence
ML	Machine Learning
MR	Mixed Reality
MUI	Metaverse User Interface/ Interaction
NPC	Non-Player Character (Non-player character)
NLP	Natural Language Processing
NUI	Natural User Interface
PVR	Persistent Virtual Reality
RVK	Reality-Virtuality Continuum
VC	Verifiable Credential
VR	Virtual Reality
WEF	World Economic Forum (Weltwirtschaftsforum)
WIMP	Window, Icon, Menu, Pointer (interaction paradigm)
WWW	World Wide Web
XR	Extended Reality

List of Figures

1 Metaverse?

The metaverse—a term that is widely known and used by many people. Nevertheless, discussions often reveal that each user has their own individual idea of what the term means. For this reason, it is essential to precisely define and consider the term metaverse as well as all related terms such as Virtual Reality (VR), Augmented Reality (AR), Mixed Reality (MR), and Extended Reality.

One main reason for the popularity of the term metaverse is probably that marketing departments of large and small companies quickly jumped on this new buzzword without really understanding what it means. These companies are now trying to use the term for their own purposes, which is understandable given the importance of the term, but it complicates the handling of the term and the topic.

There are many attempts to describe the essence of the metaverse. Such descriptions usually sound catchy and interesting, but upon closer inspection, they are at least inaccurate and often also wrong:

> "The metaverse is the moment when our digital life is worth more than our physical life"

says Shaan Puri, tech founder and former Twitch manager [ERL23].

What a sentence and what a statement! However, the question arises whether we as physical humans actually want to leave our physical life behind to move exclusively in the digital world. Although such definitions can be useful for a philosophical engagement with the metaverse, they are not necessarily helpful for the realization of the metaverse. At least they are ambiguously expressed. What Puri means is that "in the next 10 to 20 years" users' attention will focus more and more on the digital world than on the real world. This is because users will work or live with the screen even more than today. Often, however, a maximum limit seems to have already been reached, as the use of social media on mobile devices such as smartphones and tablets already makes people frequently forget their environment today.

P. Hoffmann, *Next Generation Internet*, https://doi.org/10.1007/978-3-658-46424-0_1

> "The metaverse is one of the most popular virtual worlds that exist today. It allows users to create their own avatars and explore many different environments. The platform offers hundreds of games that users can play, as well as thousands of different stores where they can buy unique things."

Such and similar definitions, which are quite obviously developed from a marketing perspective, are not helpful for the implementation approach and are also factually inaccurate.

Describing the metaverse as one of the most popular virtual worlds can certainly be criticized, as the metaverse as an independent entity does not yet exist. There are only some independent virtual worlds like Fortnite, World of Warcraft, and others that enjoy extremely high popularity. Moreover, the features of the metaverse, such as the ability to create your own avatars and explore environments, are not unique but have long been known and are now established in numerous virtual 3D platforms.

The statement that the metaverse offers hundreds of games and thousands of stores should also be viewed critically, as this cannot be considered a real peculiarity. These possibilities have long been available, quite simply through the internet alone.

At this point, it must be fairly pointed out that it is not only marketing departments that claim the term "metaverse" for themselves. Both small and large technology companies jump on the term and often hastily claim that they are now and in the future "metaverse companies" and are working to create metaverses to improve or expand people's digital and physical reality. Of course, these companies must also achieve economic success, and this is to be granted to them. However, upon closer inspection, it becomes apparent that these companies were mostly already active in the fields of 3D computing, virtual reality, or adjacent areas and are merely adding a new label to their portfolio. This is allowed, but they must now also face the criticism that they are not advancing the definition of the metaverse in this way.

Undoubtedly, many more equally inadequate definition concepts and perspectives could now be identified that deal with the term in a similarly non-committal manner. However, to enable reliable communication and discussion on the topic, the following sections will first attempt to define the environment of this planned metaverse. The goal is to present a concrete, tangible, and lasting definition in the end.

However, a step back should first be taken here. A step that leads back to today's internet.

The internet is one of the most widespread innovations of recent history on a global level. Conceived in the 1960s by ARPA, an institution of the US Department of Defense, as a decentralized and fail-safe communication network, it began in 1969 in the academic research sector. The then ARPANET functioned as an exchange platform for scientific results and was successively expanded with additional nodes as well as suitable communication protocols and applications. In the 1980s, ARPANET transformed into a global communication network. With the development of the World Wide Web by Tim Berners-Lee in 1989 and the subsequent commercialization, the internet became an omnipresent phenomenon. Over the years, the internet has gone through various development phases and has been continuously expanded with new applications, such as "user-generated content" or social networks. The timing of the next revolutionary development remains to be seen. [BRA10] Perhaps it is just around the corner with "the metaverse." Compared to the current internet, which has gradually built its economic, social, and cultural relevance over a period of three decades, the metaverse is also undergoing a continuous and progressive development. It could indeed be the Trojan horse that enables well-known technologies to break through into a new form of virtual world [SCHm21a].

But is this new virtual world, which will be significantly more interconnected and tangible than today's, really desirable? A comparison with the transformation of our geopolitical world might be helpful here. A comparison between the current younger generations of European citizens reveals that they do not know a life without the European Union (EU) and a united Europe. Although the EU is certainly not perfect, it has nevertheless created a significant economic and social space consisting of interconnected yet very different individual worlds. In the EU, it is possible and almost commonplace to travel or fly from Hamburg to Lisbon and shop in Rome, Dublin, or Athens without having to pay customs duties or pass border controls. The common currency is valid both at the northernmost point of Finland and in a mountain tavern in Crete. The Schengen Agreement has created an economic ecosystem that is greater than the sum of its parts.

The old, fragmented Europe with border posts, countless currencies, and complex customs regulations is hardly imaginable for the younger generations. The same applies to today's internet. Services like Amazon, Google, Zoom, X (formerly: Twitter), Netflix, Minecraft, and many others are simply used, but these applications, like the member countries of the EU, each stand alone and are separate from each other. For each of these places, we need a new digital identity and mostly use the two-dimensional space of our screens.

The concept of the metaverse aims to connect the various isolated elements and develop an internet capable of seamlessly linking the real and virtual spaces. The metaverse is intended to take place in real-time and parallel to the physical world. Additionally, it is supposed to have an independent economic system that allows for an unprecedented level of personal development. Furthermore, it is to evolve into a platform where digital data and goods can be exchanged without restrictions and independently of borders.

Now the question arises as to what this should mean in practice. Cathy Hackl, who will be mentioned more frequently below, has formulated a thought experiment using the example of a young woman as a user of the near-future metaverse. In her vision, Hackl sees the young woman being awakened in the morning by her virtual, voice-based assistant. She then begins her morning routine. Afterwards, she goes to her closet and looks at her volumetric representation in the form of an avatar or a hologram. She tries on clothes virtually by using the volumetric representation that takes all her measurements into account and then chooses what she wants to wear that day. The actual clothing she puts on her physical self has a digital component that transfers to her digital image. Depending on the virtual environment she is in, she can adjust the appearance of her outfit. Perhaps even digital, haptic nanoparticles are embedded in her lipstick, so she can greet her partner, who is traveling in another country, and feel his embrace. [HAC22]

There are many such—and similar—visions of life in and with the metaverse. The interesting question, therefore, is how the respective visionaries actually come to these ideas. Perhaps they are unreflectively parroting statements from other loud consultants and agencies like Axel Springer's hy: [SCHm21a]

> "Five characteristics are particularly important. The metaverse is primarily defined by the following [...]
> characteristics:
> 1. reality and virtuality are seamlessly connected,
> 2. the metaverse runs continuously and synchronously with the real world in real-time,
> 3. it spans its own economic system over the analog and digital world,
> 4. individual realization is enabled like never before, and
> 5. digital data and goods are smoothly transferable across all borders."

However, such vague statements unfortunately leave unanswered what this means technically and socially.

At least there seems to be a grounded counter-euphoria that looks at the future metaverse a bit more soberly: "A visit to one of the many NFT galleries may sound interesting at first, but once there, it quickly becomes clear that two-dimensional artworks do not benefit from the 3D world. On a website, JPG and AVI can ultimately be displayed much more sensibly. Even a virtual bar opened by the US brewery Miller Lite during the Super Bowl in Decentraland works at best as a curiosity. After five minutes at the latest, the walkable commercial has been explored, and even virtual free beer is not a really convincing reason to spend even a minute longer in the surprisingly dingy dive." [RIX22]

However, such harsh criticism of the handling of the term "metaverse" does not mean that this context should only be viewed negatively. Technology is constantly evolving. Therefore, this introductory section should be concluded with a statement from Yu Yuan, the current director of the IEEE, as a positive transition to the following considerations: [BAL22]

> "In a narrow sense, the metaverse can simply be defined as Persistent Virtual Reality (PVR). In a broader sense, the metaverse is the advanced stage and long-term vision of digital transformation."

Because that is precisely why it is so important to engage with the term, the theory, and the possible practical implementation of the metaverse.

References

[BAL22] Ball, Matthew; Furness, Thomas; Inbar, Ori; Kalinowski, Caitlin; Lange, Danny; Lebaredian, Rev; Mann, Steve; Miralles, Evelyn; Rosedale, Philip; Trevett, Neil; Yuan, Yu (14.06.2022): Metaverse decoded by top experts. In: Versemaker: Metaverse

Lands-cape & Outlook Series. Online: https://versemaker.org/download (accessed on: 10.05.2023).

[BRA10] Braun, Torsten (2010). Geschichte und Entwicklung des Internets. Informatik-Spektrum: Vol. 33, No. 2. Berlin Heidelberg: Springer-Verlag. (S. 201–207). https://doi.org/10.1007/s00287-010-0423-9.

[ERL23] Erl, Josef; Bastian, Matthias (03.09.2022): Hier sind 10 Metaverse-Definitionen, sucht euch eine aus. In: mixed.de. Online: https://mixed.de/metaverse-definitionen/ (accessed on: 10.05.2023).

[HAC22] Hackl, Cathy (29.03.2022): What is the metaverse - and what does it mean for business? Podcast: „At the Edge", McKinsey's Technology Council, hosted by: Mina Alaghband. Online: https://www.mckinsey.com/capabilities/mckinseydigital/our-insights/what-is-the-metaverse-and-what-does-it-mean-for-business.

[RIX22] Rixecker, Kim (23.02.2022): Metaverse-Selbstversuch: Wir waren da – und schwer gelangweilt. In: t3n. Online: https://t3n.de/news/metaverse-selbstversuch-decentraland-1451407/ (accessed on: 17.05.2023).

[SCHm21a] Schmidt, Cord (2021): Wie das Internet zum Metaverse wird. In: hy – the Axel Springer Consulting Group. Online: https://hy.co/2021/12/01/into-the-metaverse-oder-die-naechste-aera-des-internets/#1 (accessed on: 10.05.2023).

2 Where from ... Where to ... or: What at All

Not infrequently, the term post-Internet era is found as a synonym for the metaverse. However, this term "post-Internet" does not refer to a time after the Internet, but to our current era in which the Internet has become so ubiquitous and everyday that people hardly notice it anymore. The metaverse represents an innovation that allows the creation of online spaces where users can interact with each other multidimensionally. Instead of passively consuming digital content exclusively, users are supposed to transform into visitors of the metaverse, where they can immerse themselves in a world where the digital and the physical merge into a completely new experience [SMA20].

Although the concept of the metaverse is still relatively new, it first and foremost represents merely an evolution of augmented reality, virtual reality, and other technologies. In contrast to these technological approaches, however, the metaverse offers a new space for play, movement, or interaction for humanity, advancing to a higher level of the virtual [JIA22].

The enthusiasm surrounding the metaverse is not due to the person who first coined the term. In fact, the term "metaverse" originally comes from the science fiction novel "Snow Crash," written by Neal Stephenson in 1992. [STE92] But even though this book introduced the term, it did not trigger the hype we experience today in connection with the metaverse. Rather, it is statements like those of Mark Zuckerberg, who describes the metaverse as the future "embodied internet" and predicts in this context that in the future, the difference between the real and the virtual world in the metaverse will no longer be recognizable. This would mean a merging of reality and virtuality. However, with statements like the one quoted above, it should first be examined how users perceive real and virtual worlds at all. Because without such an understanding, the intended merging of these worlds can certainly not be successfully realized [BIT22].

> "Consensus in all discussions is that the metaverse represents a form of virtual world or virtual experience."

P. Hoffmann, *Next Generation Internet*, https://doi.org/10.1007/978-3-658-46424-0_2

However, it is important to note that the character and self-conception of virtual worlds are currently changing. These virtual worlds have existed for quite some time. Computer games are a good example of this. However, it would be a fallacy to assume that the metaverse is simply the next computer game. Especially when looking at the younger generation, virtual worlds like Minecraft, Fortnite, or Roblox have long gained new significance. They serve not only as entertainment media but also as social meeting points. It is not uncommon for people to arrange to meet in Minecraft to work together on a project like building a train station for Oberursel, as shown by the example of the platform "Oberurselcraft" [OBE20, KOM17, BOGoJ].

An approach that could be quite helpful at this point and is consciously used here is the reality-virtuality continuum (RVC) developed and presented by Paul Milgram and Akira Kishino in 1994, which is shown in Fig. 2.1. [MIL95] With this, Milgram, who should not be confused with the well-known psychologist Stanley Milgram, describes human perception or the spectrum of this perception from the perspective of the human-machine interface. He distinguishes between the extremes of 100% reality and 100% virtuality, which are separated by a broad spectrum of transition between these two aspects. This describes how humans perceive their respective environment and what this means in terms of the respective technology and technique.

So before further focusing on the metaverse itself, it should first be considered how humans and ultimately also technology perceive their respective environment. This is not yet about the often-mentioned immersiveness of virtual worlds; this will be linked later with the basics initially presented here.

2.1 Reality

The continuum spanned by Milgram and Kishino exhibits an extreme at each of its endpoints. One of these extremes is reality. This does not refer to a philosophical discussion of the concept of reality, but rather, in this context and in the entire construct of

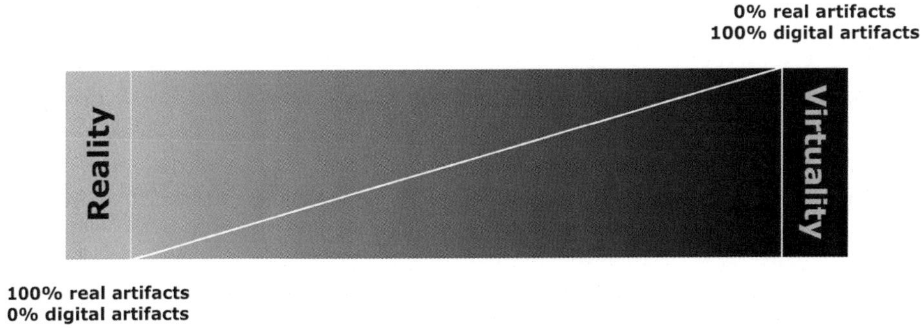

Fig. 2.1 The reality-virtuality continuum according to Milgram and Kishino. (Based on [MIL95])

the reality-virtuality continuum, it concerns the current perception of humans and their environment.

Reality in the sense of the continuum according to Milgram and Kishino means here that humans receive only real artifacts on all their available sensory channels. (see Fig. 2.2) At this point, a consideration could certainly be added regarding which sensory channels are available to humans for perceiving their environment and how these could be mapped to the technical application world. However, this will be addressed in Sect. 3.1 “Sensory Fusion”.

2.2 Virtuality

At the other end of the established continuum, according to Milgram, is the exact opposite extreme, namely one hundred percent virtuality. Here again, it means that humans perceive only virtual or digital artifacts on all their available sensory channels. That is, on this side of the continuum, humans see only digitally generated and rendered objects and hear only digitally generated audio information. However, this is only a small part of this extreme viewpoint; rather, the thought must be extended here that humans on this side of the continuum also feel, smell, and taste only digitally generated impressions. Such an extreme view must conclude that humans are completely and entirely detached from the real environment with their perception.

While the extreme of reality is technically very easy to achieve, for example, by simply turning off and removing all digital devices from the perception area, the technical effort for the extreme of virtuality is exceptionally high, as can be seen in Fig. 2.3. Although image and sound can be artificially generated in high quality and in so-called real-time, this does not apply to all other sensory channels. It is certainly conceivable to present an artificially generated smell to a user by using, for example, essential oils introduced in front of their nose. [SCH23a, LIU23] And it is certainly theoretically conceivable to address the human gustatory sense technically by targeting the taste receptors on

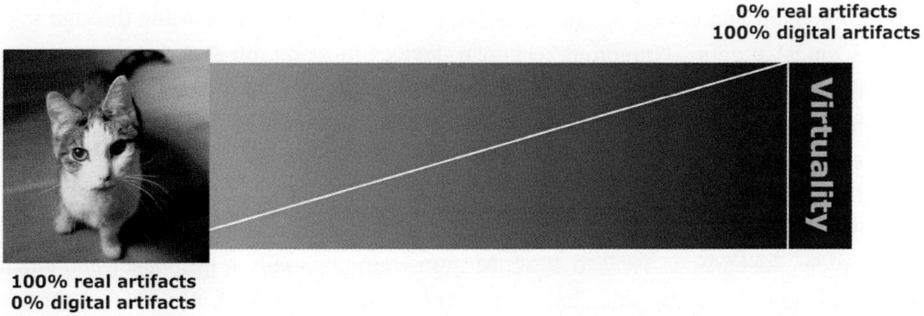

Fig. 2.2 The extreme of pure reality in the RVK. (Based on [MIL95])

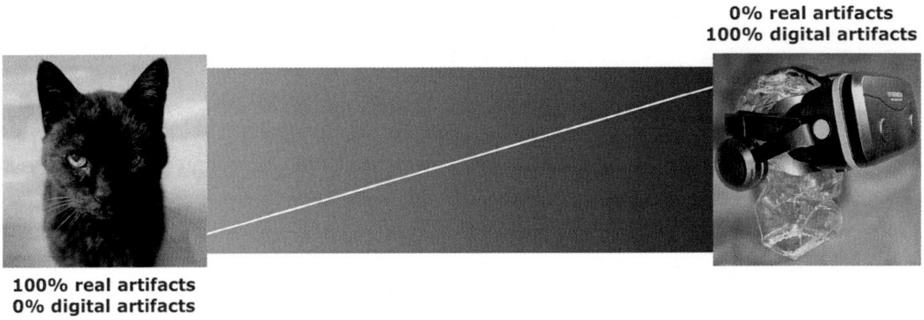

Fig. 2.3 The extreme of pure virtuality in the RVK. (Based on [MIL95])

the tongue and in the mouth area. However, whether a technical implementation would be accepted by the user is quite doubtful. In fact, there are currently very few projects that even address this problem. Of course, a potentially possible sensory activation via brain interfaces in the future is excluded here. But even here, the question would arise whether such forms of interaction devices would be accepted by the user. Likewise, the ethical questions arising in the development of brain interfaces are certainly not yet fully discussed.

In contrast, the haptic sensory channels are much easier to address. Data gloves and even entire data suits that convey mechanical or tactile impressions have been around for quite some time. Especially currently, the development of such technical devices is experiencing a significant boost. New materials open up the possibility of significantly miniaturizing the previously very bulky equipment, thus greatly improving the wearing comfort of these devices. This should ultimately also increase user acceptance. Heating and cooling elements can also be easily integrated into such suits, so that the human perception of temperature can also be artificially or technically addressed.

However, there is one sensory channel that, at least currently, cannot yet be artificially represented. This refers to the perception of gravity, which probably cannot be altered by technical devices in the foreseeable future. The potential technical possibility through the use of the brain interfaces mentioned above is explicitly excluded here.

The targeted addressing of human sensory modalities is only possible through intensive technical support. Numerous technical devices must be integrated into a system to achieve one hundred percent virtuality. Known under the umbrella term "Virtual Reality," the high degree of technologization suggests that the idea of this technology and the realized technology are novel. However, this is a misconception, as the first ideas can be traced back to the beginning of the 20th century.

Not only the ideas but also the implementations of virtual reality systems are significantly older. As early as 1957 to 1962, Morton Heilig, actually a filmmaker and cinema technician, developed the so-called "Sensorama," the precursor of all virtual reality systems known today. [HEI62, WIKoJ] However, this system was, on the one hand, far too bulky and, on the other hand, of too low a display quality to become a real success in the mass market. (see Fig. 2.4).

Since then, there have been several attempts to make virtual reality suitable for the mass market. Especially in the 1980s and 1990s, renowned companies like Sony presented a whole range of devices that were supposed to conquer the home computer or personal computer market. However, none of these attempts were truly successful. In the professional sector, on the other hand, a variety of virtual reality solutions were developed for specific applications, which were able to prove their suitability and stability. Numerically, however, their spread was quite manageable.

Whether the current new attempt with devices like the Oculus Rift, Quest, or others will be a success in the mass market this time cannot really be answered at present. However, the market still seems to be a difficult one today, as a look at the shelves of major electronics and media stores shows. Here, there is usually not a single VR headset available for sale, which suggests rather low demand.

In technical terms, a distinction must be made here once again. (see Fig. 2.5) On the one hand, there is the approach to achieve one hundred percent virtuality through the use of devices such as the already mentioned Oculus Rift and similar ones under the designation "VR headsets," which exclusively address the head senses. In combination with a suit for the physical senses, this could indeed be a way to achieve virtuality according

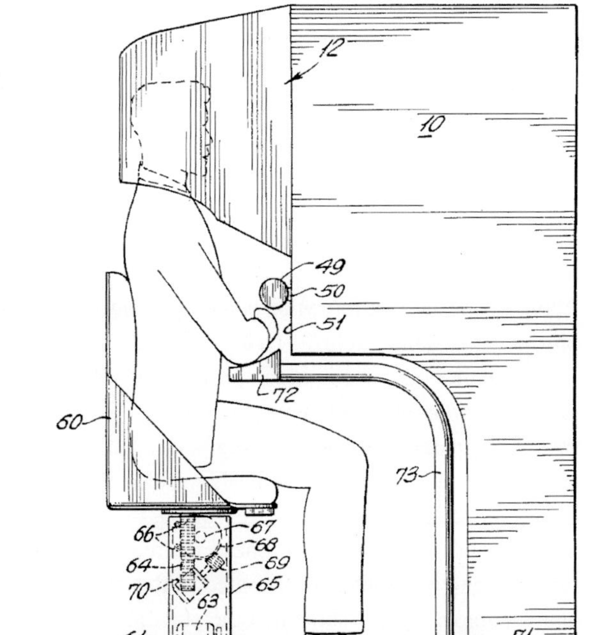

Fig. 2.4 Patent drawing of the Sensorama by Morton Heilig. (Morton Heilig: The Sensorama, from U.S. Patent #3050870)

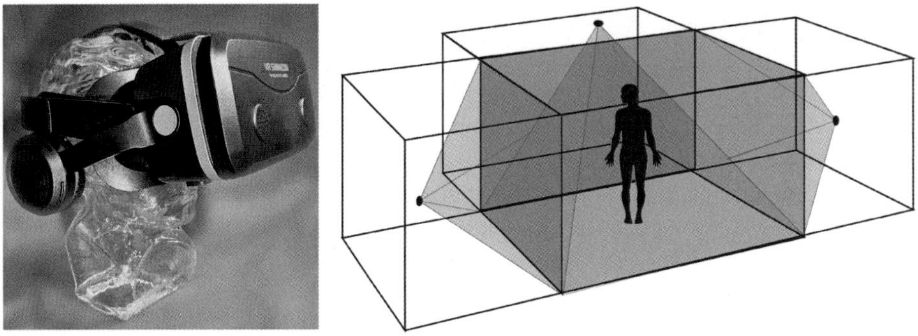

Fig. 2.5 Difference in the representation of VR: Headset vs. CAVE. (Own representation: Peter Hoffmann, Invisible Cow)

to Milgram. On the other hand, there is the approach of the so-called CAVE [CRU92, CRU93], which was first introduced in 1992.

The name CAVE, an acronym for "Cave Automatic Virtual Environment," is the program. Similar to a real cave, the user is in a completely enclosed space, on the six inner sides of which artificially generated visual information is projected. The user can move freely in this space without having to carry bulky and movement-disrupting technical devices like with a headset. This is certainly comfortable for the user; however, it seems rather unlikely that CAVE technology will establish itself in the consumer and mass market, as it would have to be integrated into the living environment of people in some form, which is significantly more complex and difficult than using a VR headset.

However, the example of the CAVE makes it clear once again that one hundred percent virtuality automatically means the almost complete decoupling of humans from their real environment.

2.3 Augmented Reality

Between the two extremes of perception, on the one hand exclusively real artifacts and on the other hand exclusively digital artifacts, Milgram and Kishino left enough room in their continuum for a wide spectrum of different, fluid gradations. Starting from the extreme of one hundred percent reality, perception is increasingly overlaid and enriched by digital artifacts, as shown in Fig. 2.6.

Milgram and Kishino divide this middle part of the continuum into two areas. The better-known of these is the area of augmented reality, in which real impressions and artifacts outweigh the digital ones in perception. It remains unconsidered what semantic meaning can or should be attributed to the digital artifacts. In their description, Milgram and Kishino simply assume that the perception of reality is enriched by artificially generated digital or virtual information and artifacts.

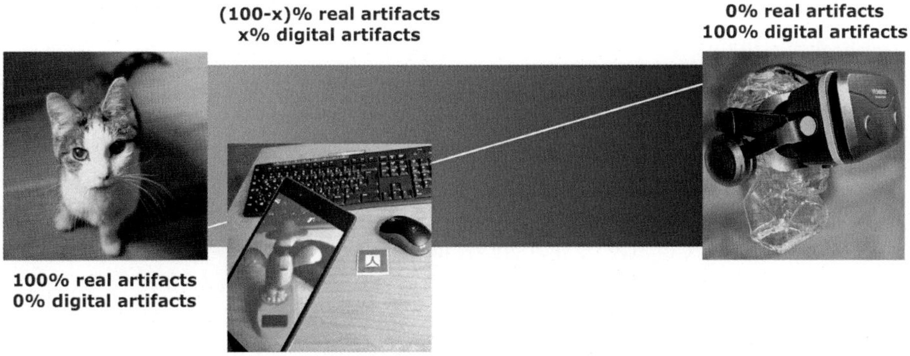

Fig. 2.6 Augmented reality (AR) in the RVK. (Own representation: Peter Hoffmann, Invisible Cow)

The idea of the reality-virtuality continuum presented here is therefore closely linked to the concept of augmented reality as it is understood today in the field of computer science. Although the history goes back further, the description of the technical foundations was first published by Ronald T. Azuma in 1993. [AZU93] According to his conception, augmented reality means that digital objects are precisely inserted into the human user's field of vision. Precise in this context means that an inserted object blends seamlessly and without a noticeable transition into the perception of the otherwise real environment. Azuma particularly refers to three-dimensional modeled digital objects [AZU95, AZU97].

From this conception, the term of accuracy must be specified:

- Geometric accuracy refers to the digital object itself, as it must correspond to reality in shape and size.
- Geographic accuracy, which derives from geometric accuracy, refers to the position of the object to be inserted. It must not only fit in shape and size but also be inserted exactly at the location expected by the user or that results from logic.
- Geographic accuracy directly leads to a third point, as the position, perspective, and (viewing) angle of the user must also be considered. This is particularly important because Azuma assumes that the user looks into reality through glasses and the digital augmentation occurs in the glasses. These glasses move with the user and their head, meaning that body movement and posture influence the orientation of the displays in the glasses.
- Temporal accuracy, or more simply, the synchronization of the rendering of the digital artifact with the user's movement and perception. This is influenced by two aspects: on the one hand, the position and posture of the user must be captured at high speed, and on the other hand, the rendering of the object to be augmented must be calculated just as quickly.

Even the smallest deviations in one aspect of the above-mentioned accuracies can easily lead to user irritation and thus to a loss of acceptance. This can be well compared to the perception of films or videos, in which, for example, the montage of an actor into a scene does not succeed optimally or in which a temporal asynchrony between the video and audio track of a film leads to a loss of lip synchronization.

An interesting thought regarding the "augmented" reality is the negation of understanding. Typically, it is assumed that in AR, perception is expanded by digital artifacts. However, this can also be thought of in the exact opposite way. If a digital artifact is introduced at a fixed coordinate in perception, it simultaneously means that part of reality is overlaid and thus no longer perceived. This thought leads to the concept of diminished reality. What may initially sound like a joke takes on a serious background, especially in terms of safety-specific questions, because what could be the consequences, for example, if a step on the user's path is covered by a digital artifact. [MAN01, HER10].

The idea of augmented reality presented by Azuma in 1994 requires the use of powerful technical systems. In Fig. 2.7, this is illustrated by a simplified system architecture. This is probably one of the reasons why augmented reality initially could not really gain traction. Nevertheless, the concept of enriching real perception with digital artifacts seems to be so significant that many approaches have been investigated to overcome the technical obstacles in other ways.

The main performance requirements could be reduced in a fairly simple way.

- First, the 3D objects were reduced to 2D artifacts, which resulted in a significant reduction in the geometric complexity of the objects.

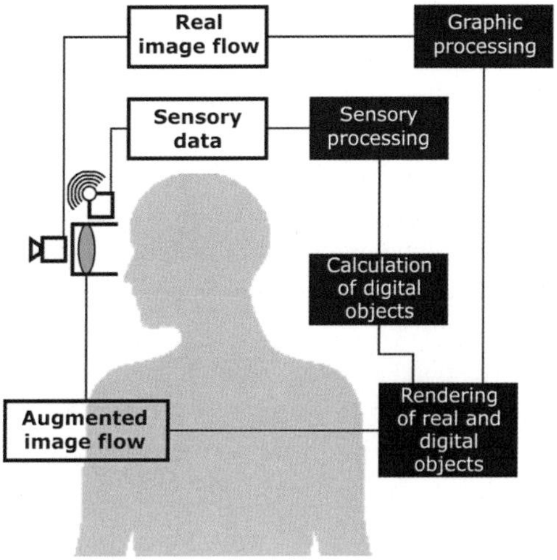

Fig. 2.7 Simplified system architecture for AR. (Own illustration: Peter Hoffmann, Invisible Cow)

- In a further step, geometric objects were often reduced to simple text fragments, which meant a further reduction in complexity.
- Finally, geographic precision was reduced, and the demand for pixel-accurate augmentation was replaced by merely location-based augmentation.

In other words, the idea of augmented reality was further developed and transferred into the now established location-based services, also known as Location Based Services. This aspect is revisited in Sect. 3.2 "Spatial Merging".

Even though current computers are naturally much more powerful due to the immense increase in performance compared to the 1990s, today's systems, especially mobile systems such as smartphones and similar devices, often still easily reach their technical limits when implementing augmented reality according to Azuma. Nevertheless, there are now numerous examples of successful 3D-based augmented reality applications. These are mainly found in professional environments, such as industrial maintenance or assembly. However, it is foreseeable that with the further increase in the performance of computer systems, more and more application examples for the private sector will be realized.

2.4 Augmented Virtuality

Milgram and Kishino developed the concept of the reality-virtuality continuum to describe the spectrum of mixed realities that range from the real world to the fully virtual world. Within this spectrum, the area of augmented virtuality (AV) is another subarea of augmentation (see Fig. 2.8), which, however, is rather rarely mentioned. In their continuum, augmented reality is closer to the real world, while augmented virtuality is more oriented towards the virtual world. In contrast to AR, perception in AV consists

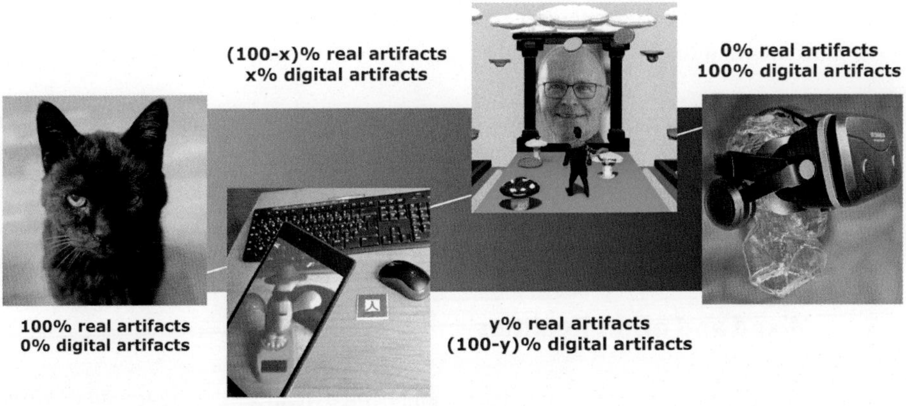

Fig. 2.8 Augmented virtuality (AV) in the RVK. (Own illustration: Peter Hoffmann, Invisible Cow)

of a computer-generated virtual world that is augmented by real objects and data. Here, digital artifacts numerically outweigh the real artifacts perceived by humans. Milgram and Kishino thus speak of augmented virtuality when reality recedes behind virtuality. However, the transition between AR and AV is fluid, as it is ultimately impossible to precisely measure when which form of artifacts appears in which quantity in perception, and moreover, the concept of predominance is highly subjective.

The significance of augmented virtuality lies in the fact that it represents an intermediate step between augmented reality and virtual reality. While virtual reality aims for complete immersion in an artificial, computer-generated environment, augmented virtuality allows the integration of real-world artifacts into this virtual environment, thereby further blurring the boundaries between reality and virtuality, but maintaining the impression of reality.

The distinction between AV and AR is therefore useful to better understand the spectrum of possible augmentations of perception and to classify the respective applications and technologies.

The idea of augmented virtual reality is currently still a rather rare concept. Nevertheless, application cases for this area of the reality-virtuality continuum can certainly be found.

- One example is undoubtedly the entertainment and gaming sector, where, for instance, a player can immerse themselves in a 3D-rendered game environment and communicate with real co-players through another sensory channel, such as the auditory channel. Likewise, real co-players can be integrated into the rendered game world via camera image.
- But even outside of game worlds, this form of telepresence of real people in virtual worlds can be applied. Ideas for implementation have been described for the field of medical applications as well as for engineering applications [GERoJ, ROS22, SHE19].
- A promising application scenario also seems to be the field of human-robot interaction [LI19, LEE21]. Here, the potential application field ranges from remote control of machines and robots to the capture and display of sensor data and images.

With the further development of the metaverse concept, the number of examples and implementations of augmented virtuality will certainly increase significantly, as AV ultimately enables enhanced interaction between real and virtual elements, thereby also enhancing the desired immersive experiences.

2.5 Mixed and other Realities

Milgram and Kishino combine the terms augmented reality and augmented virtuality under the common concept of mixed reality. However, this is where the terminological difficulties begin. Both the transition between augmented reality and augmented virtuality and the entire area of mixed reality are extremely fluid. These terminological problems are further exacerbated by the fact that many companies now use the term mixed reality as a product name or marketing buzzword.

The definition of the term mixed reality becomes even more problematic as colloquially mixed reality is often extended towards the extreme of one hundred percent virtuality and includes it. This makes a sharp definition of the term mixed reality significantly more difficult.

A comprehensible and practical approach is presented by Bellalouna et al. [BEL22] This approach is based on the work of Milgram and Kishino and defines mixed reality as the area between the two extremes of one hundred percent reality and virtuality [MIL95], but distinguishes it from the so-called extended reality (XR). The scope of mixed reality according to Milgram and Kishino thus remains unchanged. However, as soon as virtual reality is added to mixed reality, Bellalouna et al. then speak of extended reality. For understanding the concept of the metaverse, this approach seems quite sensible, as will be shown later when the merging of the real and virtual world comes into focus.

The term Mixed Reality alone does not significantly contribute to the understanding of the metaverse. Much more interesting, therefore, is the concept of Extended Reality just outlined. According to Bellalouna's understanding, Extended Reality encompasses everything that is augmented in any way by digital artifacts, and thus also includes Virtual Reality. This was previously excluded in a strict interpretation of the term Mixed Reality according to Milgram and Kishino. Thus, a truly continuous range now emerges, beginning with the first digital artifact that is inserted into perception.

Unfortunately, as mentioned above, the term Mixed Reality has now been used by many companies purely as a marketing term, most notably by Microsoft, which has almost entirely claimed the term for itself with the HoloLens. However, upon closer examination, especially considering Milgram's continuum, it becomes apparent that Microsoft's marketing also interprets the term Mixed Reality differently than described by Milgram.

This becomes noticeable when comparing the HoloLens with the definitions found in Microsoft's own publications on the term Mixed Reality. For example, it is stated here that the term Mixed Reality is understood to mean any kind of augmentation up to complete Virtual Reality. However, aside from the conflict with the reality-virtuality continuum, it is not possible to achieve this one hundred percent augmentation in the form of Virtual Reality with the HoloLens itself, as it is a device from the class of so-called see-through devices, where visual perception of the real environment is always possible.

Moreover, in the same publications about the HoloLens, it is also said that it represents a holographic display, which, according to general technical definitions, is also not correct. The HoloLens rather falls into the category of "Binocular See-through Head-Mounted Displays." For a better understanding of the various display devices, the typical categorization for such Head-Mounted Displays (HMD) is presented here, distinguishing between monocular and binocular as well as see-through and non-see-through devices. This categorization is illustrated in Fig. 2.9.

What Microsoft has implicitly created with the term Mixed Reality, namely the extension beyond the augmented areas of AR and AV towards the inclusion of complete Virtual Reality, had, as already described above, been pre-conceived by Bellalouna et al. and then called Extended Reality instead of Mixed Reality. However, this extension approach is not the only definition approach for this XR. In fact, some definitions go a considerable technical step further.

For both Augmented Reality and Augmented Virtuality, if following the classical definitions, 3D artifacts must be integrated into visual perception. These 3D objects are geometrically modeled and anchored at a location with a fixed spatial coordinate. However, a few modeling approaches provide that the 3D artifacts are not only anchored at a fixed coordinate but can also move along the three spatial axes.

This type of modeling is quite complex in itself, but it is relatively simple again because the modeling exclusively describes the digital, artificial, or virtual object and its

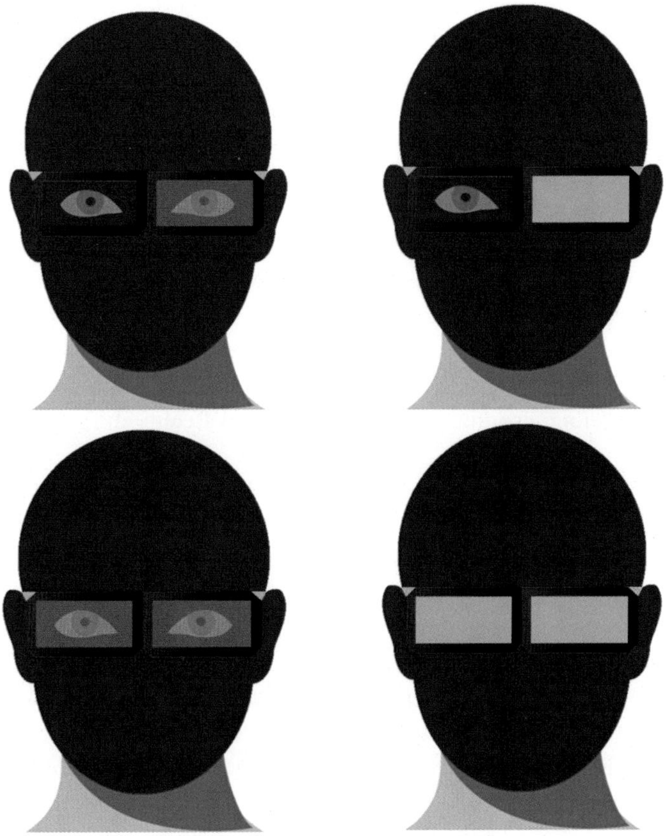

Fig. 2.9 Classification scheme for Head-Mounted Displays. top left: monocular, see-through. top right: monocular, non-see-through. bottom left: binocular, see-through. bottom right: binocular, non-see-through. (Own illustration: Peter Hoffmann, Invisible Cow)

behavior. An interesting approach to extending the concept of Mixed Reality is now the following idea:

> What happens when a digitally generated and modeled coffee cup extends reality and is positioned on a real, physical table?

In the context of Augmented Reality and thus in the context of Mixed Reality within the continuum of Milgram and Kishino, a viewer can now walk around the real table and see the precisely inserted digital cup from all perspectives through, for example, their see-through device.

However, if the viewer bumps into the table during their walk and moves it in the real world, this has no effect on the position of the digital cup. It remains unchanged at its assigned coordinates in the virtual space. In the extreme case, it can now happen that the viewer moves the table so far that the cup leaves the table and, just like Wile E. Coyote in the cartoons chasing the Road Runner, remains hanging freely in space. The difference from the real, physical world becomes very clear here. In the real world, either the cup would be moved along with the table, or if the table were actually jerked away from under it, the cup would fall to the ground and likely shatter. (see also Fig. 2.10).

The reason for this is that there is no sensory-actuator connection between the real and digital artifacts in Mixed Reality. An idea that extends MR to Extended Reality is now to create a connection between the real and digital artifacts so that the digital artifacts behave just like a real object. The digital cup would therefore either be moved with the table or it would fall off the table. This approach will be revisited and further elaborated in the later Sect. 3.2 "Spatial Merging," which also considers the modeling of the physical behavior of digital objects.

2.6 And the Metaverse?

Milgram's reality-virtuality continuum thus represents an extremely effective descriptive tool that explains the possibilities of information systems and their perception by users. This is particularly true when this tool is viewed and applied as a dynamic tool, allowing it to be correspondingly expanded. Bellalouna et al. or, albeit implicitly, also Microsoft extend the originally Mixed Reality designated inner part of the continuum and include the extreme of Virtual Reality to create an Extended Reality.

The consideration now extends from a purely real perception, which includes only physical artifacts, through any combinations of real and virtual components, to the perception of exclusively digital artifacts. However, what Milgram and Kishino did not sufficiently consider or at least did not describe in detail is that this also applies to every manifestation of the media form of digital artifacts. The perception can be enriched by a single media form, for example, merely by static images, as well as by a comprehensive media mix.

Fig. 2.10 Digital artifacts vs. the real world: Mixed Reality. (Own illustration: Peter Hoffmann, Invisible Cow)

In relation to the metaverse, however, the question now arises as to where exactly within this continuum the metaverse itself is actually located. This is not initially about the definition that Matthew Ball or Tony Parisi later attempt to formulate and establish for the metaverse, but rather the approach that Marc Zuckerberg has predicted is currently in focus. He described the metaverse as the internet of the future and, in the present context, more precisely as the "embodied internet." Ultimately, it is initially about integrating the metaverse into the user's spectrum of perception, interaction, and action.

It seems obvious that this approach excludes the extreme of perception that focuses solely on real and physical artifacts, as this cannot be part of the interpretation of the ideas of Zuckerberg and others regarding what the metaverse is supposed to be.

Although many of the presented scenarios exhibit a high degree of three-dimensionality, the extreme of one hundred percent virtuality remains ultimately quite possible, but it will probably have to be considered more as an exceptional case. This is because, in all the ideas and scenarios presented here, the interaction of real objects and people with their digital counterparts is in the foreground. This aspect will be considered in the following sections. It is assumed that the metaverse will offer the possibility that ...

- … real people can communicate, interact, and collaborate with other real people through the metaverse.
- Likewise, real people can communicate and interact with digital representations of other real people.
- Furthermore, real people can interact with digital objects, as well as …
- … digital representations of real people can interact, collaborate, and communicate with other digital representations of other real people.
- Finally, digital representations of real people can also communicate and interact with digital objects.

The transitions within the reality-virtuality continuum are fluid and influence each other. There are overlaps between the different stages, which make it possible to link them together and thereby create new applications and innovations, such as the development of Augmented Virtuality from the idea of Augmented Reality. (see also Fig. 2.11) At the same time, this also opens up the potential to create hybrid environments that combine "the best of both worlds" to develop, for example, innovative and immersive learning or working environments. Additionally, the merging of virtual and real environments can also be used for novel forms of entertainment and art.

However, linking the different levels of the continuum also brings challenges. Data protection and security aspects are of great importance, especially when combining virtual and real environments. The integration of technologies also requires close cooperation between different industries and disciplines, as well as the joint development of standards to ensure smooth integration and interoperability.

Another problem regarding the connection of the different levels is the complexity and unpredictability of the technology. When introducing new technologies to the market, it is always difficult to predict how they will interact with existing technologies. It is

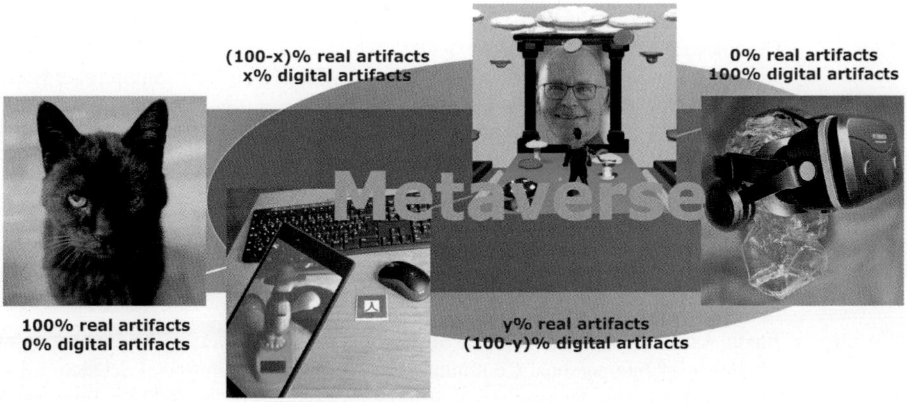

Fig. 2.11 The positioning of the metaverse in the RVK. (Own illustration: Peter Hoffmann, Invisible Cow)

also difficult to foresee the impact of this integration on the user experience and society as a whole.

References

[AZU93] Azuma, Ronald T. (1993). Tracking Requirements for Augmented Reality. In: Communications of the ACM 36, 7 (July 1993), 50–51.

[AZU95] Azuma, Ronald T. (1995). Predictive Tracking for Augmented Reality. Ph.D. dissertation. UNC Chapel Hill Department of Computer Science technical report TR95-007 (February 1995).

[AZU97] Azuma, Ronald (1997). A Survey of Augmented Reality (PDF). Presence: Teleoperators and Virtual Environments. MIT Press. 6 (4): 355–385. https://doi.org/10.1162/pres.1997.6.4.355. S2CID 469744. Retrieved 2 June 2021.

[BEL22] Bellalouna, Fahmi; Langebach, Robin; Stamer, Volker; Zipperling, Franco (2022). Use Cases für industrielle Anwendungen der Augmented Reality Technologie (Use Cases for Industrial Applications of Augmented Reality Technology). In: HMD Praxis der Wirtschaftsinformatik. 59. https://doi.org/10.1365/s40702-021-00824-x.

[BIT22] Bitkom (2022). Wegweiser in das Metaversum – Technologische und rechtliche Grundlagen, geschäftliche Potenziale, gesellschaftliche Bedeutung. In: Bitkom e. V., AG Metaverse Forum, Projektleitung: Dr. Sebastian Klöß. Online: https://www.bitkom.org/Bitkom/Publikationen/Wegweiser-Metaverse (accessed on: 10.05.2023).

[BOGoJ] Bogatzki, Josef Heinrich (o.J.). Oberurselcraft. Online: https://thejocraft.de/obuc/ (accessed on: 17.05.2023).

[CRU92] Cruz-Neira, Carolina; Sandin, Daniel J.; DeFanti, Thomas A.; Kenyon, Robert V.; Hart, John C. (1 June 1992). „The CAVE: Audio Visual Experience Au-tomatic Virtual Environment". Commun. ACM. 35 (6): 64–72. https://doi.org/10.1145/129888.129892 [Titel anhand dieser DOI in Citavi-Projekt übernehmen] . ISSN 0001-0782. S2CID 19283900.

[CRU93] Cruz-Neira, C., Sandin, D. J., & DeFanti, T. A. (1993). Surroundscreen projection-based virtual reality: The design and implementation of the CAVE. Proceedings of the 20th Annual Conference on Computer Graphics and Interaktive Techniques, 135–142.

[DER19] Dernbach, Beatrice; Godulla, Alexander; Sehl, Annika (08.01.2019). Komplexität im Journalismus. Springer Fachmedien Wiesbaden GmbH, ein Teil von Springer Nature. https://doi.org/10.1007/978-3-658-22860-6_8.

[GERoJ] Geriatronics (o. J.). Forschungszentrum Geriatronik der TUM, München. Online: https://geriatronics.mirmi.tum.de/ (accessed on: 17.05.2023).

[HEI62] Heilig, Morton (1962). The Sensorama. US Patent #3,050,870.

[HER10] Herling, Jan; Broll, Wolfgang (2010). Advanced self-contained object removal for realizing real-time Diminished Reality in unconstrained environments. International Symposium on Mixed and Augmented Reality. 207–212. https://doi.org/10.1109/ISMAR.2010.5643572.

[JIA22] Jiaxin, Li; Gongjing, Gao (2022). Socializing in the Metaverse: The Innovation and Challenge of Interpersonal Communication. In: Advances in Social Science, Education and Humanities Research, volume 664. Proceedings of the 2022 8th International Conference on Humanities and Social Science Research (ICHSSR 2022).

[KOM17] Kommune 21 (31.08.2017). Oberursel: Stadtentwicklung mit Minecraft. Online: https://www.kommune21.de/meldung_27130_Stadtentwicklung+mit+Minecraft.html (accessed on: 17.05.2023).

[LEE21] Lee, Lik-Hang; Braud, Tristan; Zhou, Pengyuan; Wang, Lin; Xu, Dianlei; Lin, Zijun; Kumar, Abhishek; Bermejo, Carlos; Hui Pan (2021): All One Needs to Know about Metaverse: A Complete Survey on Technological Singularity, Virtual Ecosystem, and Research Agenda. In: Journal of LaTex Class Files, Vol. 14, No. 8, September 2021 1.

[LI19] Li, Yang; Huang, Lin; Tian, Feng; Wang, Hong-An ; Dai, Guo-Zhong (2019). Gesture interaction in virtual reality. In: Virtual Reality & Intelligent Hardware, Volume 1, Issue 1, 2019, Pages 84–112. ISSN 2096-5796, https://doi.org/10.3724/SP.J.2096-5796.2018.0006.

[LIU23] Liu, Yiming; Yiu, Chun, Zhao, Zhao; Park, Wooyoung; Shi, Rui; Huang, Xingcan; Zeng, Yuyang; Wang, Kuan; Wong, Tsz; Jia, Shengxin; Zhou, Jingkun; Gao, Zhan; Zhao, Ling; Yao, Kuanming; Li, Jian; Sha, Chuanlu; Gao, Yuyu; Zhao, Guangyao; Huang, Ya; Yu, Xinge (2023). Soft, miniaturized, wireless olfactory interface for virtual reality. Nature Communications. 14. https://doi.org/10.1038/s41467-023-37678-4.

[MAN01] Mann, Steve; Fung, James (14.03.2001). VideoOrbits on Eye Tap devices for deliberately Diminished Reality or altering the visual perception of rigid planar patches of a real world scene. In: International Symposium on Mixed Reality ({ISMR} 2001).

[MIL95] Milgram, Paul ; Takemura, Haruo; Utsumi, Akira; Kishino, Akira (1995). Augmented reality: a class of displays on the reality-virtuality continuum. In: Proceedings of SPIE 2351, Telemanipulator and Telepresence Technologies. 21. Dezember 1995, S. 282–292.

[OBE20] Oberursel im Dialog (28.08.2020). Oberurselcraft Wettbewerb. Jetzt mitmachen! Von: Stadt Oberursel (Taunus). Online: https://www.oberurselimdialog.de/post/oberurselcraft-wettbewerb-jetzt-mitmachen (accessed on: 17.05.2023).

[ROS22] Rosenberg, Louis (24.07.2022). Medicine and the metaverse: New tech allows doctors to travel inside of your body. In VentureBeat. Online: https://venturebeat.com/datadecisionmakers/medicine-and-the-metaverse-new-tech-allows-doctors-to-travel-inside-of-your-body/ (accessed on: 17.05.2023).

[SCH23a] .Schlott, Karin (10.05.2023). Wenn die Computerblume duftet. In: Spektrum.de. Online: https://www.spektrum.de/news/virtuelle-realitaet-wenn-die-computerblume-duftet/2137641 (accessed on: 17.05.2023).

[SHE19] Sherman, W. R.; Craig A. B. (2019). Chapter 1 – Introduction to Virtual Reality. In: Sherman WR, Craig AB (Hrsg) Understanding Virtual Reality (Second Edition), Second Edition. Morgan Kaufmann, Boston, pp 4–58.

[SMA20] Smarzoch, Raphael (22.02.2020). „Miss Anthropocene“ von Grimes: Verlorene Zukunft. In: Deutschlandfunk: Raphael Smarzoch im Kollegengespräch mit Fabian Elsäßer. Online: https://www.deutschlandfunk.de/miss-anthropocene-von-grimes-verlorene-zukunft-100.html (accessed on: 10.05.2023).

[STE92] Stephenson, Neal (1992). Snow Crash. Blanvalet, München 1995. ISBN 978-3-442-23686-2, Kap. 37. Englisches Original: Snow Crash. New York, 1992.

[WIKoJ] Wikipedia (o. J.). Sensorama. Online: https://en.wikipedia.org/wiki/Sensorama (accessed on: 10.05.2023).

3 The Merging of Worlds and … of Immersion

During the presentation on the renaming of the Facebook corporation to "Meta", Marc Zuckerberg said the one sentence that sparked the hype around the topic of the metaverse: [BLU21]

> "You can think of the metaverse as an embodied internet where you are not just looking at content, but you are in it and immersed in it."

In order to "immerse" in content or "be in it," the perception aspects from reality to virtuality considered in the previous chapters must be linked with another aspect that is not taken into account in the RVK: immersion!

The term "immersion" originally comes from the Latin word "immersio". Typically, the concept of immersion is mainly discussed in the field of communication sciences and characterizes the feeling of deep immersion in media content. Recently, however, immersion is also gaining increasing importance for and in interactive systems. [DER19] Without explicitly addressing the term immersion, Ludwig Kapeller, a journalist for the magazine UHU in 1926, characterized the "radio of tomorrow" as a comprehensive, multimedia sensory experience. [DER19] In this context, he illustrated his individual impressions and the potential he recognized in the then-emerging television transmission technology.

In a more recent context, immersion is considered a kind of quality criterion for video games. Jan-Noël Thon, a professor of media studies at the Norwegian University of Science and Technology, developed an immersion model that describes four different forms of immersion in video games: [ASC12]

- *Spatial Immersion:* This refers to an effect in computer games where the player's attention gradually shifts from their real environment to the fictional game world presented to them by the game. In this process, the player takes on the role of an

P. Hoffmann, *Next Generation Internet*, https://doi.org/10.1007/978-3-658-46424-0_3

avatar representing them and gains immediate access to the events within the game. [THO06]

- *Ludic Immersion:* This also involves a comprehensive focus of the player's attention on the presented game events. In contrast to spatial immersion, the focus here is on interaction with the virtual environment, control of the avatar, and the challenges posed by the game. A balanced equilibrium of these challenges is the crucial factor for the emergence of ludic immersion. Overwhelming the player can quickly lead to frustration, while underwhelming them can cause boredom. [THO06]
- *Narrative Immersion:* The inclusion of additional sequences of events between the various game phases can lead to an improved design of the fictional game environment. If this successfully generates tension and directs the player's concentration to the course of the plot and the characters appearing in it, it is referred to as narrative immersion. [THO06]
- *Social Immersion:* While narrative immersion primarily focuses on single-player games, multiplayer games further promote the emergence of social immersion. By bringing avatars together in virtual environments, players have the opportunity to interact with other participants. To enable this, online games typically have communication functions such as text chat or voice transmission. [THO06]

However, immersion is not only the goal in the context of games. In general, immersion as a concept for storytelling (multi-) media systems is also gaining importance. The particular challenge in this context is that the plot should be logical in its progression, exciting for the individual audience, and at the same time allow the user the highest possible degree of interaction freedom. These different dimensions often stand in diametric opposition to each other, which complicates the development and production of such systems. [HOF10] This is exemplarily illustrated in Fig. 3.1.

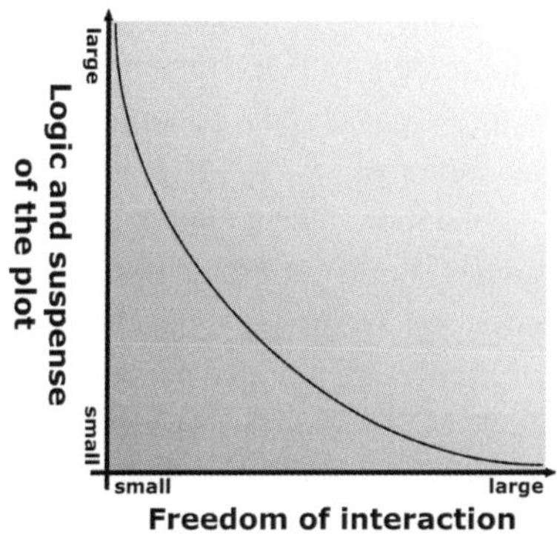

Fig. 3.1 Logic and excitement of the plot vs. freedom of interaction. (Own illustration: Peter Hoffmann, Invisible Cow)

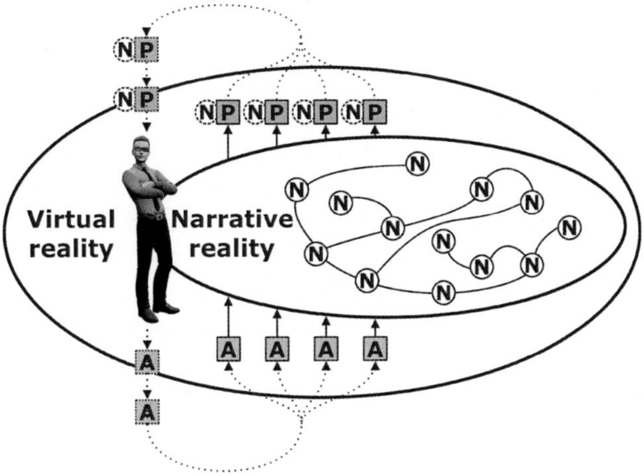

Fig. 3.2 The dimension of narrative reality. (N)—Narratem (atomic action unit); (P) Presentation object; (A) (User) action. (Own representation: Peter Hoffmann, Invisible Cow)

In cases of strong immersion, a narrative reality can embed itself into a virtual reality, as shown in Fig. 3.2. In this case, the user does not only immerse technically and interactively into the virtual world. Rather, supported by the interactive freedom offered to him, he immerses himself into the narrative events in the virtual world. [HOF10]

To develop a manageable definition of the metaverse, the path through the reality-virtuality continuum offers a good starting point. From a marketing perspective, for example, Mark Zuckerberg explains, as already mentioned, that the metaverse represents the embodied internet of the future. However, the central aspect remains the question of how the user should and can perceive this new embodied internet.

The term "embodied internet" indicates that in the metaverse, the physical world of the body and the digital world of the internet are supposed to come together and, in extreme cases, merge into a new application and information world. The continuum presented by Milgram can provide a helpful foundation for this. Between the two extremes of pure reality and pure virtuality, the continuum is dedicated to enriching the worlds with opposing artifacts.

It is precisely this merging in its original form, especially with the extension through the introduction of the term Extended Reality, that contributes to the idea of the metaverse being located in the perceptual world of humans and should be. However, a complete merging of virtuality and reality, as a true embodiment of the internet requires, is far from being achieved with the perceptual focus of the continuum alone.

Rather, a whole range of other perspectives arise in which the real world and the digital world can or even must merge to fully realize this embodied internet. In addition to perception, aspects such as the following must also be included in the overall picture:

- The sensory merging as a basis for perception.
- The spatial merging, as already hinted at with Extended Reality.
- The semantic, i.e., the content merging, which builds on perception, sensory, and spatiality.
- Derived from this, the merging of interactions in the real and digital world into a combined new form of interaction, also in reference to the term Extended Reality.
- A temporal merging with the goal of synchronizing the actions and behaviors of artifacts in the real and digital world.
- As well as the sociocultural merging, when digital twins of real persons communicate, interact, and collaborate with other digital twins of real persons or with the persons themselves.

All these aspects, which are also listed in Fig. 3.3, will first be considered individually and discussed in terms of their impact and issues. Subsequently, they will be brought together to create a fully embodied new medium. In doing so, the technical challenges should not be overlooked.

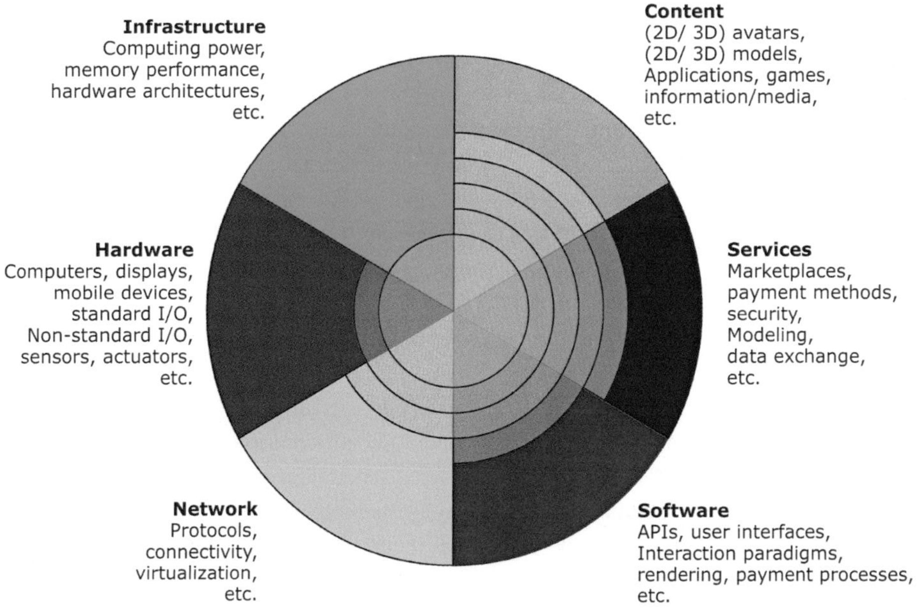

Fig. 3.3 Technical sub-aspects of merging. (Based on [BIT22])

3.1 Sensory Merging

If the merging of the perception of reality and virtuality is to be considered as the basis for the metaverse, as can certainly be derived from Milgram's continuum, then the first essential step must be to analyze which sensory channels humans use or can use to perceive their environment. This concerns both the real, physical environment and the digital, virtual environment.

The basis for the perception of the real physical environment relies on human sensory channels. (see Fig. 3.4) Typically, these classical modalities include the visual, auditory, haptic-tactile, olfactory, and gustatory channels. This traditional perspective is often supplemented by additional sensory modalities. For example, Ayres also introduces the vestibular and proprioceptive channels in this context, i.e., the sense of balance and deep sensitivity. [AYR79, AYR13] Furthermore, Ayres expands the consideration of the tactile modality by attributing surface sensitivity to this channel. Finally, nociception, i.e., pain reception, is also included in this area. However, this latter aspect remains largely unconsidered in the use of the metaverse or generally in the digital world, and hopefully will continue to be so. A rare exception, besides presumably occurring research in the military sector, is the entertainment sector, as evidenced by the so-called Painstation [MOR01] or more recently the "Feelbelt" [DAN21].

What already applies to the general design of interaction must also be applied to a fusion with the goal of the metaverse, namely the transfer of human modalities to their digital and technical counterparts. For example, visual media are required so that the human user can perceive artificial or virtual graphic and visual information, just as auditory media are needed for the perception of artificial sound and noise. Furthermore, it is

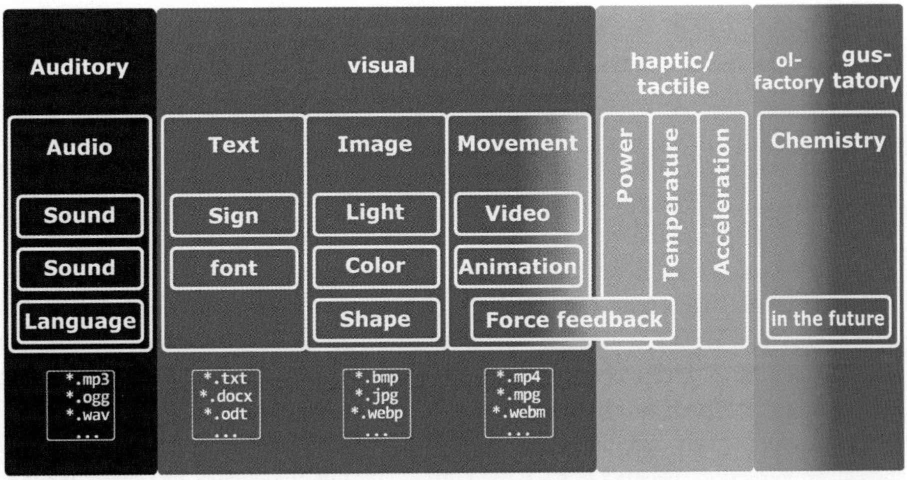

Fig. 3.4 A systematics of perception in HCI. (Own illustration: Peter Hoffmann, Invisible Cow)

also necessary to find such counterparts for all other sensory channels. As just hinted at, this is easily possible for the visual and auditory channels, as there are numerous modeling approaches and established media and data formats for these channels, with which the content in these forms can be described, stored, and transmitted. Established here means that a very large number of technical standards already exist and are usable in this area.

However, the situation proves to be more problematic for the haptic-tactile channel. On the one hand, there are numerous applications, especially in the entertainment sector, that show that haptic and tactile information can indeed be artificially generated and transmitted. Examples of this are the tactile feedback in many games, which can be experienced via joystick or gamepad, or even more clearly the tactile feedback in professional simulation environments, such as the three-axis trainers of the aerospace industry. What these approaches have in common is that there are no widespread established standards, and instead, a proprietary solution approach is pursued for each individual solution. They also all share the fact that they are technically extremely complex.

Technically, the stimulation of the gustatory and olfactory sensory channels is considerably less complex, as the use of aromatic oils, for example, which are nebulized in the area of the nose or mouth, would suffice. There are also research works and individual solutions for these approaches, which, although not particularly demanding technically, have not yet been widely adopted or established in broad application [LIU23, SCH23a].

In the previous consideration, it was tacitly assumed that the technical infrastructure, i.e., the computer systems used, would be supplemented by technical extensions. However, if the term embodiment of the internet is taken literally, this implicit assumption could also be expanded or even reversed, by not supplementing the technical system or the technical infrastructure, but rather the human being, thus extending their immediate biological-human sensory perception.

Although this sounds extreme, this process actually began some time ago, not least through the constant accompaniment of devices such as smartphones or devices from the field of wearable computing. Especially in this context, the human user perceives not only their immediate sensory environment but also the digital environment with the help of the digital senses of their accompanying devices. The term "environment" should initially be considered metaphorically here and will only come into sharper focus in the following Sect. 3.2. Nevertheless, the human user perceives things and information through these technical devices that do not originate from their immediate physical perception.

The consideration of the course of technical development, as well as human creativity and willingness, suggests that it will not stop at the addition of supplementary devices that accompany humans as accessories. Rather, there are tendencies towards the development of the critically discussed concept of the cyborg. Research and developments by serious scientists, such as Steve Mann and Thad Starner, show that it is already technically possible today for humans to have technical devices implanted for perception and later interaction. [MAN13, KRE13] Ultimately, this is actually just another logical step, as the example of technical development reveals. For a long time, people have been implanted with devices such as pacemakers or insulin pumps, and prosthetics also show great progress in the field of supporting the mobility-impaired.

In addition to such serious approaches to the immediate support and assistance of humans, research and development are also being conducted in many places on the so-called direct brain interface. At this point, no philosophical-ethical discussion about these developments will be initiated, even though this would certainly be justified—and interesting. That this does not fall into the realm of fiction is demonstrated by examples from the field of so-called transhumanism, such as the artist Stelarc or, even more clearly, Neil Harbisson. The ultimate merging of sensory perception from the real physical and digital virtual world is shown in his non-removable implant, which offers him a new sensory channel. In this way, color information that Harbisson cannot perceive due to his color blindness is converted into haptic-tactile information. [DON17] At this point, it must be emphasized that an extreme case like Neil Harbisson's will certainly represent only a rare extreme case of sensory merging and enhancement of humans in the near future. It is to be expected that the metaverse will be experienceable and usable for the average human user even without such extreme interventions. Whether this will change in the distant future cannot be said with certainty today.

3.2 Spatial Merging

Engaging with the metaverse reveals characteristics at certain points that can be considered schizophrenic or at least inconsistent. On the one hand, as in previous discussions, it is claimed that the metaverse will be the embodied internet and therefore merge the digital and physical worlds. On the other hand, some sources, upon closer examination, say exactly the opposite. Statements can be found such as: [THEoJ]

> "A new cult is born, the digital world is coming, and we are no longer bound to physical space."

This view initially has no connection with merging, as digitality and physical reality are clearly separated here. However, this has no impact on the discussions that were started in the previous Sect. 3.1 "Sensory Merging" regarding sensory perception. Ultimately, whether merged or not, both areas must be captured and sensorially perceived by the user. Obviously, two definitional approaches contradict each other here.

It becomes particularly interesting and amusing when—even though this represents a small preview of later sections—potential business models are already considered here. On the vast majority of platforms that call themselves metaverse platforms, the user can only become truly active once they acquire a plot of land located in the digital world of the respective platform. So, we leave the physical space to act in the digital space, separated but parallel, with equally spatial metaphors such as dimension of areas and distances between locations. This type of marketing argumentation is further driven in statements like: [STO22]

> "Compared to the physical world, virtual worlds are not bound by the laws of physics. […] Logistics, travel time, waste, or environmental pollution do not exist in the metaverse."

Waste and environmental pollution in terms of sustainability will not be further discussed here. However, the denial of logistics and travel time is ultimately a fallacy. If there are plots with spatial dimensions, these dimensions and distances must also be overcome. Certainly, it could now be argued that the metaverse is supposed to be the internet of the future and thus naturally also brings with it the characteristic of today's internet, where all information is only a click away—with one click, the user moves from the Tokyo Dome in Japan to the Tuileries in Paris and to the Statue of Liberty in New York. [HOF21] However, this characteristic renders the concept of distance associated with the plot absurd, and this mental misdirection goes even further. Because the user's representation in the virtual world of the metaverse is the avatar, which moves on the plot or between the plots. If the avatar moves in the same way as the human in the physical world, then the supposedly saved travel time suddenly becomes significant again.

So, the question arises as to how spatial merging is actually supposed to take place and whether this should or must be a real goal of the development of the metaverse.

A central challenge in merging the spatial properties of real and virtual worlds lies in connecting the movements of objects in both worlds. A typical example often presented as a possible realization of the metaverse is the virtual world "Oasis" from the novel [CLI11] and the film "Ready Player One" [SPI18]. In this world, the main character takes on the role of a player who wants to achieve a goal in the Oasis. To do this, he controls an avatar in the virtual game world. He controls this by wearing a full data suit in the real world, which transfers the movements of the human user to the avatar. This works both in the book and film as well as in real-world application practice, as such data suits do exist and are usable in practice. However, the use cases behind them are quite specific [LEE20b] and the price of these suits will not be further considered here, as it currently significantly exceeds the price for the general consumer market.

Such a suit enables the transfer of the full-body movement of the human user to a three-dimensional avatar in a virtual world. This also applies to the movement of the avatar: The user's step movements can also be transferred to the avatar to move it from one place to another.

The exciting question now is how avatar and human are actually linked or merged in the virtual and real world. Nowadays, humans move on so-called treadmills on a movable surface or in a sphere, without moving from their current position in the real world, while the avatar changes its location in the virtual world. [WEH20] This means that there is no merging connection in the direction from real to virtual. Likewise, there is no such connection in the opposite direction from virtual to real, as any movement of an avatar in the virtual world and the associated change in position or location has no impact in the real world: The user remains standing in the place where they previously stood. Therefore, at this point, it cannot be said that there is a real merging.

Apart from the lack of connection between the virtual avatar and the real human, the idea of a spatial merging of avatar and human user carries a not insignificant potential danger for the user in the real world. The fundamental question is: To what extent do the real and virtual worlds match?

- If both worlds are completely aligned and fit perfectly, the potential danger for the user in the real world would probably be rather low. In the case of a change in the avatar's position, for example, if it wants to cross a street, the process should hopefully be similar to that in the real world: The avatar approaches the street, waits until it is clear, and then crosses it without being hit by a (virtual) vehicle.
- However, if the real and virtual worlds do not match and fit perfectly, and the avatar crosses a large open area, it can only be hoped for the user in the physical world that this large open area also exists in the physical world and that the human user's path does not intersect with the path of a car on a street.

The confrontation and solution of this spatial merging represent a significant challenge for the acceptance of the metaverse. Although there is often talk of the so-called digital twin of the user, of other real objects, or even of digital twins of entire manufacturing plants and entire cities, if there will indeed be a walkable, 3D-modeled world, this will probably be just one of many application scenarios. It is more likely that the 3D-modeled worlds will be designed quite differently in their dimensions, distances, and especially in their structure than the real world. The metaverse will not depict the real world in a 3D model, as the goal is to create new worlds in which innovative solutions and interaction possibilities can be modeled and represented.

Although the previous discussion of the merging of the spatial properties of the physical and virtual worlds tended to be critical, it must be acknowledged that this aspect of merging will be a fundamental aspect of the future metaverse. After all, internet-based services already respond quite naturally to the user's current location today. This must also be ensured in the future metaverse. For example, if the user moves from one place to another, such as in the pedestrian zone of a city center on the way from one store to another, their avatar as their digital twin should be informed about this change in position. Only in this way can location-based services and transactions be initiated or used in the virtual world. Without a spatial merging, however it may ultimately look and be, the metaverse as the embodied internet of the future would be unthinkable.

3.3 Semantic Merging

It is easy to claim that the features of merging the spatial, physical world with the digital, virtual world presented at the end of the previous Sect. 3.2 "Spatial Merging" have already been solved for some time. For a long time, users have been accompanied by mobile devices on their way through the physical world. In the process, the respective own location is now mostly captured, forwarded, evaluated, and transactions are initiated in response, without the user having to explicitly allow this—although from a security perspective, it would often certainly be better for the user to decide for themselves.

In addition, the user is provided with current data and information about their respective location, as shown in Fig. 3.5 as an example. Examples of this are apps on mobile devices for public transportation, which show the user the next stop and list the departure times at that stop.

It is true that this type of content or semantic support has long been known and available as location awareness. The example above of enriching the real world with location-based information such as the next stops of public transportation or those of surrounding retail stores illustrates this. (Fig. 3.5).

However, a closer look at the situation depicted in reality quickly reveals something else: Usually, it is individual applications that respond to the user's current location as position or location information. Moreover, these individual applications act exclusively selectively and extremely limited. The respective reaction of the application is always based on only one single piece of information about the user—their location. Only a few apps include additional information to be able to make more precise statements.

For example, if a user is walking through the city center and has the public transportation application installed, it does not help them if they suddenly crave a local delicacy. But even within its own application context, such as here in the area of public transportation, these applications quickly reach their limits. Most of these applications internally list the last or preferred stops more or less obviously for the user, as seen in the image of

Fig. 3.5 Semantic merging as a location-based service. (Own representation: Peter Hoffmann, Invisible Cow)

the DB and SBB app in Fig. 3.6. However, they generally do not make proactive statements about how the user can get from the Eiffeltower in Paris to Notre Dame or to Sacre Coeur. Such assisting information cannot be extracted from location information alone. Rather, a multitude of additional context information would need to be linked and connected here.

The difficulty of context formation is already evident in everyday use of the internet. Here too, attempts are often made to recognize a context to support or unobtrusively assist the user, for example in e-commerce applications on the web. However, such information often limits itself to aspects that are only conditionally really helpful. In a virtual bookstore, it can still make sense to present the potential customer with information like "Readers who bought this book also bought the following." However, if a suggestion for the purchase of the next set of winter tires is generated from the purchase history of a user who has just bought a set of winter tires for their vehicle, it certainly cannot be considered helpful assistance and good context recognition. How difficult it is to recognize the user's context on the web has already been demonstrated by Ziegler, Lohmann et al. [ZIE05].

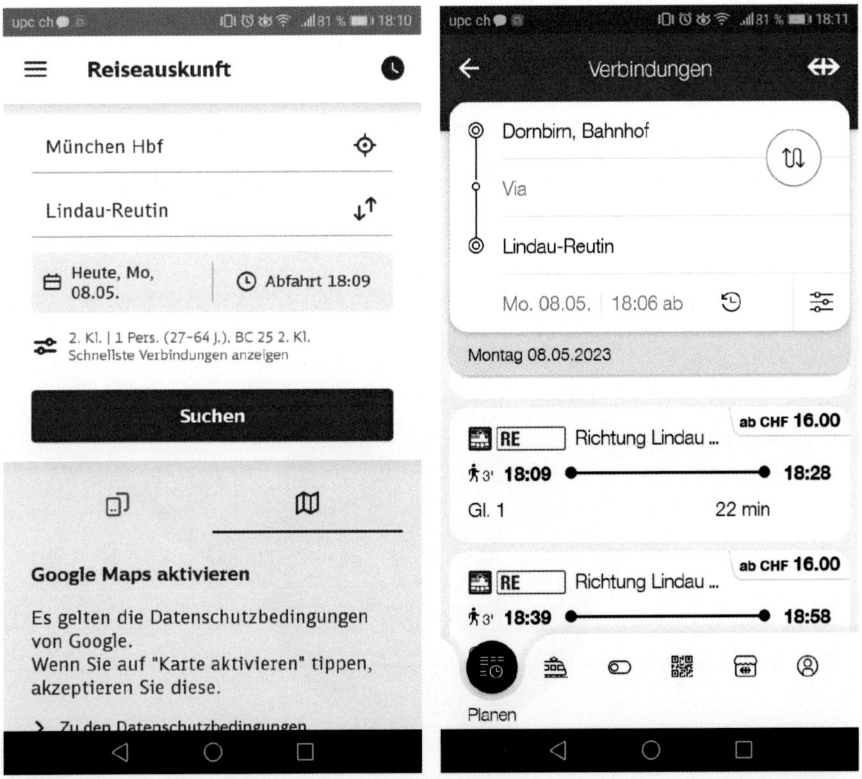

Fig. 3.6 Screenshots of the mobile apps of DB and SBB

Context initially consists of three separate semantic areas. (see Fig. 3.7) The fundamental part is, of course, the technical system. However, this is also the area from which information can most easily be derived for context recognition. The system knows itself, its functions in general, as well as the functionalities available in the current state. Ultimately, all this information can be derived from the system's self-monitoring and kept constantly up to date.

The other two sub-areas, which influence each other, are the human and the physical environment in which the human user moves and is active. To establish an accurate action and assistance context, it must first be recognized in what state the human user currently is. This includes general information such as location, but also often medical and other information. In the broadest sense, this also includes parameters such as hunger or thirst.

To increase complexity, this also includes data about the user's mental state, such as current stress factors or the current stress level the user is experiencing. Many mobile devices, such as a whole range of wearable devices, are capable of recording medical data. Thus, it is quite possible to determine pulse, blood pressure, and partially even blood sugar levels and similar parameters with smartwatches and similar devices. At this point, the accuracy of these measurements is not considered, as it is not about preventive medical goals. However, from a combination of such values, a somewhat accurate

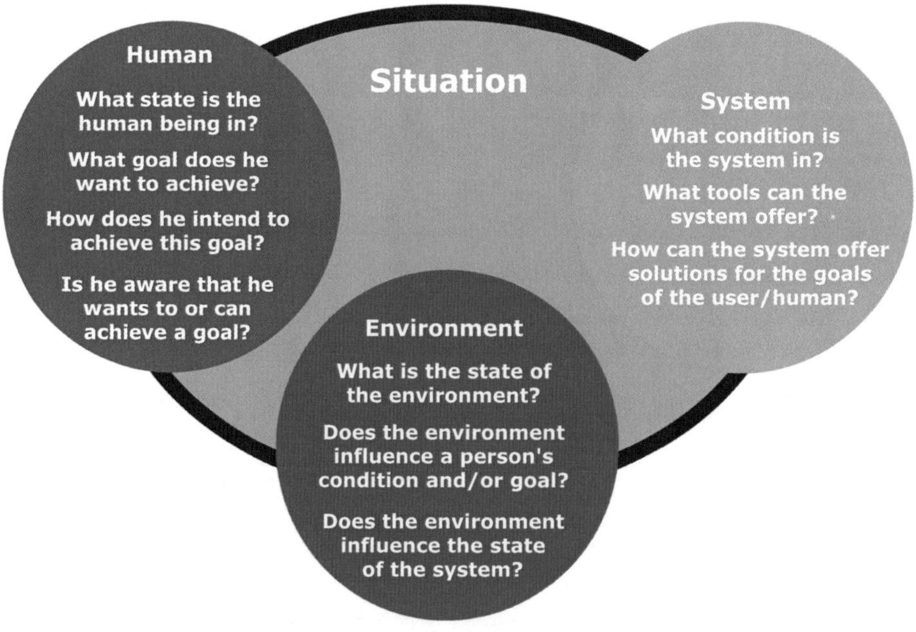

Fig. 3.7 Sub-aspects of context formation. (Own representation: Peter Hoffmann, Invisible Cow)

statement about the user's mental state can be derived, and thus, for example, the aforementioned stress level can be inferred.

The third area is the environment in which the human and the system are located. The state of the environment has a significant influence on how the current context is built. The underlying information here is even more heterogeneous than the information in the human sub-area. The latter generally consists of the two mentioned subcomponents, medical and mental. The state of the environment, however, can depend on a variety of different parameters, starting with simple meteorological parameters such as temperature, air pressure, rain, and sun. Additionally, the current traffic situation and the number of people currently active in the vicinity may also be considered. Noise, smell, general hustle and bustle caused by nearby people in the environment, and many other factors must be considered here to determine an overall impression and state of the environment.

Individually, this information is certainly tangible. While meteorological information can be captured through simple sensory measures, other information, such as the traffic situation or other more advanced statements, may require less easily accessible sources. For example, traffic density could be determined by linking information from many individual devices accessible at the location. The heterogeneity of information sources on the one hand and data protection on the other hand pose a considerable challenge for context acquisition of this kind.

As usual, capturing the state of the sub-areas human, system, and environment in this approach is merely a simplified representation, as each aspect has been considered individually so far. However, reality is, as always, much more complex, as the three subareas are in constant close interaction with each other.

The system may perhaps have the least influences to process from the other two subareas. Humans and the environment, on the other hand, are closely linked; the state of humans is closely dependent on the state of the environment. Extreme heat, heavy traffic, or a high activity level of neighboring people can easily lead to an increase in an individual's stress level. Similarly, the state of the system can lead to such an increase in stress levels—who does not know the often aggressive reactions when a technical system or application once again does not respond as the user expects?

This means that to capture the entire context from the three subareas, a description must be found that shows how these three subareas are interconnected and influence each other.

At this point, it is necessary to consider another aspect as a fourth subarea: the temporal, i.e., the situational aspect. The capture of the state of the individual subareas and their respective evaluation must be continuously carried out in temporal synchronization and actuality. The circumstances and states of the individual subareas can change significantly over time. Neglecting temporal synchronization could easily lead to an incorrect context being assembled. This requirement also poses a significant challenge from a technical perspective for the acquisition and generation of context information.

The central aspect of assistive help for humans has not yet been sufficiently considered despite the elaborate construction of the context through the situational and synchronous interplay of the three subareas. The fundamental question for assistive help is what task the user is currently pursuing or what goal they want to achieve with their activities. It is assumed that the user does not always and constantly actively communicate their goal to the system or even want to communicate it actively. Rather, the system must be able to recognize this goal independently. For this, a further analysis of the already examined subarea "human" is necessary. It is neither effective nor sufficient to try to recognize the human user's goal merely from a history. Instead, various information sources must be combined to identify such a goal precisely and correctly.

Without sophisticated context recognition, the semantic merging of the digital and physical worlds is doomed to fail from the outset. Because the great goal, which is already being pursued with the Internet and which the metaverse aims for even more, is ultimately that the user immerses in this metaverse not just figuratively but actually. This means, in turn, that the user does not want to be distracted by constantly having to make inputs to communicate their current state or momentary goal to the system. At this point, it must be admitted that this is not just a single problem of the metaverse and its implementation but ultimately the fundamental problem for all active and proactive assistance systems.

3.4 Temporal Merging

The aspect of semantic merging examined in the previous Sect. 3.3 probably represents the central point when it comes to how the physical and virtual worlds can be combined and to what extent they should merge. Within the semantic consideration, the synchronization of the three subareas—system, human, and environment—is the core question. This synchronization, in turn, is also part of another merging perspective. If the physical and digital worlds are to merge, this process must also occur in temporal synchronization. Therefore, it is imperative to consider how the temporal behaviors of the real and digital worlds can be put into synchronous relation. In this context, at least three different approaches exist:

- The first perspective concerns the synchronization of the temporal behavior of physical and virtual objects, also considering whether an asynchronous temporal relationship might be possible in certain situations or contexts.
- The continuation of this perspective is the second consideration of the temporal behavior of merged physical and virtual worlds, namely the continuous temporal flow of both realities. In the real world, the state continuously changes through interactive and proactive behavior as well as through the inherent behavior of all objects, even if the individual human as part of this world is not currently present. For example, a bus travels from stop A to stop B, regardless of whether a human passenger is on board or not. This second perspective also raises the question of whether there can or even

must be an interruption of the respective continuous temporal flow in certain contexts or situations.
- The third perspective in examining temporal behavior does not touch the time flow itself but raises the question of whether temporal processes could be shifted against each other. This approach aims to re-examine or re-experience certain events in the virtual world in the sense of a replay, as known in the video or film world. This goes so far that past events could be represented again through a decoupling of the temporal processes between the real and virtual worlds. Such possibilities would be of particular interest, for example, for teaching and learning purposes or for simulations.

The internet is to be understood as a document-centric network. Ultimately, it can be considered a large, interconnected document or medium. Although this document is continuously worked on in countless places, resulting in constant changes to its content and state, these changes are relatively negligible compared to the scope and size of the overall content. [HOF21] Changes occur in two ways:

- The first approach is to add or remove a domain or subdomain on the internet, or to add or remove a document to or from a subdomain or domain. This represents the classic method of editing the internet.
- The second approach refers to the editing of a single document. This can be seen as a characteristic feature of the so-called Web 2.0, i.e., the web with user-generated content.

Although the share of user-generated content has increased significantly in recent times, as can be easily seen, for example, from the development of YouTube's upload numbers [STA23], the share of this content remains significantly smaller in scope than the static share. Even considering social media platforms like YouTube or Instagram, changes on the internet occur only in a limited area, which hardly affects the rest of the area. Consequently, the internet or its content changes little or not at all during a user's absence. Of course, it may happen that a document is no longer accessible after the user's absence because it has been deleted, or that the content of a document has changed due to editing by another user. However, when these changes are set in relation to the unchanged content, this confirms the initially asserted view that the classic internet is document-centric and can be treated as such.

Consequently, it can be stated that the internet can be considered a network with mainly static content. Here, temporal aspects play only a subordinate role, as no comprehensive temporal synchronization between the user's real world and the virtual world of document content is necessary. However, this static perspective changes in the context of the metaverse. The metaverse can be seen as an actor-centric network. Drawing on software development and the tools used there, such as UML, the entirety of the metaverse arises from the interaction of various actors. These actors can be divided into six groups:

- The first group consists of human users who are anchored in the physical world.
- The second group consists of avatars, which are digital twins of human users anchored in the digital world.
- The third group includes the real physical world with its objects.
- The fourth group consists of digital twins of real objects. Just like the avatars, these digital twins are also anchored in the digital world.
- A fifth group of actors includes objects that exist exclusively in the virtual world. These can be further divided into …
  - … objects that describe the digital world, such as a door as a portal leading to another virtual room, or a chair on which the virtual avatar can sit, as well as …
  - … information objects that are comparable to the documents of the classic internet.
- The sixth group of actors includes objects that serve exclusively for communication between the virtual and physical world and vice versa. These can be distinguished according to their main communication direction into …
  - … communication objects for communication from the digital to the real world and …
  - … those for communication from the real to the digital world.

In particular, group 5b can be compared to the classic internet in terms of its content. The actors within this group exhibit no or only very minimal change behavior over time, much like the documents on the classic internet, which also do not change over time.

This temporal behavior can be transferred to a part of the actors in group 5a. Certainly, the previously mentioned chair, on which the avatar normally does not sit by itself, will also not move, change, or disappear on its own. This means that such objects also exhibit no or only very minimal change behavior over time. Nevertheless, in group 5a, there can also be objects or actors that change independently without requiring physical or virtual user interaction. The most illustrative example of this is probably a vehicle or a virtual animal that exists exclusively in the virtual world and has no real twin.

Even in this subgroup of group 5a, it becomes clear that when merging the physical and virtual worlds into a metaverse, the different temporal flows must be considered. Also, in groups 3 and 4, there are objects that do not change in the temporal flow, as well as those that exhibit their own dynamics or interaction-driven dynamics and thus change in the temporal flow.

Although the third and fourth groups of actors are listed separately, they are closely connected, as one group represents the respective twin of the individual objects in the other world. In doing so, there will certainly also be objects that do not have their own dynamics and are thus static actors of their respective world. However, a look into the physical world shows that such static objects are rather rare, because the aspect of dynamics affects not only characteristics such as position or size but all states in which individual objects can be in each world. Such state changes also leave traces in the temporal flows of the respective world, regardless of whether it is physical or virtual.

It becomes clear that the compulsion for temporal merging exists in groups 1 and 2, as these involve humans as actors. In group 1, the human user, through his own behavior and drive, forces his digital twin as an actor in group 2 to change. However, the reverse effect relationship is also conceivable, namely from the digital twin as an actor in group 2 to the human user as an actor in group 1. For example, the digital twin in its virtual environment could be addressed or otherwise influenced by another actor, regardless of its group affiliation. In this case, the virtual actor from group 2 must transmit this influence or its consequences to its twin actor in group 1 to trigger a reaction in group 1.

		Entity	Anchored in the …	Role	Change/Example
1		Human user	Physical world	The independently acting user	Self-driven change of states of all kinds (position, movement, gesture, information curiosity, etc.)
2		Digital twin of a human user (avatar)	Virtual world	The representative of the physical user in the virtual world	Driven by its physical twin
					Can also be driven by its own autonomous behavior
3	**a**	Physically existing object	Physical world	Represents as a physical twin a digital object of the virtual world	Can be static
					Can be externally prompted to change its own state in all kinds (size, position, own behavior, etc.)
					Can independently change its own state in all kinds (size, position, own behavior, etc.)
	b	Physically existing object	Physical world	Exists without a digital twin exclusively in the physical world	
4	**a**	Digital object	Virtual world	Represents a real object of the physical world as a digital twin	Can be static
					Can be triggered from the outside from the physical world to change its own state in all ways (size, position, own behavior, etc.)
					Can independently change its own state in all ways (size, position, own behavior, etc.)

		Entity	Anchored in the …	Role	Change/Example
	b	Digital object	Virtual world	Exists without a physical twin exclusively in the virtual world	–
5	**a**	World-describing objects	Virtual world	Contribute to the construction and understanding of the virtual world. Usually have no representative in the "other" world	No own effort to change the state (e.g., digital chair in a (virtual room))
					Low own effort to change the state (e.g., a cup falling from a table)
					Independent change of its own state even without physical or virtual interaction from users or other objects (e.g., an autonomous virtual vehicle or a virtual living being)
	b	Information objects (documents)	Virtual world	Present static and dynamic media and their information content	e.g., virtual screens without the ability to change themselves
					Can be triggered from the outside from the virtual world to change its own state in all ways (size, position, own behavior, etc.)
					Can independently change its own state in all ways (size, position, own behavior, etc.)
6	**a**	Communication objects	Physical world	Communication from the physical to the virtual world	e.g., physical devices for interaction like keyboard, mouse, etc.
	b		Virtual world	Communication from the virtual to the physical world	e.g., virtual tools for communication like chats, etc.

From the above-mentioned examples, it becomes clear that synchronization of temporal processes and flows is absolutely necessary. For example, if a virtual actor wants to initiate communication with the real user via the digital twin of a user, this must necessarily occur in temporal synchronization. This is because it can generally be assumed that communication between avatars and their "real twins" will take place in the form of a conversation and not in an asynchronous form, such as in a text chat or an email thread.

The example of communication just used illustrates the discussion from the perspective of viewpoint 1. Communication between human users, avatars, or the interaction between humans and avatars can occur both synchronously and asynchronously. However, synchronous communication necessarily requires the simultaneous presence or at least accessibility of the involved actors.

The email thread, as an example of asynchronous communication, detaches from viewpoint 1 and transitions to viewpoint 2. Of course, both actors involved in the communication can be present simultaneously and still communicate asynchronously. However, it is also possible that the actors are not present in their respective worlds at the same time. The temporal process in the respective world continues nonetheless, even if a state of static pause is currently reached in the communication flow. The state of the respective world continues to change continuously, even if the communication process or flow is not currently changing.

Even if it may not seem obvious at first glance, viewpoints 1 and 2 require an extremely sophisticated technical implementation of the metaverse. The technical hurdles and challenges arising from viewpoint 1 were already addressed in the earlier Sect. 2.5 "Mixed and other Realities" during the analysis of the concept of mixed reality. The example there was the virtual coffee cup placed on a table. The idea of mixed reality was interpreted such that if the real table moves away from under the virtual cup, the virtual cup does not float in space but falls in the virtual world just like its analog twin. This is also an aspect of temporal merging, because naturally, the virtual cup should only fall when the real table has moved away from under it and not earlier. However, it should also not hover in virtual air for seconds before accelerating towards the ground in the virtual world. To realize this temporal merging in this synchronous form, it must be known where and in what state of motion both the table in the real world and the virtual cup in the virtual world are located.

In the case of the virtual cup, it could be said that this is a natural part of the cup's data model. However, this also results in the requirement that the state in the cup's data model must always be persistently stored and retrievable. This is a purely data-driven problem. The real table in the real world, however, poses significantly higher technical requirements. Although it can also be said here that the position and movement information of the table must be stored in its data model alongside its shape, size, and color as other characteristics. The real challenge, however, lies elsewhere: How or who observes the table, records the position and movement of the table, and stores this information? Is it the table itself, which is a smart table and monitors itself in terms of its own state in the physical world through sensors? Or is it the world that observes the objects residing in it, including the table? Both approaches require immense technical infrastructure, which is theoretically solvable. This is certainly an aspect considered in the extensive research field of the Internet of Things. However, the realization poses an exceptionally high technical hurdle. Ultimately, every single real object that is to have a twin in the virtual world must either be observed or be smart and intelligent itself. Whether and to what extent this meets the newly demanded requirements of sustainability is not to be discussed here. Furthermore, another question arises: Should there be objects in the real world that do not leave a digital imprint in the virtual world, or does this contradict the required principle of (complete) persistence of the metaverse?

The technical requirements and challenges hinted at above, which already appear in perspectives 1 and 2, particularly come to light in perspective 3. In this context, it is about the temporal sequences of the real and virtual worlds being shiftable against each other. However, this implies that at least for the time axis that is to be shifted, comprehensive information about the historical states of the involved actors must be available. Otherwise, it would not be possible to restart the temporal sequence and consider the individual time-dynamic behaviors of the actors.

In this context, the term "historical" remains vague, as do the requirements for data quality. If only the last communication sequence is to be repeated, both the scope of information and the temporal reach are comparatively small. However, if actual historical events are to be reconstructed, such as the Battle of Waterloo or the first moon landing, this requires a significant leap on the time axis in terms of history as well as the amount and quality of data necessary to describe the respective situation. For the depiction of the first moon landing, information about the landing capsule Eagle and the two astronauts Neil Armstrong and Edwin "Buzz" Aldrin is initially sufficient. In contrast, a realistic reenactment of the Battle of Waterloo would require an enormous amount of information, for example, about as many involved soldiers as possible, their weapons, movements, as well as the state of the environment, landscape, and buildings. However, it is unlikely that such data about the Battle of Waterloo exists or can be generated at all, as neither all involved soldiers nor their individual movements and behaviors are known. Similar information is often not available for historically closer points in time or situations. Therefore, we encounter both historical and general technical as well as data-technical limits here.

3.5 The Merging of Interaction

In Sect. 3.1 "Sensory Merging," the sensor technology necessary to generally capture the environment was already examined. In the first step, it is irrelevant whether it is the virtual or the real environment that is to be captured. However, since the metaverse aims to merge virtuality and reality, it is not enough to merely consider the two extremes of 100% reality and virtuality, as discussed in Sect. 2.6 "And the Metaverse?" during the discussion and localization of the metaverse in the reality-virtuality continuum. There, it was initially important to conduct a more detailed examination of the perception channels. This approach should and must now also be continued in this section, which deals with the question of how the user should interact with and in the combined environment in the metaverse.

The term "interaction" is defined and used very differently in many disciplines. In the context of the present considerations of the metaverse, various aspects of interaction are to be brought together. First, it is important to clarify the possible forms of interaction of the human user: How can he actively intervene in his environment? Usually, the focus here is on the "actuators" of the human user. However, it must not be overlooked whether interaction refers to social interaction, such as communication with other people, or to the influence on objects or the surrounding world.

In the completely real environment, without digital artifacts, humans have various tools for interaction.

- The strongest tools are undoubtedly the hands in connection with the arms. They serve both as gripping tools to touch, move, and change objects in the real world, and for communication, such as through pointing gestures.
- Additional human interaction tools are feet and legs, which are used for locomotion.
- However, humans do not only interact with their extremities but also use their face and sometimes the entire body for communication and interaction with their social environment. Gestures, facial expressions, and body posture serve to convey various information.
- Not to forget speaking as probably the strongest form of communication tools.

It is already apparent here that interaction must never be considered in isolation. Rather, it is necessary to always consider the context and the goal that is to be achieved through an interaction. From the list of interaction channels, three different target areas can therefore be derived:

1. The change of the environment and the objects within this environment.
2. The adjustment of the position of the human within the environment.
3. The direct and indirect communication with the environment, especially concerning other human interaction partners.

Of course, this consideration merely forms the general basis for human interaction with technical devices and environments. However, it is even more relevant for the design of human interaction with information technology devices. Unlike the classic machines of the analog and physical world, computers are not only pure work tools but also interaction tools for communication between people. Moreover, they are currently developing more and more into proactively communicating partners and thus also into autonomous interaction partners, as can be seen in numerous more or less intelligent chatbots. Furthermore, with the approach of merging reality and virtuality, the distance between humans and their digital tools is decreasing.

With the completion of the final step, the full immersion, this distance no longer exists. The computer and the application become independent interaction and communication partners, ideally behaving just as autonomously. However, this means that new ways must be found for designing the interaction, as the classic interaction paradigms still separate the entities of human and computer. Therefore, it seems highly relevant for the goal of the merged metaverse to follow Steve Mann's suggestion and not merely design Human Computer Interfaces (HCI), but rather consider this interface from the aspect of Humanistic Intelligence. This should not be confused with the typical ideas of Artificial Intelligence (AI). With this term, Mann wants to conceptually indicate that the separation between human and machine will not be helpful in future IT systems. Incidentally, this term, which Mann first coined in 1998 in the context of wearable computing, also shows that the idea of merging reality and digitality is actually not as new as it is often described nowadays [MAN91, MIN13].

For the design of the metaverse, it is necessary to develop at least one new interaction paradigm for IT, as the previous paradigms, as already shown above, are insufficient for this. This new interaction paradigm will, in contrast to the previous paradigms, focus less on the technical possibilities and characteristics of the interface. Instead, this novel interaction paradigm will be a multidimensional paradigm into which various aspects must be integrated:

- The consideration at the beginning of this section, which was also used in sensor technology, initially focused on the examination of individual interaction channels. In the real, natural world, however, human interaction usually does not take place through just one channel, but people generally interact with a combination of different channels simultaneously. In computer science, this phenomenon is referred to as "multimodal interaction." As early as 1978, an example of this was presented at MIT (Fig. 3.8), the so-called "Put-that-there" scenarios, where pointing gestures were combined with voice commands. [BOL80]
- The next challenge in developing the new paradigm is to combine the dimension of multimodality so that it can be effective synchronously "cross-media" as well as "cross-world." An interaction in the physical world can either refer exclusively to the physical environment or also influence the virtual environment. At the same time, an interaction in the virtual environment can either refer exclusively to this virtual environment or also influence the physical environment. In this context, the physical and digital worlds are considered as medialities.
- Furthermore, another challenge for the new paradigm is emerging. The merging of reality and digitality also leads to a merging of application worlds, processes, and transactions. Classic interaction paradigms always refer exclusively to a single application or a single process. An interaction is started in the context of an application and also refers exclusively to it. Although these applications can be of varying complexity, they remain self-contained. An example is the interaction in a word processor, which changes the textual information or, in the extreme case, saves this information. Other information, however, is not addressed here. This perspective can also be transferred to the context of operating systems, as starting or closing an application happens in the context of the individual installation of the operating system. In the classic application world, the direct influence of one application by another on the same level, for example within the ISO-OSI model, is still quite rare. In the environment of the future metaverse, however, this will be the norm. Interactions carried out in a virtual space

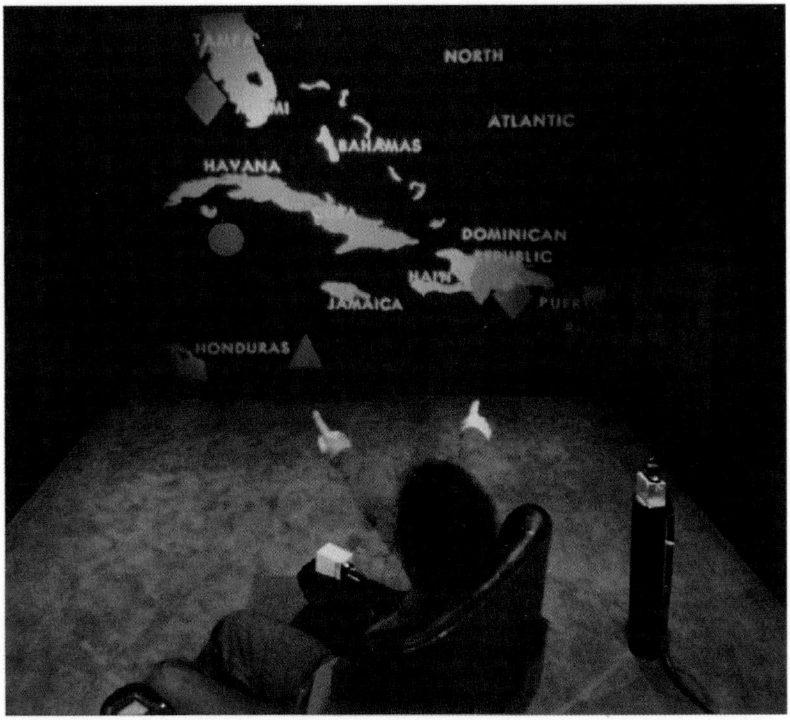

Fig. 3.8 Multimodal interaction: "Put that there" [BOL80]

will influence the physical environment or other virtual spaces and the transactions and events taking place there.

An example should illustrate this. If the avatars of two people are facing each other and one avatar points to an accessory of the other avatar and says: *"That is a nice bag. Hello, metaverse, I would like to have that for myself too,"* this has an impact on a whole range of different applications running in the background:

- First, the multimodal interaction of pointing and speaking in the current virtual space must be correctly interpreted. It must be recognized which accessory—in this example, the bag—is being referred to and in which store this bag can be purchased.
- In this store, the purchase transaction must be initiated.
- Along with this, the virtual inventory management and virtual payment must take place in the store.
- The latter entails that banking sub-transactions must also be processed.
- And finally, the newly acquired virtual bag must be added to the avatar of the purchasing person.

This collaboration of the various processes and transactions must occur automatically, without the transitions between the individual transaction threads needing to be confirmed in detail. For this, in turn, would negatively affect the immersion of the real person in the virtual environment.

- The final challenge for the new interaction paradigm lies in its technical implementation. After all, both the initiation of the interaction itself and all subsequent processes must be possible on a variety of devices or device types. In current web design, this approach is known under the term responsive design. However, responsiveness becomes significantly more complex in the context of the metaverse. While in classic web design, mainly different screen sizes and orientations need to be considered, the goal for the realization of the metaverse is to map the entire reality-virtuality continuum. This means that both classic, display-based devices such as smartwatches, smartphones, tablets, laptops, and desktop PCs, as well as VR devices, data glasses, CAVEs, and all augmented reality or augmented virtuality devices must be taken into account.

The above representation aims to combine and ideally synchronize the effects of an interaction in the physical and virtual world. The temporal effects that need to be considered in this context were already discussed in the previous Sect. 3.4 "Temporal Merging." However, this is only one of the target aspects of such a new interaction paradigm. Another aspect, which ultimately underlies all other interaction paradigms, is to provide the user with the interaction with a machine, an application, or the entire world as simply as possible. In some places, this is referred to as a Natural User Interface (NUI) [JAI11, BLA13].

On the one hand, this certainly brings advantages for the user, because the more natural an interaction is designed, the more "intuitive" it will be and the easier it will be to understand. However, whether this can actually be achieved remains to be seen, because every time a new technology comes to market, it takes time for people to accept it as potential users. For example, the introduction of graphical user interfaces (GUI) according to the WIMP paradigm with the first mouse by Douglas Engelbart at the end of the 1960s was impressive but not necessarily successful [ENG65].

Apart from the insufficient computing power for such interaction systems at that time, users faced an immense mental challenge. Understanding that moving a real physical object on the desk would cause a graphical pointer on the screen to move accordingly required a high level of abstraction. For the users of these early computer systems, this was a significantly high hurdle. Similar hurdles were also evident with each newly introduced interaction paradigm or new interaction technique. Only when users are accustomed to it or willing to get accustomed to it does a new paradigm spread in society and only then does it become the new normal [NEXoJ].

It can currently be observed that in the case of the metaverse, the foundation for a metaverse-related interaction paradigm has been laid by the numerous VR and AR applications now available and certainly also by the many games that use these techniques. However, it must also be considered that the users who have become accustomed to these technologies so far mainly come from a few, rather narrow niches such as gaming or individual construction domains, and the mass market has not yet been truly reached.

Another exciting challenge, especially for interaction designers, will be usability or rather the user experience. For these two aspects are also influenced by the merging of reality and virtuality. It is no longer just about designing the user interface behind the digital boundary, but rather usability must be considered across boundaries. The person moves in the physical world and initiates an action in the digital world. For example, Tauziet says: [TAU16]

> "The higher the person has to raise their arm to perform an interaction, the faster this interaction should be to avoid fatigue."

From this initially quite simple-sounding sentence, Tauzier develops a series of challenges [TAU16]:

- Fatigue from raising the arm without body contact at the elbow
- Challenge in interacting with moving user interfaces (e.g., watch), especially during fast actions
- Difficulties in visually perceiving depth;
  this requires time and practice as (still) VR object manipulation is often unknown
- Grasping objects while sitting close to the virtual body can become problematic
- Visually realistic hands can cause discomfort;
  especially in cases of errors such as penetrating physical objects
- Familiar objects provide clues for handling,
  e.g., the expectation that weapon-shaped props can be used for aiming
- Different physics for physical objects necessary;
  should, for example, a pen go through a table or instead bounce off it
- Loss of awareness of the real environment when staying in VR;
  hand movements could lead to collisions or loss of controllers

Examples of technical solutions could possibly come from the vast field of telepresence [LEE20a]. Particularly illustrative examples include the so-called ActiTouch [ZHA19] and the PocketThumb [DOB17].

The ultimate pinnacle is finally achieved through the interplay of the fusion of interaction PLUS the fusion of sensor technology PLUS inclusion AND accessibility. As described in the visionary design of human-city interaction [LEE20a], the design of mobile AR/MR user interaction in urban environments should consider various stakeholders. The metaverse should also include all members of the community, regardless of ethnicity, gender, age, and religion, including children, the elderly, disabled persons, and so on. Different content can appear in the metaverse, and it must be ensured that this is suitable for a wide range of user groups. Furthermore, it is important to consider personalized content presentations for users [LAM21] and to promote the fairness of recommendation systems to reduce biased content and thus influence user behavior and decision-making [LAN18].

3.6 All-together—The Path to Socio-cultural Fusion

The metaverse, according to the vision of the driving forces behind it, is destined to become an even more central component of future human life worlds than the internet ever managed to be. Whether the end result will actually look like Neal Stephenson envisioned in "Snow Crash" [STE92], Ernest Cline in "Ready Player One" [CLI11], or William Gibson in "Neuromancer" [GIB84] remains open at this point. A compelling look at history shows that new technologies and especially new media forms can influence the social and societal environment of humans—starting with the first media revolution by Johannes Gutenberg and the introduction of the printing press with movable type in the 15th century, through the introduction of electrically operated media and communication technologies such as the telegraph, telephone, radio, and television at the beginning of the 20th century, to the not too distant introduction of PCs, the internet, and the World Wide Web. Each of these new media and communication technologies has more or less radically changed the way people communicate with each other, how information is conveyed, and ultimately also the social structures and social interactions. [MCL64] A similar development is therefore likely to be brought about by the metaverse, provided it is realized in the intended form.

3.6.1 The Real-Life Connector—A New Interaction Paradigm?

The importance of the fusion of the virtual and real world was exemplified in the previous sections. The focus was always on individual aspects, which were considered and evaluated separately. The possibilities of each individual aspect alone are already impressive, possibly also daunting in some places, and certainly technically demanding overall. But it is important to consider that these aspects will not exist in isolation from each other. Rather, it is to be expected that they will continue to develop in parallel, albeit perhaps at different speeds. To gain at least a somewhat realistic perspective on the future possibilities and impacts of the metaverse, it is necessary to connect the individual aspects—a process that will be examined more closely in this section.

The world is neither monomedia nor monomodal—this applies to both the real and the virtual world. For this reason, it is necessary to unite the various aspects of the above consideration. Therefore, a Real Life Connector will be systematically developed here, which is presented in Fig. 3.9 and aims to achieve the most comprehensive representation possible of the fusion of the virtual and real world.

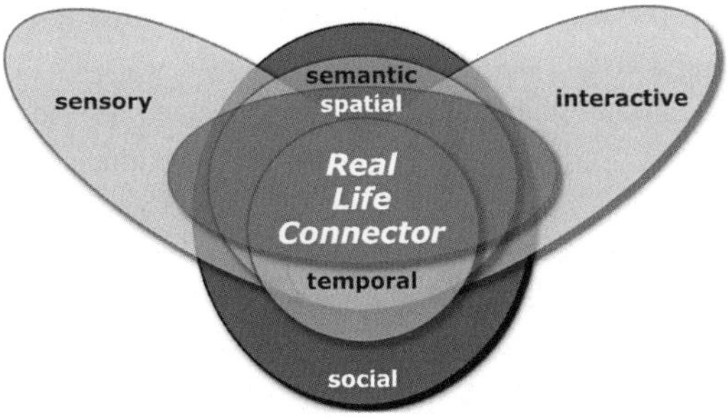

Fig. 3.9 The Real-Life Connector. (Own illustration: Peter Hoffmann, Invisible Cow)

- *Step 1:* Since the metaverse is also a computer-controlled application at its core, it is essential in this context that the user has the ability to interact with the metaverse just as they would with any other application.

At this point, it should be noted that the term "user" as a designation for someone who visits the metaverse may not be optimally chosen. It remains questionable whether it can actually be said that someone really "uses" the metaverse. Other terms might be more appropriate, but each brings its own difficulties. For example, instead of "user," the term "viewer" could be used, although this implies a passivity that excludes other activities and thus does not do justice to the active experience of the metaverse. The most fitting alternative term would probably be "visitor," as this most closely corresponds to the intended immersion in the metaverse or a virtual world. Despite this terminological issue and the widespread anchoring of the term in IT, the term "user" will continue to be used here.

To enable the user to actively participate in the "Metaverse" application, it must be ensured that they can not only perceive the metaverse but also become active themselves. This must also be considered by the intended *Real Life Connector*. Therefore, the first step is to consider the merging of sensory perception and interaction, as detailed in Sect. 3.1 "Sensory Merging" and 3.5 "The Merging of Interaction." Without the perception of the real world in synchronization with the perception of the virtual world, the user remains anchored solely in their real environment. However, mere perception would push the user into the previously mentioned passivity and make them a spectator. For this reason, the possibility of interaction in the real world must be combined on the same level with the possibility of interaction in the virtual world. Only in this way can it be achieved that the user can actively participate in both worlds. The technical challenge at this lower level of the Real Life Connector is thus the bidirectional synchronization of the two mentioned aspects.

- *Step 2:* In the first step, it was ensured that the user could both perceive the two sub-worlds of reality and virtuality sensorily and interact with the existing real and virtual artifacts simultaneously. Therefore, the second step must aim to connect the perception and interaction possibilities both spatially and temporally with the user. Currently, it is unclear whether a separation of spatial from temporal coupling is sensible, which is why both aspects should be considered together in this first generation of the Real Life Connector description.

The spatial coupling of perception and interaction to the user in the metaverse is fundamental, as in the real world, both perception and interaction are always related to the user's immediate surroundings: We see the things that surround us at our current position and interact with those that enable interaction. This also applies to the virtual world in the context of the metaverse. Therefore, the results of sensory and interactive merging must necessarily be coupled to the user's current spatial location. Regarding perception, this probably does not pose a significant challenge, as the user always wants to perceive both reality and virtuality on all sensory modalities: In the real world, we do not usually turn off our visual perception at one place to turn it on again at another, unless special circumstances or disturbances require it. Similarly, we will also try to receive information on all accessible sensory channels at any place and at any time in the virtual world. Interaction might be somewhat different, as it is conceivable that interaction possibilities depend on the current position. Simply because the interactively influenceable artifacts vary at different locations, there is often a need in the real world to use different tools for interaction. For example, switching from voice input to keyboard input when it is too loud at a position for the application to correctly capture the user's voice input. Sensory and interactive merging are thus directly coupled to the user and their spatial position.

Sensory and interactive merging are also closely coupled from the user's temporal perspective. It can be assumed that it is normal for the user to perceive the current situation in both the virtual and real environments. Likewise, it is likely that the user wants to interact with the artifacts currently surrounding them. In a normal situation, it seems rather unusual for the user to interact with an artifact that was present or accessible at the current position at an earlier time. Certainly, examples could be found for such states, for instance, if an earlier state of a digital artifact is offered. In this case, however, the user would need to be informed about the earlier state of the digital artifact. This means, concerning the user, that sensory and interactive mergings are both spatially and temporally bound to them, their position, and possibly additionally to their current state.

Spatial and temporal mergings can, however, be extended further, as they do not only relate to the user but also to all other artifacts. Artifacts that exist independently of the user in both the real and virtual worlds and act proactively or interactively are conceivable. In such cases, the perception and interaction of these artifacts must be spatially and temporally synchronized.

In addition to the joint spatial and temporal coupling, it is also conceivable that sensory and interactive mergings are either only spatially or only temporally coupled.

- *Step 3:* In steps 1 and 2, the focus was on merging and coupling, which were directly related to the user and the artifacts by considering them as objects. These objects were reduced to their individual significance, which emerged from the object itself. However, considering the spatial and temporal connections between the user and artifacts can extend this self-reference. In this way, a semantic meaning can be assigned or emerge from the object itself. Nevertheless, such semantic meaning is not conceivable without the situational, i.e., the temporal and spatial level. Likewise, for this semantic meaning, a perception must be present that considers the state of the world and the current situation. Interaction can, but does not necessarily have to, play a role on this semantic level.

With steps 1 to 3 and the integration of sensory, interactive, semantic, as well as spatial and temporal fusion, a technical foundation for the Real Life Connector was initially created. It is now important to take a look at the interaction paradigms that have been valid so far to determine whether they meet the requirements arising from the connection of these various merging aspects. Considering the peculiarity that the metaverse is supposed to be both highly interactive and highly immersive, these two aspects must be included in the requirements for the Real Life Connector. From the dimension of immersion, three different levels of immersion can be identified for the metaverse:

- If the metaverse is considered a classic internet, it corresponds to typical desktop applications.
- If the metaverse is seen as pure virtual reality, technical VR manifestations apply here, such as access via VR headset or access using a CAVE.
- Between these two extreme levels of immersion lies the area of enrichment, which includes AR and AV and is characterized by the user experiencing a perception of reality enriched by digital artifacts.

Regardless of the dimension of immersion, there are currently three well-known interaction paradigms for the dimension of interaction:

- The currently most widespread interaction paradigm is terminal or WIMP interaction with keyboard, mouse, or, depending on the manifestation, possibly also with touch input or stylus. This paradigm is predominant in desktop workplace situations.
- From some specialized workplace situations, but especially from entertainment and gaming applications, the paradigm of direct interaction is known. Here, the interaction does not take place via a writing tool like the keyboard or pointing gesture devices like a mouse or touchpad, but the user takes control of digital artifacts with specialized controllers. In the most technically advanced case, this can extend to data gloves or even a full data suit. This second paradigm is significantly less common compared to WIMP and terminal.
- Possibly, the currently increasing prevalence of voice interaction could be included as another interaction paradigm in the future.

It is now necessary to reconcile the two dimensions to determine whether the current interaction paradigms can meet the requirements of the metaverse. The question arises whether the current, predominant interaction paradigms are sufficient to cover the broad spectrum of immersion necessary to interact effectively with the metaverse:

- Terminal and WIMP were specifically developed for the desktop environment and have always been geared towards this purpose.
- Direct interaction in the desktop environment is only possible with significant limitations. Of course, it can be argued that the input and editing of text or image files on the desktop represent direct interaction with these texts and images. However, this is rather an exceptional form of direct interaction. Direct handling of a three-dimensional digital artifact, on the other hand, is very difficult or even impossible with a keyboard or classic mouse, which usually only moves in the two-dimensional plane of the desk.
- However, terminal and WIMP are unsuitable for both augmented reality (AR) and virtual reality (VR). Immersion in VR would be significantly disrupted by the need to focus attention on a keyboard to perform an interaction. This applies equally or perhaps even more to AR, as the user is in the physical world and is usually not at the desktop. Of course, similar to the often-cited example of Tom Cruise in Minority Report, a keyboard could be displayed in the user's field of view. [SPI02] Nevertheless, even here, immersion would be disrupted by the necessary attention to the keyboard.
- Just as terminal and WIMP were developed for the desktop environment, the paradigm of direct interaction is specifically designed for use in virtual realities.
- For augmented reality, direct interaction is at least partially fundamental, as the representation of digital artifacts, which are tied to a spatial situation and position, directly depends on the position and viewing vector from which the user perceives this digital artifact. If the user changes their position or viewing direction, the representation also changes. A direct connection between the user and the artifact is therefore essential here. However, whether the user can also "touch" or "manually manipulate" the digital artifact is not necessarily guaranteed.

It can currently be said that some aspects of interaction and immersion are technically feasible, but there are still significant gaps in many areas and across all levels of immersion. Therefore, it seems necessary to develop a new, independent interaction paradigm for the metaverse as a fused medium. What this paradigm specifically looks like can probably only be described once the requirements for and of the fused metaverse are known. Such a new interaction paradigm must incorporate the known advantages and disadvantages of the previous interaction paradigms. There have already been studies for some time on the well-known GUI as the embodiment of the WIMP interaction paradigm, analyzing how the use of keyboard and mouse influences cognitive processes in our brain, particularly concerning interaction with the environment and other people

[DOU01]. The basic idea is that human cognitive development is significantly shaped by physical and social interactions with objects and living beings. The findings of such studies expand the concept of paradigms.

For some time now, there has been the term Reality-Based Interaction, coined by Jacob et al. [JAC08], and in their description, they also included approaches of the so-called multimodal interaction, which was already introduced in 1978. Although Jacob et al., with Reality-Based Interaction, remain technically focused like other interaction paradigms, some developments, such as Reiterer's Blended Interaction, take a significant step further by leaving the purely technical context [DOU01] and also considering how much workflows, business processes, or handling in the entertainment sector influence the design of interactions.

Thus, numerous foundations have already been laid for a new, let's call it merged, interaction paradigm that is aligned with the upcoming metaverse (see Fig. 3.10).

Fundamentally necessary for the development of a Metaverse User Interaction Paradigm (MUI) is therefore to consider both the technical and user-oriented aspects, such as the integration of business processes into the design process and context. Furthermore, the novel interaction must not only be accepted by the user but, above all, understood. It is essential to include all insights from interaction design that are common in the fields of User Interaction Design or Usability. These can generally be traced back to Don Norman and his seminal work "The Design of Everyday Things" [NOR02], although many others have also contributed to this field.

3.6.2 The Social and Societal Merging

As already emphasized above, the previous analysis of the mergers focuses on individual, independent aspects. Such isolated considerations are initially helpful as they are easier to handle. However, these are not sufficient if the metaverse is to be implemented as the future embodied internet and thus as the future form of human life and coexistence [JIA22]. Instead, something is needed that was referred to above as the "Real Life Connector" and in which the various aspects are brought together. It is important to note that this is not only about technical aspects but also about human and social dimensions. The metaverse, as it is currently conceived, is intended to enable a new experience of virtual realities in connection with "real reality." This includes not only individual experiences but also social interactions and different areas of life of individual users, such as learning, traveling, or cultural experiences [BIT22]. To avoid a purely virtual parallel world that merely represents another perspective of today's mobile internet, the metaverse must rather be a logical further development of it. This can only succeed if the networking of the various aspects is successfully implemented.

Of course, the entire concept is initially based on the fact that each individual aspect can actually be implemented and exist independently. This means that methods must first be developed to perceive the new combination of physical and virtual reality at all, as well as approaches to interact with these new reality combinations. Here, the technical aspects are initially in the foreground.

Regardless of sensor and interaction technology, solutions must be developed to unite the spatial sub-aspects and challenges from both realities so that, for example, the movements of objects can take place in all combined sub-realities.

At this point, the necessity becomes clear to move away from a purely technical perspective of the merger. As mentioned in the previous Sect. 3.6.1 "The Real-Life Connector—a new interaction paradigm?", the area of interaction not only includes the immediate interaction with visible objects in the various realities but also the interaction of applications with each other in terms of a process- or transaction-oriented thinking and design approach. Although technical interfaces are required for these process-spanning interactions, a fundamental understanding of the processes in the metaverse itself is initially essential [BAL20].

Already in this first step, a combination takes place by considering both the states of physical and digital reality together. The realization of the connection between sensor technology and interaction concerning spatiality is usually only possible if temporal or temporal aspects are also taken into account.

It is this holistic integration that will ultimately characterize the metaverse. Multimodal interaction alone is no more the metaverse than multimodal sensor technology alone. Only the interplay of all aspects will lead to an innovative medium that can meet the expectations currently placed on the idea of the metaverse.

At this point, the question must certainly be asked: What is all this for? Why do we need such an inflated, technically-technological network?

First, the thread begun above can be picked up again. The future metaverse is intended to be open to all people and, not least, to serve the purpose of designing all the barriers we face in everyday life—such as in daily mobility, at work, and also in leisure—in such a way that no one is actually excluded. The great aspiration here is

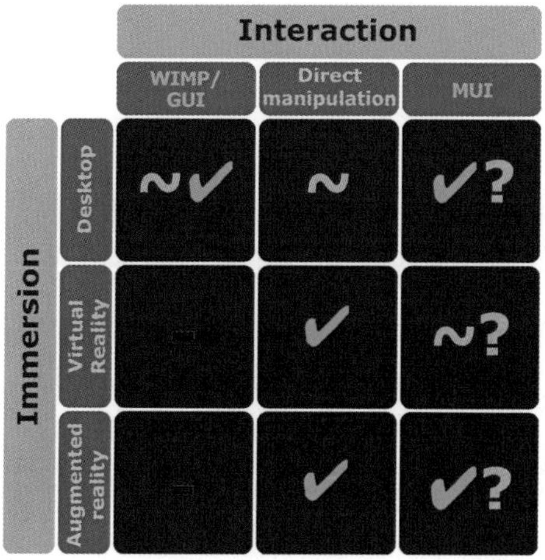

Fig. 3.10 Immersion of Interaction Paradigms: Metaverse User Interaction (MUI). (Own illustration: Peter Hoffmann, Invisible Cow)

practical accessibility. What initially sounds like a contradiction, namely that many different aspects must be thought of and combined together, which will naturally be an immense technical and technological effort, is not a contradiction at all. Because it is precisely through this pronounced combination that accessibility will be much easier to achieve.

The limitations of people regarding their different abilities, such as in vision and hearing or in mobility or in mental or cognitive perception, can be compensated for by a combination of various synchronous channels in the sense of redundancy. Challenges here include the diversity of different limitations as well as the lack of generally accepted standards. Although there are a number of frameworks for accessible design in general web design, these are relatively rarely used and, if at all, often not consistently and thoroughly. The number of accessible solutions for the VR sector is even significantly lower. The number of accepted established standards in this area is manageable. There is no need to even talk about the AR sector at this point, as the number of publications from practical projects here is already approaching zero.

In addition to this technically driven, practical, or user-centered approach that is supposed to enable the metaverse, there is another, possibly equally practical approach. If the previous technical development with a focus on the internet is considered, it is obvious and unmistakable that the introduction of the internet and especially the World Wide Web has significantly changed the way people live. Both the working world and the procurement and handling of information, as well as the entire leisure behavior today, are fundamentally different from what they were a few decades ago. Certainly, other technologies have also contributed to this, such as mobile telephony. Ultimately, however, this technology also culminates in the current mobile internet and shapes our present way of life. How could a metaverse, considering the previously mentioned merging aspects, influence our way of life in the future? The already mentioned Cathy Hackl, a not entirely unknown blogger and journalist in the field of IT, web, and metaverse, has given a very illustrative example of this: [HAC21].

At the beginning of this example, it should be emphasized that the reader of this book is probably somewhat older than the main character in the said example. But each of these readers can undoubtedly remember their first concert visit. It does not matter whether it was the concert of a small local band in a small venue around the corner or a large multi-day festival. We all still remember how it felt to stand in reality with other euphoric people, often literally body to body, in front of the stage, to see, hear, feel, and possibly also smell the neighbor. This aligns with the memories of Cathy Hackl, who, however, reports on the first concert visit of her ten-year-old son. He attended the performance of Lil Nas X, which, due to the then rampant coronavirus pandemic, did not take place in a real location but in the virtual world of Fortnite. Unlike the crowd in the mosh pit in front of a real stage, Cathy Hackl's son enjoyed the concert from home through a VR headset. Although it was a purely digital experience, it was no less real for the young man.

This is underscored by the behavior Cathy Hackl shows in another example. During the pandemic, she hosted a birthday party for her son in the virtual world of Roblox as well. [HAC21] Just as almost every (not only) teenager in the real world would do, Cathy Hackl's son also placed great importance on how his avatar should appear at this party. The design and appearance of the avatar were just as important to him as a shirt or blouse is to real-world guests.

Such and similar examples illustrate an important insight: VR, AR, or MR do not constitute the essential core components of the approaching metaverse. Rather, the central element lies in the possibility of social interaction within the virtual world. If this option is not implemented and made available to users, the upcoming metaverse would merely correspond to an ordinary virtual world, as known from classic entertainment and gaming environments or as depicted in numerous dystopias. The most popular example of such a dystopian implementation is the often-mentioned "Ready Player One" [CLI11], in whose OASIS people primarily immerse themselves to experience better living conditions. However, this also shows that this very OASIS cannot be a true implementation of the metaverse. Because users lose themselves in the OASIS and simultaneously escape reality, which fundamentally contradicts the definition of the metaverse.

The fact that technology recedes into the background and social and cultural aspects come to the forefront presents a major challenge for users. If the metaverse is indeed realized in the merged form envisioned here, significant impacts on the social interaction of users are to be expected, and significant changes will be initiated. Such changes are well known when considering the history of computers, the internet, and especially the World Wide Web. Both the computer itself and the internet initially carried a stigma upon their introduction. The broad population in society saw the use of computers and later the internet as primarily wasted and even antisocial time. The destigmatization of both the computer or PC and the internet took a very long time. Even today, about 30 years after the introduction of the internet, the use of this medium is still viewed critically in part—which is certainly partly justified.

Exactly this can also be expected for the new metaverse. Probably even worse than in the classic internet, as the typical user—the surfer in the media worlds—is usually not isolated from their environment on the internet. They typically sit in front of the screen and are fundamentally approachable, even when they are looking into the cyberspheres through the window of their screen. [BAL22] In the metaverse, however, there is a danger that the user will actually disconnect from the real world by using devices like VR headsets and similar, and thus will presumably no longer be directly approachable.

The early adopters could be confronted with this stigma in the foreseeable future. However, it is possible that the period until this negative view of the metaverse is transformed into a neutral or even positive perspective will be shorter than it was for the internet. After all, the metaverse is already known to many users and generally in society, as numerous people are already active in VR or 3D worlds when they immerse themselves in game worlds [BAL21b].

The real challenge arising from the merging is thus not technical but sociocultural in nature. On the one hand, the emerging metaverse and its users must be in harmony with pure real reality, because only if widespread acceptance is achieved can this metaverse successfully establish itself. However, other sociocultural observations from the World Wide Web can be transferred to the upcoming metaverse. It is now undisputed [DÖR10] that the establishment of the internet had and still has a significant impact on society and social interactions. Behaviors, forms of expression, and expectations regarding communication and communication structures have changed compared to the paper-based analog era, not least due to the media break. But even within the medium of the internet or the WWW, new social forms have established themselves. For example, the manners in social media differ from those in classic forums of the early internet. Even within social media, there are different communication and manners. Communication on channels like Twitter (now: "X") or Telegram is characterized by a high level of directness, which, for example, is not found in this form on professional platforms like LinkedIn. This aspect can also be transferred to other media forms like wikis, which are characterized by collaboration, and even more so to media forms like gaming platforms. In these, although playing against each other, it often happens within social structures like gaming clans and similar.

If pseudo- or partial societies and sociocultural currents already form in the "classic" internet, where there is no merging of digitality and reality, it is very likely that new sociocultural currents will also emerge in the environment of a new medium, where exactly this merging is the focus and is being pursued. The great challenge is that in this metaverse, there will no longer be any possibility to rely on physical experiences as humans have made them so far in and through the real environment and their social surroundings. Even if it may be unpopular, it is a fundamental human behavior that we automatically categorize a counterpart based on the first visual and auditory impression. Different character traits are attributed to a Eurasian-looking person than to an African-looking person or an Asian-looking person. Of course, such initial categorizations are not always accurate and are usually corrected through longer interactions. However, in the fully merged environment of the metaverse, the user can no longer rely on such perceptions in any way.

Users immerse themselves in the metaverse and use avatars that they can usually design completely freely. This refers not only to the appearance but also to the behavior of the avatar, which can also be scripted. So the question arises as to which category we should assign the Gorgon covered in purple plush, who stands before us hopping on one of its seven legs with a huge axe in hand. How do we communicate with an avatar that has such an absurd and certainly no longer natural form and possibly also behavior? In the real world, we would certainly be extremely cautious and reserved in such a situation at first, as we would assume that this being is not well-disposed towards us. Who knows what will happen if our digital counterpart suddenly gets the idea to swing its axe and injure or even kill our avatar, which—as we have read above—is our digital twin. After all, as a real person, we are merged with our digital avatar. Such situations can indeed have different impacts, not only in terms of personal behaviors and patterns but also generally in terms of the structure and behavior of individuals in social groups. If we think positively, we could hope that the metaverse gives us the opportunity to leave all these prejudiced ways of thinking and thought structures behind. However, where it leads if we think negatively, the reader may imagine for themselves at this point.

Problems related to sociocultural merging in the metaverse can also reveal themselves from another perspective. In the future, it will probably be rather unusual or possibly even not occur that we immerse ourselves in the metaverse and the virtual world we enter is a digital clone or twin of our real world. Of course, there will be such applications, because, for example, in the tourism industry, it would be quite desirable to have a digital twin of a holiday paradise, as will be considered in Sect. 4.5.6 "Tourism". In these, we could not only immerse ourselves from home but also directly on-site to enrich our perception with virtual information. Typical examples of this are classic augmented reality projects, such as visiting an archaeological site, where we can bring the ruins back to life with the help of AR.

In the metaverse, commercially operated platforms will also establish themselves, presenting innovative virtual worlds independent of the real world, into which one can immerse from any location in the real world. Here too, a comparison can be drawn to our experiences in the real world: When we board a plane in the real world and visit a remote location in a different cultural area, be it the Nepalese highlands or a remote island in Polynesia, we have an idea of the cultural world we are entering upon leaving the plane. Based on this, we usually draw conclusions about how we should or should not behave. However, in a freely designed virtual world that we enter, as in the case of the aforementioned Gorgon avatar, we cannot draw such conclusions. If we consider it consistently, we enter the creator's fantasy in such a freely designed virtual world. In such a world, the typical laws of the real world do not necessarily have to apply. The word "laws" here refers to both sociocultural rules and actual legal regulations. Furthermore, it also includes physical and other scientific rules. Indeed, a visitor in such a freely designed virtual world cannot be sure whether …

- … the laws of nature, such as gravity or similar, also apply in this virtual world, …
- … what the spatial structure of the world is like and how the visitor can orient themselves within it, as well as …
- … how the present avatars will ultimately react to their presence and behavior.

For this reason, the user is initially helpless without any information and must explore the world and its rules on all levels. While some users find this easy because they are more open and possibly playful, the initial helplessness can be problematic for other users and deny them easy access to this world.

The integration of the real world with virtual worlds brings significant challenges for the legislative, judicial, and executive branches, especially in the area of sociocultural fusion, but also in other areas such as economic fusion, which will be examined in more detail in the following major Sect. 3.4. Approaches to these challenges can already be recognized and derived from the current handling of the internet. However, these challenges will be much greater in the metaverse. For example, the question arises as to which legal rules actually apply in a virtual world. Let us take as a thought experiment that two avatars meet in the digital world and both perform the same action. In the physical origin of the real twin of one avatar, this action is allowed, while in the physical origin of the real twin of the other avatar, it is forbidden. What implications does this have for the virtual world? What rules and laws apply here?

The term "action" was deliberately chosen in this context because it can encompass both a social action and any other type of action, such as an economic action, as already indicated above. Henz illustrates this problem very clearly: [HEN22]

> "Even if a metaverse platform is used globally, users must comply with the laws of the physical region. This is important because crimes also occur in virtual reality, such as harassment, stalking, theft, elimination, or kidnapping of an avatar. If potential perpetrators and victims come from different countries, additional laws may apply. This depends on a country's ability to extend its legal system internationally. The avatar can be perceived as a unique part of the user; any kind of violence against it would have relevant impacts on the person, even if it were committed while the user was offline and the avatar was acting semi-autonomously. The perceived safety of staying in the metaverse, but also in combination with the consequences in the physical world, is essential to encourage users to stay."

3.6.3 The Fusion in Everyday Life: Leisure, Culture, Art ...

While the previous Sect. 3.6.2 examined the user both individually and from a societal perspective as a social being, this section will focus on the practical everyday life of this social being. The range of individual topics that open up here is, of course, so broad that ultimately a separate book would not suffice to delve into these topics in depth. Nevertheless, an attempt will be made at this point to at least provide a brief impression and insight into various areas of everyday life. For this purpose, an application world will be presented for each of the three major everyday topics of leisure, art, and culture.

The attentive observation of leisure activities has shown for some time that technologies such as VR and AR are increasingly establishing themselves in this area. For example, a growing number of offerings can currently be found that further develop the now established numerous leisure activities such as escape rooms and laser tag arenas. These are often based on the CAVE idea, where, as already introduced above, the visitor enters a space similar to a squash box, in which the projection of a VR world can be seen on every wall as well as on the floor and ceiling. The visitor is thus literally standing in the middle of the VR world. Before entering the world, the visitor puts on equipment equipped with sensors that allow the visitor's movements to be captured and translated into position changes and interactions. The visitor is therefore not only passive but can move freely in the world projected around them and interact with various digital artifacts. However, since the projection here only occurs on the walls around the user, interaction with the artifacts is still relatively limited. Another technical approach goes a step further, where the visitor also enters a room, but the projection of the virtual world is done via a VR headset that the visitor must wear in addition to the sensor-equipped equipment. This is actually a similar scenario to what many players already know from home when they have expanded their game consoles with a VR headset. However, professional leisure installations offer a significant added value in that the user can actually move within the installation, which is often not possible or only extremely problematic at home due to the cramped space in one's own apartment. Additionally, in these professional environments, the powerful computer systems installed make it possible to experience the selected VR world collaboratively. This often already resembles the frequently cited example of OASIS from Ready Player One. The goal here is either action games or escape room scenarios, which can be offered in various themes, suitable for almost all age groups.

The leisure activities just mentioned are entirely based on virtual reality. However, when talking about the merging of the virtual and real world, especially in the leisure sector, another trend that is significantly older than the VR offerings described above must not be overlooked. This involves the real integration of digital leisure activities into real presence, in the form of digital or virtual games that are played in the real world.

The best-known example of this form of merging with a focus on leisure is likely Pokémon Go, developed by Niantic and published by Nintendo in 2015. In a very short time, the game became a huge success, bringing hundreds of thousands of players worldwide to chase after virtual Pokémon figures. Thus, Pokémon Go is the first game that managed to merge the real world with a digital game world and virtual content and become known to a large public. [REI15] Although there were already some predecessors, such as the game Ingress, on which Pokémon Go is actually based, this was primarily a technical feasibility study and not a game for the general public.

The example of PacManhattan from 2004, initiated by the Tisch School of the Arts at New York University, shows that the idea of combining virtual worlds known from computer games with the real world is much older than Pokémon Go. In this urban game, the rectangular arrangement of the streets of Manhattan served as the basis for transferring the Pac-Man game into the real world. In this implementation, a human player took on the role of Pac-Man, and other players took on the role of the hostile Pac-Man ghosts chasing the player. These ghosts received instructions on where they had to or should run from a central location, where the respective positions of the human players in the real environment were managed and where it was decided in which direction the Pac-Man ghosts should run. Although the degree of digitization was relatively low here, the degree of merging the real world and the game world was quite high. This is shown not only by video recordings but also by reports about the game [LAN09, LANoJ].

But even PacManhattan is not the first example of the merging of the real and digital world. As early as 1996, an attempt was made with a significantly higher degree of digitization to integrate a virtual game world into the real world. Students from the School of Computer and Information Science at the University of South Australia attempted to transfer the then very popular shooter game Quake to the university's parking lot using augmented reality. Considering the computing power available at the time, the results are still quite impressive even today [PIE02, PIEoJ].

It seems quite relevant to use the merging of the real and virtual world not only for the procurement and processing of information but also with the aim of experiencing games in this way. This is currently evident on a larger scale in the entertainment sector. Here, not only the VR-based installations presented above but also renowned amusement parks are increasingly relying on this merging. The brand term "Coastiality" gives a hint of the goal of these efforts [COAoJ], namely to further enhance the experience of roller coaster rides with VR technologies. The passengers sit in the coaster, i.e., the roller coaster train, and wear VR headsets during the ride. Thus, they are visually disconnected from the real environment and visually immersed in a virtual world. The other sensory modalities remain unaffected, meaning the physical sensations of a typical roller coaster ride, such as acceleration, the wind, and also the laughter and screams of fellow riders, come from the real world and are perceived as such [PLOoJ].

For the passengers, it may be a physical challenge to wear a VR headset with the current usual dimensions and weight during the accelerations of a roller coaster ride. However, the necessary registration of the passenger is significantly lower compared to AR games such as the aforementioned AR Quake. The registration can be done here through the installation of sensors on the ride, which are adapted to the respective environmental situation. This increases the accuracy of the registration. Additionally, the graphical representation, i.e., the rendering of virtual artifacts, is significantly simpler here. Since the entire world in which the passenger immerses is depicted, no virtual artifacts need to be precisely integrated into the passenger's visual perception. The world's first ride experience enriched in this way was the Galaxy Express at the Space Center in Bremen (Germany), which was introduced in 2003. It was an indoor steel roller coaster, where the ride was supported by screens embedded in the passenger gondolas that rendered the VR effect. The result was said to be quite impressive, which unfortunately can no longer be verified as the Space Center in Bremen was closed again after a short time [AIR14].

Although the Galaxy Express was not successful, the technology on which it was based could serve as a foundation for further developments. The developer and manufacturer Mack GmbH & Co. KG has been designing and building roller coasters since 1921 and has been closely associated with Europa-Park in Rust (Germany) since 1975, which was also founded by the Mack family. The area around this park has now developed into a mecca for the combination of VR, AR, and amusement park technologies. In addition to virtually enriched roller coasters in the park, there are also dedicated VR experiences in the immediate vicinity, where research and development in this area are conducted and transferred into application and operation. Some of these developments and attractions are technically connected beyond the usual standard today, such as the possibility of experiencing VR in and under water in a virtual snorkeling and diving experience.

The enrichment of roller coasters and other rides with VR and AR technologies is not only interesting for passengers but also a significant economic factor for the operator. Equipping an existing ride with VR technology opens up the possibility of changing the experience for the passenger without having to alter the mechanical construction. Typically, such rides also have a limited acceptance period and must be replaced by new or different rides at regular intervals to maintain their attraction. VR technology offers the possibility of exchanging the virtual world in which the ride is embedded around the constructions in the real world, thus offering a novel ride experience. However, there are no long-term studies yet on how long the operating time of the mechanical constructions can be extended with the use of VR and AR.

In the field of cultural entertainment, especially in pop culture, there are more and more active examples indicating that a fusion of the virtual and real world will also be of interest in this area. The approach, however, is different. An example of this is the thought experiment by Cathy Hackl, where artists from the real world perform in the virtual world. A long list of artists now performs in virtual worlds such as Fortnite, Decentraland, and Roblox. The concert by Ariana Grande in 2021 in Fortnite is said to have activated about 78 million viewers [WEB21] and generated revenues of about 20 million euros [DAI21]. Various video recordings on YouTube and other video platforms [MEI21] also show a quite large number of active avatars during the virtual performance. Here, even if 78 million avatars are not clearly visible, it can still be considered a successful event. Although not every virtual concert event can be seen as such a success, the event by Ariana Grande shows that success is indeed possible. However, this does not apply to every virtual concert event. At the Decentraland Metaverse Music Festival 2022, which is shown again in Fig. 3.11, opinions on success and failure differ significantly. Although the platform operator speaks of a successful event in company-related blogs and publications, which activated many virtual visitors and generated revenues, there are also other sources that do not have a good word to say about the event. For example, about 100 students from the fields of computer science, business informatics, and digital transformation at the FOM University in Munich (Germany) were asked to participate in the event [HOF22]. The impressions gathered and discussed afterward ranged from incomprehension to horror regarding the quality of the graphical rendering and the few visible user avatars. None of the students, who must be considered the target group for such platforms and events due to their technical background and age, rated the event positively or indicated that they could imagine attending music festivals in this way in the future. Reports from established magazines such as Metal Hammer [GER22] go in the same direction.

The recently mentioned Decentraland Metaverse Music Festival 2022 clearly highlights the issues of such events, especially in comparison to events like the aforementioned Fortnite concert by Ariana Grande. Due to the few avatars present, no typical festival atmosphere could arise, as visitors of events like Rock am Ring or Wacken Open Air know. The olfactory and haptic perceptions typical of festivals were not addressed. Additionally, the technical implementation of this event was questionable. Decentraland must therefore ask itself whether it is really necessary to model and implement a three-dimensional virtual venue if only YouTube videos or livestreams are shown on virtually installed screens. Wouldn't it have been better to show these videos directly on a screen? This example also shows that big names alone do not guarantee success. The not unknown Ozzy Osbourne tried to market his renowned metal festival Ozzfest as part of the DMMF 2022 virtually. For this, a separate virtual festival venue was modeled and implemented. But here too, mainly videos of well-known metal bands were shown. However, the marketing of this virtual Ozzfest went a step further by having Ozzy Osbourne himself and the already deceased Lemmy Kilmister of Motörhead rock on the virtual stage as avatars. Yet, these virtual performances can also be described as unsuccessful. The modeling of the avatars was more reminiscent of the graphic quality of early computer games from the 1980s, and the movements of the avatars were limited and not synchronized with the music or singing [GER22, HOF22].

At this point, another discussion point must be mentioned, which is independent of the discussed DMMF events and the platform. The question arises as to what extent interaction devices like the VR headset impair immersion, even if the graphical rendering and photorealistic modeling of the musicians' avatars were of the highest quality. Despite good wearing comfort, the weight of these devices is noticeable and affects the users' mobility. It is assumed that the typical physical behavior in music genres like metal is impaired. Headbanging with a VR headset will probably only become a reality when these devices become significantly smaller and lighter than they are today.

In addition to the technical discussion and criticism points mentioned in connection with the implementation of virtual music events in the form of the DMMF, some of the subsequently interviewed visitors began a rather ethical debate. The serious question was raised whether it is justifiable to let deceased artists, who have not given their consent, perform posthumously as avatars and especially to use them for commercial purposes. While the real twin of Ozzy Osbourne was still alive at the time of the DMMF 2022, Lemmy Kilmister had already passed away in December 2015. It is likely that this question cannot be answered universally. However, there are now a number of events where deceased artists perform together with living musicians in front of a real audience in the real world. Examples of this are the hologram shows of Ronnie James Dio [BLI19, BAK21], Michael Jackson [FEE14, VIB23] and other artists. The main argument for this merging of real worlds with virtual artifacts is often that this way, younger people can also experience concerts with these artists. The hologram technology provides an impressive experience, especially since it addresses not only the visual and auditory modality, as is the case with virtual concert experiences, but it is a concrete and real concert experience.

In this way, not only deceased artists can be brought to the stage, but it is also possible to experience living artists in action in this way. A quite impressive example of this is the Swedish group ABBA, which had its own concert hall built in London in 2022, where the so-called "Abbatars" perform in a show as virtual twins of the band members. [ASW23, ABB23] Interestingly, the digital twins in this case were rejuvenated and do not correspond to the actual age of the real persons. This broadly corresponds to the idea

Fig. 3.11 The Decentraland Metaverse Music Festival 2022. (Screenshots: DMMF 2022, Peter Hoffmann, Invisible Cow)

of temporal merging, which was considered in Sect. 3.4 and where initially the temporal courses between the real and virtual world were changed and only then merged.

The idea of merging real and virtual elements can, however, be taken even further by completely dispensing with human participation on stage. The successful and usually sold-out concert events of Hatsune Miku are an excellent example of this. Originally designed in 2007 as a drawn mascot for a software synthesizer, this figure quickly developed into a singer with the artificially synthesized singing voice of the software, releasing singles and albums in the J-Pop genre that were quite successful. [REH21] Just under a year after the first album release, Hatsune Miku performed live for the first time virtually on a video screen at Japan's largest anime music concert. The positive response to the concert and the music releases led to Hatsune Miku performing every year in August in Japan as a hologram in front of a real audience under the name Magical Mirai since 2013 and now also going on a world tour under the name Miku Expo [CLI20].

At this point, the circle undoubtedly closes, which began with Cathy Hackl's concert description in the previous Sect. 3.6.2: The merging of the virtual and real world in the field of concert events can now be considered established and successful. However, the limit of creativity and possibilities has certainly not yet been reached here. Further developments are emerging in the extremely vibrant pop culture of South Korea. In the K-Pop business, the Korean counterpart to J-Pop, the metaverse is specifically addressed and considered in the planning and design of new groups. Thus, there are now a whole series of bands in South Korea that, like Hatsune Miku, are purely virtual. For example, the K-Pop girl group Eternity, introduced in 2021, consists of 11 members, all of whom are only virtual characters. [BBC22] In contrast to the manually modeled avatars of Lemmy Kilmister and Ozzy Osbourne mentioned above, the characters of this group are photorealistic thanks to AI rendering. The formation of such bands, at least in the case of Eternity, is not artistically motivated. Rather, it is argued here that especially in the K-Pop industry, human stars often reach their physical and mental limits, as the demands of perfectly choreographed performances and the number of events these groups have to perform at are extreme. Virtual characters have significant advantages over human persons in this regard. [YOU23, MUR22, NOO22, BUS23] Although these purely virtual groups are highly accepted by the audience, even the minds behind the industry and these groups say,

that they would probably prefer the real groups: [BBC22]

> „Honestly, if someone asks me, „Do you want to watch Billlie on the metaverse for 100 minutes or in real life for ten minutes?", I'll choose to see Billlie for ten minutes in real life."

Another approach to merging real and virtual presence is pursued by the South Korean label SM Entertainment with the group aespa. This group consists of four real members, for whom digital twins were developed and presented at the time of their formation. In various forms, the human members interact with their digital counterparts. The possibility is also utilized that the virtual twins can represent the group independently of the human members, thus contributing to the reduction of the physical and mental strain on the individual members. [STEoJ] Moreover, these digital band members are also interesting from an economic perspective, as they can be used as a basis for collection and merchandise strategies.

The design of 3D worlds itself, but especially that of 3D avatars, whether created using AI-supported tools or entirely manually in the traditional way, requires not only extensive technical knowledge and skills. Rather, many examples of such 3D models are characterized by a high artistic standard. Not least, digital art has now become an acknowledged direction within the art world. Here, there is an overlap with renowned computer artists such as Herbert W. Franke [FRA01], Frieder Nake [DIE86] and others, who already in the early days of computer development tried to establish a connection between new technology and art. This increasingly close connection between art and technology can be traced back to 1979 at Ars Electronica, which has now established itself as one of the leading platforms and annual events for electronic art in the broadest sense [FORoJ, ARSoJ].

A brief look at the art objects and performances presented over time shows that in this environment, artistic engagement and exchange with the metaverse and associated technologies have been taking place for a long time. The examples range from exploiting the interaction possibilities between visitors and artistic artifacts to proactive 3D installations and augmenting the real world with digital art artifacts. It is interesting that even before the introduction of the term metaverse, artistic experiments with the merging aspects described above were being conducted. This extends to artworks that play with the temporal relationship between the visitor and the artwork. This artistic environment represents a space where things and ideas can simply be tried out without having to fulfill a direct economic or other purpose. It could also be seen as a playground for technical ideas that may flow into serious applications at an unspecified time.

It is not really surprising that in examining the connection between the art world and the metaverse, the current metaverse, much like its predecessor Second Life about 20 years ago, is considered by many exhibitors and museums as a potentially significant place for future presence. However, the development in the context of the metaverse goes significantly beyond what was possible in Second Life. [SECoJ, HUA14] While in Second Life, museums and exhibitions were almost exclusively designed by their real-world counterparts, i.e., the museums in the real world, the metaverse, through its openness and the significantly easier possibilities for designing one's own worlds on numerous platforms, offers anyone interested the chance to design their own virtual museum or virtual exhibition. For this purpose, there are special platforms such as Spatial.io, which pursue exactly this goal [SPAoJ].

3.6.4 The Fusion in Everyday Life: Work Environment

Another fundamental aspect of human everyday life is undoubtedly the work environment. In this area as well, the term metaverse will gain increasing importance in the future. However, it should be emphasized here that the connection between the metaverse and the workplace is already an established and widespread application.

Although the term "metaverse" has not been mentioned too often in this context so far, the associated technologies have been the subject of research and development for use in the work environment for some time. There are numerous examples of the implementation and use of virtual reality for a wide variety of applications, as well as for the use of augmented reality. Furthermore, it has been common practice for many years for production lines and manufacturing halls to have a digital twin. This twin is used to analyze the installation of fixtures and production machines, as well as workflows and potential hazard areas. Due to this fact, this area will not be further elaborated here, but instead, reference is made to the extensive publications by, for example, Bitkom and other industry associations and research institutions.

At this point, it is also deliberately put up for discussion whether the vision of future workplaces, which Mark Zuckerberg so impressively presented during his announcement of the renaming of the Facebook corporation to Meta, is actually realistic. It will only become apparent in future work scenarios whether typical office workplaces, where ERP systems, spreadsheets, or word processing are used, are suitable work environments that can be transferred to the metaverse or at least transformed by AR and VR. This also applies to other workplaces, situations, and industries. Presumably, the aforementioned question also arises for retail or craft businesses such as hairdressers or the electrical trade. Fundamentally, it will depend on how the term metaverse is defined in the future. The support of work through augmented and virtual reality technologies can certainly be successful in the future. However, whether this will actually be the case remains uncertain at the moment, even though numerous research projects in this area are active.

3.6.5 Or the Opposite: The Dissolution of …

If fusion represents such a central element in the establishment of a metaverse, which can be viewed from various perspectives mentioned above, the question arises whether the opposite, i.e., a "dissolution" and thus a targeted separation of certain aspects, is conceivable and in some situations possibly even advantageous.

The first thought that probably plays a role in this context is that the user sends their digital twin into the metaverse with a task to complete independently. A vivid example of this is again the concert situation. The user wants to spontaneously attend a metaverse concert that includes both real and virtual elements but does not yet have a ticket. While they make their way to the real venue in the real world, they instruct their avatar in the virtual space to independently visit the virtual concert location and purchase tickets there. This allows the user to focus on traffic and transportation in the real world without having to worry about buying tickets themselves. Ultimately, this idea is not new but merely an evolution of the already existing assistance solutions in the workplace.

However, this dissolution does not have to be limited to the separation of virtual and real artifacts. Rather, it can be particularly useful in the virtual environment to deliberately introduce the idea of separation. Again, the concert situation can serve as a basis for a vivid example. The concert by Ariana Grande on Fortnite mentioned in Sect. 3.6.3 "Fusion in Everyday Life: Leisure, Culture, Art …" was attended by about 78 million guests according to the organizers. [WIC21, WEB21] Even today's computing power of mainframes does not allow each of these guests to bring their own virtual avatar to such an event, as registration and rendering are highly computationally intensive. The

IT infrastructure would quickly reach its limits here. Additionally, even in the virtual world, each avatar needs a place to stay, just as a human guest in the real world needs a place from which to view the concert. One of the largest concerts in the real world was the Rolling Stones' performance in Rio de Janeiro in 2006 during their "Bigger Bang" world tour. About 1.5 million visitors are said to have gathered at Copacabana for this. [ROH06] They spread out over the approximately 4 km long beach. Assuming that an avatar in the metaverse needs about as much standing space as a human in the real world, one can imagine the dimensions of a concert venue that would accommodate 78 million guests. Therefore, it makes sense, both for reasons of computing capacity and user experience, to separate the event and hold the concert in various parallel sessions. That this works and is accepted by visitors is demonstrated by the concert of the artist Marshmello, which also took place in Fortnite in 2019. Although only 11 million guests attended this concert in the metaverse, computing power and the virtual space situation would certainly have stood in the way of a high-quality concert experience here as well. Fortnite divided this concert into 100,000 instances, each with only about 100 visitors. Users accepted this situation and this dissolution, even though they saw and interacted with only a few of the other guests. However, the concert itself became a pleasant experience for each visitor [WEB19, RUB19].

In addition to the already mentioned technical-practical aspects, there are certainly additional considerations where certain aspects can be viewed separately. In some situations, it might be quite interesting or simply advantageous to perform a temporal dissolution to place the human and the digital twin on separate timelines. On the digital twin's timeline, the sequence of time could then be accelerated or slowed down. Ultimately, such a thought moves in the direction of the previously considered virtual assistance.

References

[ABB23] ABBA (2023). Voyage. Online: https://abbavoyage.com/ (accessed on: 19.05.2023).

[AIR14] Airtimers (03.08.2014). Galaxie Express [2003/04] Space Center Bremen. In: Airtimers. Online: http://forum.airtimers.com/index.php%3F/topic/3807-galaxie-express-200304-space-center-bremen/ (accessed on: 22.05.2023)

[ARSoJ Ars Electronica (o. J.). Ars Electronica. Online: https://ars.electronica.art (accessed on: 10.05.2023).

[ASC12] Ascher, Franziska (27.08.2012). Immersion – Die Faszinationskraft virtueller Welten. In: Paidia Zeitschrift für Computerspielforschung. Online: https://www.paidia.de/immersion (accessed on: 17.05.2023).

[ASW23] Aswad, Jem (02.05.2023). ABBA's 'Voyage' Virtual Concert to Go on Tour 'Around the World'. In: Variety. Online: https://variety.com/2023/music/news/abba-voyage-virtual-concert-tour-1235541368/ (accessed on: 19.05.2023).

[AYR13] Ayres, Anna Jean (2013). Bausteine der kindlichen Entwicklung – Sensorische Integration verstehen und anwenden. Heidelberg: Springer, 5. Auflage.

[AYR79] Ayres, Anna Jean (1979). Sensory Integration and the Child. Los Angeles: Western Psychological Services.

[BAS22] BaselLive (16.05.2022) ARTour – Digitale Kunst in einer neuen Dimension. Online: https://basellive.ch/blog/artour-digitale-kunst-in-einer-neuen-dimension-entdecken/wf6w (accessed on: 10.05.2023).

[BAK21] Baker, Danica (05.04.2021). Ronnie James Dio's hologram for 'Dio Returns' cost $2.6 million. In: Tone Deaf. Online: https://tonedeaf.thebrag.com/widow-reveals-price-of-dio-hologram/ (accessed on: 19.05.2023).

[BAL20] Ball, Matthew (13.01.2020). What It Is, Where to Find it, and Who Will Build It. Online: https://www.matthewball.vc/all/themetaverse (accessed on: 17.05.2023)

[BAL21b] Ball, Matthew (28.06.2021). Evolving User + Business Behaviors and the Metaverse. In: The Metaverse Primer. Online: https://www.matthewball.vc/all/userbehaviors-metaverse (accessed on: 17.05.2023)

[BAL22] Ball, Matthew; Furness, Thomas; Inbar, Ori; Kalinowski, Caitlin; Lange, Danny; Lebaredian, Rev; Mann, Steve; Miralles, Evelyn; Rosedale, Philip; Trevett, Neil; Yuan, Yu (14.06.2022): Metaverse decoded by top experts. In: Versemaker: Metaverse Lands-cape & Outlook Series. Online: https://versemaker.org/download (accessed on: 10.05.2023).

[BBC19] BBC (24.05.2019). Mona Lisa 'brought to life' with deepfake AI. In: BBC Tech. Online: https://www.bbc.com/news/technology-48395521 (accessed on: 10.05.2023).

[BBC22] BBC (12.12.2022). K-pop: The rise of the virtual girl bands. In BBC Asia. Online: https://www.bbc.com/news/world-asia-63827838 (accessed on: 19.05.2023).

[BIT22] bitkom (2022). Wegweiser in das Metaversum – Technologische und rechtliche Grundlagen, geschäftliche Potenziale, gesellschaftliche Bedeutung. In: Bitkom e. V., AG Metaverse Forum, Projektleitung: Dr. Sebastian Klöß. Online: https://www.bitkom.org/Bitkom/Publikationen/Wegweiser-Metaverse (accessed on: 10.05.2023).

[BLA13] Blake Joshua (12.08.2013). Einführung in natürliche Benutzeroberflächen (NUI) und Kinect – Kinect für Windows: Blog für Entwickler. In: Microsoft Shows. Online: https://learn.microsoft.com/de-de/shows/k4wdev/introduction-to-natural-user-interfaces-nui-kinect (accessed on: 21.05.2023).

[BLI19] Blistein, Jon (09.04.2019). Ronnie James Dio Hologram to Tour U.S. In: Rolling Stone. Online: https://www.rollingstone.com/music/music-news/ronnie-james-dio-hologram-us-tour-dates-820040/ (accessed on: 19.05.2023).

[BLU21] Blug, Finn (14.10.2021). Immersion: Eintauchen ins Metaverse. In: ada. Online: https://ada-magazin.com/de/immersion-eintauchen-ins-metaverse (accessed on: 17.05.2023).

[BOL80] Bolt, Richard A. (1980). Put that there: Voice and gesture at the graphics interface. In: SIGGRAPH '80: Proceedings of the 7th annual conference on Computer graphics and interactive techniques; July 1980 Pages 262–270https://doi.org/10.1145/800250.807503)

[BUS23] Buse, Keskin (16.03.2023). Metaverse K-pop girl band MAVE goes viral on social media. In: Reuters, Daily Sabah. Online: https://www.dailysabah.com/life/science/metaverse-k-pop-girl-band-mave-goes-viral-on-social-media (accessed on: 19.05.2023).

[CLI11] Cline, Ernest (2011). Ready Player One. Blanvalet Verlag, München 2014, ISBN 978-3-442-38030-5.

[CLI20] Cliff, Aimee (12.01.2020). Hatsune Miku review – hologram star fires up crowd-sourced power pop. In: The Guardian. Online: https://www.theguardian.com/music/2020/jan/12/hatsune-miku-review-london-02-academy-brixton-london (accessed on: 19.05.2023).

[COAoJ] Coastiality (o.J.). Coastiality – Entdecke neue unglaubliche Welten. Online: https://coastiality.com/ (accessed on: 19.05.2023).

[DAI21] Daily Local (04.08.2021). Ariana Grande to earn more than ‚$20m“ for virtual Fortnite concert. In: Daily Local News. Online: https://www.dailylocal.com/2021/08/04/ariana-grande-to-earn-more-than-20m-for-virtual-fortnite-concert/ (accessed on: 19.05.2023).

[DAN21] Danneberg, Benjamin (19.09.2021). Feelbelt im Test: Zwischen Sound-Wucht und Haptikbrei. In: Mixed. Online: https://mixed.de/feelbelt-test/ (accessed on: 20.05.2021).

[DER19] Dernbach, Beatrice; Godulla, Alexander; Sehl, Annika (08.01.2019). Komplexität im Journalismus. Springer Fachmedien Wiesbaden GmbH, ein Teil von Springer Nature. https://doi.org/10.1007/978-3-658-22860-6_8.

[DEC23] Decentraland (27.02.203). Tradition and Innovation Collide: Decentraland Metaverse Fashion Week 2023. In: Announcements. Online: https://decentraland.org/blog/announcements/tradition-and-innovation-collide-decentraland-metaverse-fashion-week-2023 (accessed on: 17.05.2023).

[DIE86] Dietrich, Frank (1986). Visual Intelligence: The First Decade of Computer Art (1965–1975). In: Leonardo, vol. 19, no. 2, 1986, pp. 159–69. JSTOR, https://doi.org/10.2307/1578284. (accessed on: 19.05.2023).

[DOB17] Dobbelstein, David; Winkler, Christian; Haas, Gabriel; Rukzio, Enrico. (2017). PocketThumb: a Wearable Dual-Sided Touch Interface for Cursor-based Control of Smart-Eyewear. Proceedings of the ACM on Interactive, Mobile, Wearable and Ubiquitous Technologies. 1. 1–17. https://doi.org/10.1145/3090055. Online: https://www.researchgate.net/publication/318071779_PocketThumb_a_Wearable_Dual-Sided_Touch_Interface_for_Cursor-based_Control_of_Smart-Eyewear (accessed on: 17.05.2023).

[DON17] Donahue, Michelle Z. (09.11.2017). Ein farbenblinder Künstler wurde zum ersten Cyborg der Welt. In: National Geographic. Online: https://www.nationalgeographic.de/wissenschaft/2017/04/ein-farbenblinder-kuenstler-wurde-zum-ersten-cyborg-der-welt (accessed on: 21.05.2023).

[DÖR10] Döring, Nicola (2010). Sozialkontakte online: Identitäten, Beziehungen, Gemeinschaften. Handbuch online-kommunikation 1 (2010): 159-183.

[DOU01] Dourish, P. (2001). Where The Action Is: The Foundations of Embodied Interaction. MIT Press, Cambridge, MA, USA

[DRA22] Draht, Moritz (24.11.2022). “Danke für den guten Deal” Bored Ape für fast eine Million US-Dollar verkauft. In: BTC-Echo. Online: https://www.btc-echo.de/schlagzeilen/nft-dauerbrenner-bored-ape-fuer-fast-eine-million-dollar-verkauft-155084/ (accessed on: 17.05.2023).

[ENG65] Engelbart, Douglas C.; English, W. K.; Huddart. B. (1965). Computer-aided display control Final report. In: NASA Technical Documents, 1965.

[FEE14] Feeney, Nolan (19.05.2014). Watch a Michael Jackson Hologram Moonwalk at the Billboard Music Awards. In: Time. Online: https://time.com/104725/michael-jackson-hologram-billboard/ (accessed on: 19.05.2023).

[FORoJ] Forum OÖ Geschichte (o. J.). Ars Electronica Festival. Online: https://www.ooegeschichte.at/archiv/themen/kunst-und-kultur/musikgeschichte-oberoesterreichs/musikforschung-und-musikpflege/ars-electronica-festival (accessed on: 10.05.2023).

[FRA01] Franke, Herbert W. (2001). Wege zur Computerkunst – ein Rückblick In: Murnau Manila Minsk – 50 Jahre Goethe-Institut. 2001, ISBN 3-406-47542-6.

[FRI09] Frieling, J. (2009). Zielgruppe Digital Natives: Wie das Internet die Lebensweise von Jugendlichen ver „ndert: Neue Herausforderungen an die Medienbranche. Diplomica Verlag.

[GIB84] Gibson, William (1984). Neuromancer. Ace.

[GER22] Gerber, Lothar (15.11.2022). Das Ozzfest im Metaverse: was für ein überflüssiges Event. In: Metal-Hammer. Online: https://www.metal-hammer.de/das-ozzfest-im-metaverse-was-fuer-ein-ueberfluessiges-event-1992083/ (accessed on: 19.05.2023).

[HAC21] Hackl, Cathy (27.10.2021). The metaverse is coming. Cathy Hackl explains why we should care. In: Freethink. Online: https://www.freethink.com/hard-tech/building-the-metaverse-cathy-hackl-gives-us-a-glimpse-of-the-future (accessed on: 21.05.2023).

[HEN22] Henz, Patrick (2022). The societal impact of the metaverse. In: Discov Artif Intell 2, 19. https://doi.org/10.1007/s44163-022-00032-6 (accessed on: 19.05.2023).

[HOF10] Hoffmann, Peter (01.12.2010). „Narrative Realitäten": Informationspräsentation über multimediales, programmiertes Geschichtenerzählen. In: Berichte aus der Informatik. Shaker, Düren.

[HOF21] Hoffmann, Peter (04.12.2021). Beyond Hypermedia – Interaktion in Hypermedia neu gedacht. bifop-Verlag, Bremen. ISBN: 978-3-948773-27-4.

[HOF22] Hoffmann, Peter (16.11.2022). Lemmy würde …! Virtual Headbanging beim #DLM-VMF Ozzfest. In 1E9, Community #Metaverse. Online: https://1e9.community/t/lemmy-wuerde-virtual-headbanging-beim-dlmvmf-ozzfest/18268 (accessed on: 19.05.2023).

[HUA14] Huang, Yu-Chun; Han, Sooyeon (2014). An Immersive Virtual Reality Museum via Second Life Extending Art Appreciation from 2D to 3D. Communications in Computer and Information Science. 434. https://doi.org/10.1007/978-3-319-07857-1_102.

[HUG23] Hughes, Rebecca Ann (15.02.2023). Do You Have To Pay To Visit Venice? Here's What To Know About The Entry Fee. In: Forbes. Online: https://www.forbes.com/sites/rebeccahughes/2023/02/15/do-you-have-to-pay-to-visit-venice-heres-what-to-know-about-the-entry-fee/ (accessed on: 10.05.2023).

[JAC08] Jacob, Robert; Girouard, Audrey; Hirshfield, Leanne; Horn, Michael; Shaer, Orit; Solovey, Erin; Zigelbaum, Jamie (2008). Reality-based interaction: A framework for post-WIMP interfaces. CHI '08: Proceeding of the Twenty-Sixth Annual SIGCHI Conference on Human Factors in Computing Systems, Florence, Italy, 5–10 April 2008, ACM, New York, NY, pp 201–210.

[JAI11] Jain, Jhilmil; Lund. Arnold; Wixon, Dennis (07.05.2011). The future of natural user interfaces. In: CHI EA '11: CHI '11 Extended Abstracts on Human Factors in Computing Systems May 2011 Pages 211–214https://doi.org/10.1145/1979742.1979527.

[JIA22] Jiaxin, Li; Gongjing, Gao (2022). Socializing in the Metaverse: The Innovation and Challenge of Interpersonal Communication. In: Advances in Social Science, Education and Humanities Research, volume 664. Proceedings of the 2022 8th International Conference on Humanities and Social Science Research (ICHSSR 2022)

[KRE13] Kress, Bernard; Starner, Thad (2013). A review of head-mounted displays (HMD) technologies and applications for consumer electronics. In: Proceedings of SPIE – The International Society for Optical Engineering. 8720. 87200A. https://doi.org/10.1117/12.2015654.

[KER21] Kerris, Richard (Juni 2021). The Metaverse Begins: NVIDIA Omniverse and a Future of Shared Worlds. Von: Nvidia. Online: https://www.nvidia.com/en-us/on-demand/session/computex2021-com2104/ (accessed on: 17.05.2023).

[LAM21] Lam, Kit Yung; Lee, Lik Han; Hui, Pan (21). A2w: Context-awarerecommendation system for mobile augmented reality web browser. InACM International Conference on Multimedia, United States, October2021. Association for Computing Machinery (ACM)

[LAN09] Lantz, Frank. (2009). PacManhattan. https://doi.org/10.1007/978-3-7643-8415-9_94.

[LAN18] Lanette, Simone; Chua, Phoebe K.; Hayes, Gillian; Mazmanian, Melissa (2018). How much is 'too much'? the role of a smartphone addictionnarrative in individuals' experience of use. Proc. ACM Hum.-Comput. Interact., 2(CSCW), November 2018.

[LANoJ] Lantz, Frank (o.J.). Pacmanhattan. In: New York University NYU ITP/IMA. Online: https://www.pacmanhattan.com/about.php (accessed on: 22.05.2023)

[LEE20a] Lee, Lik-Hang; Braud, Tristan; Hosio, S.; Hui, Pan (2020). Towards augmented reality-driven human-city interaction: Current research and futurechallenges. ArXiv, abs/2007.09207, 2020.

[LEE20b] Lee, Shaun; Teh, Pei-Lee (2020). "Suiting Up" to Enhance Empathy Toward Aging: A Randomized Controlled Study. Frontiers in Public Health. 8. 376. https://doi.org/10.3389/fpubh.2020.00376.

[LEWoJ] Lewis, Irene (o.J.). Augmented Reality in the Furniture Industry: 5 Benefits of Using AR for Shopping Apps. In: CGIFURNITURE. Online: https://cgifurniture.com/augmented-reality-in-furniture-industry/ (accessed on: 10.05.2023).

[LIU23] Liu, Yiming; Yiu, Chun, Zhao, Zhao; Park, Wooyoung; Shi, Rui; Huang, Xingcan; Zeng, Yuyang; Wang, Kuan; Wong, Tsz; Jia, Shengxin; Zhou, Jingkun; Gao, Zhan; Zhao, Ling; Yao, Kuanming; Li, Jian; Sha, Chuanlu; Gao, Yuyu; Zhao, Guangyao; Huang, Ya; Yu, Xinge (2023). Soft, miniaturized, wireless olfactory interface for virtual reality. Nature Communications. 14. https://doi.org/10.1038/s41467-023-37678-4.

[MAN13] Mann, Steve (01.03.2013). My „Augmediated“: Life What I've learned from 35 years of wearing computerized eyewear. In: IEEE Spectrum. Online: https://spectrum.ieee.org/view-from-the-valley/consumer-electronics/portable-devices/steve-mann-the-man-who-invented-wearable-computing (accessed on: 21.05.2023).

[MAN91] Mann, Steve; Wyckoff, Charles (1991). Extended Reality, MIT 4–405, 1991, Online: http://wearcam.org/xr.htm (accessed on: 17.05.2023).

[MAR15] Marshall, Cain (10.092015). Pokémon go is brought up into the real world through iOS and Android. In: GeekSnack. Online: https://web.archive.org/web/20150912184201/http://www.geeksnack.com/2015/09/10/pokemon-go-is-brought-up-into-the-real-world-through-ios-and-android/ (accessed on: 21.05.2023).

[MAR20] Martens, Todd (13.05.2020). Epic's Tim Sweeney reveals a more connected, 'Fortnite'-driven, game-unified world. In: Los Angeles Times, Entertainment & Arts. Online: https://www.latimes.com/entertainment-arts/story/2020-05-13/epic-games-outlines-a-fortnite-driven-more-connected-future (accessed on: 10.05.2023).

[MCL64] McLuhan, Marshall (1964). Understanding Media: The Extensions of Man. McGraw-Hill, New York.

[MEI21] MeinMMO (07.08.2021). Fortnite: So lief das Ariana Grande Konzert ab – Lasst es euch nicht entgehen. In:. MeinMMO. Online: https://mein-mmo.de/fortnite-so-lief-das-ariana-grande-konzert-ab-lasst-es-euch-nicht-entgehen/ (accessed on: 19.05.2023).

[METoJa] Metamandrill (o. J.). Metaverse Werbung; Arten von Metaverse Marketing & Beispiele. In: metamandrill metaverse information. Online: https://metamandrill.com/de/metaverse-werbung-2/ (accessed on: 17.05.2023).

[METoJb] Metamandrill (o. J.). AR-Marketing; Top-Beispiele für Augmented-Reality-Marketing. In: metamandrill metaverse information. Online: https://metamandrill.com/de/ar-marketing/#great-examples-of-ar-marketing (accessed on: 17.05.2023).

[MOR01] Morawe, Volker; Reiff, Tilman (2001). Painstation. In: Kunsthochschule für Medien zu Köln. Online (Memento des Originals vom 28. September 2007 im Internet Archive): https://web.archive.org/web/20070928103548/http://www.khm.de/~morawe/painstation/PainStation_ger.pdf (accessed on: 20.05.2021).

[MIN13] Minsky, Marvin; Kurzweil, Ray; Mann, Steve (2013). „The society of intelligent veillance." 2013 IEEE International Symposium on Technology and Society (ISTAS): Social Implications of Wearable Computing and Augmediated Reality in Everyday Life. IEEE, 2013.

[MUR22] Murray, Sean (28.01.2022). South Korea Is Planning A 'K-Pop Metaverse' With Full Government Support. In: The Gamer. Online: https://www.thegamer.com/south-korea-k-pop-metaverse/ (accessed on: 19.05.2023).

[NET18] netzreich GmbH (16.04.2018): Augmented Bier – Die neue Version ist online. Online: https://www.youtube.com/watch%3Fv%3DEpPaQ9Qfci4 (accessed on: 10.05.2023).

[NEXoJ] Next Meet (o. J.). Will Metaverse Change How People Interact With The World I Metaverse The Technology Of Future. Online: https://nextmeet.live/people-interacting-in-metaverse-metaverse-the-technology-of-future/ (accessed on: 17.05.2023).

[NOR02] Norman, Donald A. (2002). The Design Of Everyday Things. Basic Books (Perseus).

[NOO22] Noor, Jasmine; Putri, Andhreta (04.03.2022). A World Beyond: Metaverse and the K-pop Industry. In: Center for Digital Society. Online: https://cfds.fisipol.ugm.ac.id/2022/03/04/a-world-beyond-metaverse-and-the-k-pop-industry/ (accessed on: 19.05.2023).

[PIE02] Piekarski, Wayne & Thomas, Bruce. (2002). ARQuake: The Outdoor Augmented Reality Gaming System. Commun. ACM. 45. 36–38. https://doi.org/10.1145/502269.502291.

[PIEoJ] Piekarski, Wayne (o. J.). The Wearable Computer Lab at the School of Computer and Information Science, University of South Australia. In: tinmith. Online: https://www.tinmith.net/arquake/ (accessed on: 22.05.2023)

[PLOoJ] Ploog, Keno (o. J.). Die Entwicklung von VR in Freizeitparks. In: Coasterfriends. Online: https://coasterfriends.de/joomla/magazin/15-sonstige/2934-die-entwicklung-von-vr-in-freizeitparks (accessed on: 19.05.2023).

[REH21] Rehagen, Tony (05.05.2021). One of Japan's most beloved pop stars is a hologram. In: experience magazine. Online: https://expmag.com/2021/05/one-of-japans-most-beloved-pop-stars-is-a-hologram/ (accessed on: 19.05.2023).

[REI15] Reilly, Luke (10.09.2015). Pokémon GO Coming to Smartphones - Pokémon goes mobile. IGN Entertainment. Online: https://www.ign.com/articles/2015/09/10/pokemon-go-coming-to-smartphones (accessed on: 20.11.2023).

[ROH06] Rohter, Larry (19.02.2006). The Stones Rock 1.5 Million in Rio Days Before Carnival. In: The New York Times. Online: https://www.nytimes.com/2006/02/19/world/americas/the-stones-rock-15-million-in-rio-days-before-carnival.html (accessed on: 10.05.2023).

[RUB19] Rubin, Peter (05.02.2019). Fortnite's Marshmello Concert Is the Future of the Metaverse. In: Wired. Online: https://www.wired.com/story/fortnite-marshmello-concert-vr-ar-multiverse/ (accessed on: 10.05.2023).

[SCH23a] Schlott, Karin (10.05.2023). Wenn die Computerblume duftet. In: Spektrum.de. Online: https://www.spektrum.de/news/virtuelle-realitaet-wenn-die-computerblume-duftet/2137641 (accessed on: 17.05.2023).

[SECoJ] Second Life (o. J.). Museen. In: Second Life. Online: https://secondlife.com/destinations/learning/museums (accessed on: 10.05.2023).

[SER18] Seraphin, Hugues; Sheeran, Paul; Pilato, Manuela. (2018). Over-tourism and the fall of Venice as a destination. Journal of Destination Marketing & Management. 9. https://doi.org/10.1016/j.jdmm.2018.01.011 (accessed on: 10.05.2023).

[SIR22] Sirisha (29.07.2022). You Can Be Monalisa in Seconds, Thanks to this Deepfake Tech. In: Analytics Insight. Online: https://www.analyticsinsight.net/you-can-be-monalisa-in-seconds-thanks-to-this-deepfake-tech/ (accessed on: 10.05.2023).

[SPAoJ] Spatial.io (o. J.). Unlock Your Imagination. Online: https://www.spatial.io/ (accessed on: 10.05.2023).

[SPI02] Spielberg, Steven (Regie) (2002). Minority Report. 20th Century Fox.

[SPI18] Spielberg, Steven (Regie) (2018). Ready Player One. Warner Bros. Pictures.

[STA23] Staista ()2023). Hours of video uploaded to YouTube every minute as of February 2022. In: Statista. Online: https://www.statista.com/statistics/259477/hours-of-video-uploaded-to-youtube-every-minute/ (accessed on: 21.05.2023).

[STE92] Stephenson, Neal (1992). Snow Crash. Blanvalet, München 1995. ISBN 978-3-442-23686-2, Kap. 37. Englisches Original: Snow Crash. New York, 1992.

[STEoJ] Stern, Bradley (o. J.). aespa Is Leading Us Into the Metaverse. Get in loser, we're going to the SMCU. In: MuuMuse. Online: https://muumuse.com/2021/11/aespa-metaverse-sm-entertainment.html/ (accessed on: 19.05.2023).

[STO22] Stoyanov, Nadine; Moser, Christian; Kwiatkowski, Marta (2022). Extended Retail – Die Zukunft des Handels ist grenzenlos. Zühlke und GDI/Studie zu «Extended Retail». Von: – Zühlke Engineering AG. Online: https://www.zuehlke.com/de/extended-retail-die-zukunft-des-handels-ist-grenzenlos (accessed on: 17.05.2023).

[TAU16] Tauziet,Christophe (15.12.2016). Designing for Hands in VR – The next step in buil-ding natural human-machine interactions. In: Design at Meta, Medium. Online: https://medium.com/designatmeta/designing-for-hands-in-vr-61e6815add99 (accessed on: 17.05.2023).

[THEoJ] The Fabricant x DapperLabs (o. J.): Iridescence. Online: https://www.thefabricant.com/iridescence (accessed on: 10.05.2023).

[THO06] Thon, Jan-Noël (2006). Immersion revisited. Varianten von Immersion im Computerspiel des 21. Jahrhunderts. In: Christian Hißnauer/Andreas Jahn-Sudmann (Hg.): Medien – Zeit – Zeichen. Beiträge des 19. Film- und Fernsehwissenschaftlichen Kolloquiums. Marburg: Schüren 2006. S. 125–132. Online: https://www.academia.edu/3414149/Immersion_revisited_Varianten_von_Immersion_im_Computerspiel_des_21_Jahrhunderts (accessed on: 17.05.2023)

[WEB19] Webster, Andrew (21.02.2019). Fortnite's Marshmello concert was the game's biggest event ever. In: The Verge. Online: https://www.theverge.com/2019/2/21/18234980/fortnite-marshmello-concert-viewer-numbers

[WEB21] Webster, Andrew (09.08.2021). Ariana Grande's Fortnite tour was a moment years in the making. In: The Verge. Online: https://www.theverge.com/2021/8/9/22616664/ariana-grande-fortnite-rift-tour-worldbuilding-storytelling (accessed on: 10.05.2023).

[WEB22] Weber, Urs (11.10.2022). ARTour – Kunstspaziergang durch Basel mit Augmented Reality. In: Tourismuspresse, Schweiz Tourismus. https://www.tourismuspresse.at/presseaussendung/TPT_20221011_TPT0004/artour-kunstspaziergang-durch-basel-mit-augmented-reality-bild (accessed on: 10.05.2023).

[WEH20] Wehden, Lars-Ole; Reer, Felix; Janzik, Robin; Tang, Wai Yen; Quandt, Thorsten (17.04.2020). The Slippery Path to Total Presence: How Omnidirectional Virtual Reality Treadmills Influence the Gaming Experience. In: Media and Communication (ISSN: 2183–2439) 2021, Volume 9, Issue 1, Pages 5–16. https://doi.org/10.17645/mac.v9i1.3170.

[WEI22] Wei, Hongtao; Tang, Lei; Wang, Wenshuo; Zhang, Jiaming (26.05.2022). Home Environment Augmented Reality System Based on 3D Reconstruction of a Single Furniture Picture. In: Sensors 2022, 22(11), 4020; https://doi.org/10.3390/s22114020.

[WIC21] Wickes, Jade (09.08.2021). Inside Ariana Grande's Fortnite virtual concert. In: The Face. Online: https://theface.com/music/ariana-grande-fortnite-rift-tour-performance-gaming-vr-mac-miller-travis-scott-lil-nas-x (accessed on: 10.05.2023).

[VIB23] Vibe (05.05.2023). Michael Jackson Most Requested Artist for a Hologram Concert in Canada. In: Vibe. Online: https://www.mjvibe.com/michael-jackson-most-requested-artist-for-a-hologram-concert-in-canada/ (accessed on: 19.05.2023).

[YOU23] Young, Jin Yu; Stevens, Matt (29.01.2023). Will the Metaverse Be Entertaining? Ask South Korea. In: The New York Times. Online: https://www.nytimes.com/2023/01/29/business/metaverse-k-pop-south-korea.html (accessed on: 19.05.2023).

[ZHA19] Zhang, Yan; Kienzle, Wolf; Ma, Yanjun; Ng, Shiu S.; Benko, Hrvoje; Harrison, Chris (2019). ActiTouch: Robust Touch Detection for On-Skin AR/VR Interfaces. In: UIST '19: Proceedings of the 32nd Annual ACM Symposium on User Interface Software and Technology, October 2019, Pages 1151–1159 https://doi.org/10.1145/3332165.3347869

[ZIE05] Ziegler, Jürgen; Lohmann, Steffen; Kaltz, J. Wolfgang (2005). Kontextmodellierung für adaptive webbasierte Systeme. In: C. Stary (Hrsg.): Mensch & Computer 2005: Kunst und Wissenschaft – Grenzüberschreitungen der interaktiven ART. München: Oldenbourg Verlag. 2005, S. 181–189

4 Another Dimension: Economic Merging

If the metaverse is considered an evolution of the internet, its development technically dates back to 1968 when the ARPANET was created. However, the theory underlying the internet, and especially today's World Wide Web, has its roots much earlier. [REDoJ] As early as 1948, Vannevar Bush introduced the theoretical idea of a networked information management and research system in his article "As We May Think" in The Atlantic magazine. [BUS45] At that time, his considerations were still based on static documents that existed in two-dimensional form as text and images. However, Bush already saw the necessity of not only storing the documents themselves but also the work on them for future research purposes. The user interface he outlined would still correspond to current systems today, although the Memory Expander alias "Memex" could not be technically implemented at that time. Nevertheless, the theoretical idea was revolutionary at that time.

It is unproven whether or to what extent Vannevar Bush's Memex was considered in the conception of the ARPA network. However, the goal and content of the ARPA network corresponded quite well to the Memex concept, as it aimed to create a decentralized network for communication and data exchange between U.S. universities and research institutions. The first email was also sent over the ARPA network in 1972, and it slowly developed into a precursor of today's internet. Although only 400 computers were connected to the network in 1983, the number increased significantly afterward until the internet was released for commercial use in 1989/1990. [HRZoJ]

Around the same time, Tim Berners-Lee began his hypertext project at CERN in Zurich (Switzerland), which was eventually published as the WWW in 1991 and from which today's World Wide Web developed. It thus forms both the theoretical and technical foundation for the future metaverse. Interestingly, the development of the WWW parallels the current discussion about the metaverse. [BER89] While tech-savvy nerds support and advance the idea, others dismiss it as a useless hype that will not last. In

P. Hoffmann, *Next Generation Internet*, https://doi.org/10.1007/978-3-658-46424-0_4

the case of the WWW, there were voices like those of Bill Gates and Ron Sommer who believed that the internet and the WWW were merely a passing trend that would not play a role for their companies. Such voices can also be found in the current discussion about the metaverse.

In the early days of the World Wide Web, the content focus was on documents and information. The idealistic notion that the web would facilitate access to information and thus improve access to education and political information to strengthen democratic structures was established. (see also Fig. 4.1) However, it was soon recognized that the web also offered economic potential. The possibility of consumption was integrated into the web, and paper catalogs were transferred into electronic form. Although a media break initially had to be overcome for ordering, and the order-relevant information had to be sent either by phone, fax, or email, this did not stand in the way of the rapid establishment of the economic use of the web. The situation at that time, in which all information and thus also the catalog contents were freely accessible and retrievable, laid the foundation for the development and success of the web.

With the beginning of the 2000s, a significant change in the web compared to the earlier version took place. Thanks to new technologies, programming languages, and concepts, the originally static web could be further developed into an interactive medium under the label Web 2.0. A central role was played by the development of wikis. Although users could already save contributions in forums in the early web, applications like wikis significantly expanded the interaction possibilities of users with the web's content. In Web 2.0, users could now directly work with the content, for example, by changing texts in a wiki or uploading their own content to make it available to other users. The static web, which only served to consume content or process orders, transformed into an interactive web in which every user could participate directly. The economic potential of this participation was also quickly recognized, and attempts began to monetize the content. However, this was difficult due to the technology, as digital artifacts and information as content of Web 2.0 could not really be protected, and users had become

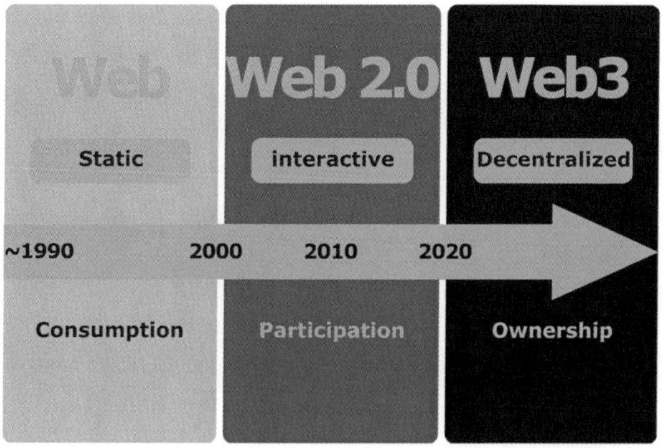

Fig. 4.1 Web 1–2–3. (According to [SCHm21a])

accustomed to accessing content on the web for free. This "free mentality" is still deeply ingrained in users' minds, and it remains extremely difficult to get them to pay for content even in Web 2.0. This aspect will be repeatedly addressed in the following sections.

The original idealistic goals of the early internet have obviously not been fully realized. The freedom of access to any information is now restricted and controlled from many sides. Furthermore, the underlying technology is a point of criticism and also a security risk for certain users, as it is often difficult or even impossible to operate on the internet without disclosing personal data. Additionally, it is gradually being recognized that not every content can be free. The production of media and high-quality journalistic content requires payment for the effort and work involved. For this reason, since the beginning of the 2020s, work has been underway on developing a decentralized internet based on the idea of ownership, which is intended to replace the interactive Web 2.0. This development is accompanied by new technological approaches such as blockchain, smart contracts, and NFTs and is intended to form the foundation for the metaverse.

In the metaverse, a significant part revolves around the ownership and trade of virtual goods and artifacts. Therefore, it is important that the concept of copyright and intellectual property is established in the virtual space to enable ownership and property. [BIT22] This contrasts with the usual understanding that digital artifacts can be infinitely duplicated, as enabled by typical copy & paste. Blockchain and NFT now at least offer approaches to assign a unique owner to digital items. This is particularly essential in the field of cryptocurrencies, as the simple copying of payment units would be economically fatal. The same applies to digital artifacts such as virtual artworks. Without economic security, the metaverse cannot develop into an independent economic system.

According to Chris Dickson of Andreesen Horowitz, it is essential that the metaverse develops into a full-fledged economic system that corresponds to our physical life. [SCHm21a] In this context, users should have the opportunity to create, acquire, own, sell, or otherwise manage digital artifacts. The example of Second Life shows that paid work is also possible in such a context. [SEC19, LAY07] Therefore, it is absolutely necessary that applications in a metaverse or in various parallel metaverses exhibit the highest interoperability, including interoperability between technical platforms, commercial applications, and the digital and real world [BAL20].

4.1 The Analog Economy of the "Classic Value Chain"

If the metaverse is considered an economic system that connects the real and digital economies, the value chain must be adapted to the new environment. An independent economy has already developed on the internet, which has evolved into a platform economy, particularly through the widespread use of social media and platforms. If this is also to play an important role in the metaverse, individual transactions and business models must be able to merge across the boundary between the real and virtual worlds. The German industry association Bitkom emphasizes in its "Guide to the Metaverse" that the role of market participants will change to the point where separate roles can be taken over by a single company or a single person. [BIT22]

To better understand these changes within the value chain in the metaverse, the following sections will first adopt a highly simplified view of this value chain, as shown in Fig. 4.2, and then compare and expand it with existing theories and models of business and economics. The goal is to at least obtain a basic understanding of the new value chain in the metaverse. The simplification consists of reducing the value chain to three participants:

- the producer, who offers a product or service,
- the consumer, who wants to consume the product or service, and
- the distributor as an intermediary.

Although the roles and tasks of the producer and consumer will also change, the role of the distributor and its tasks will undergo a much stronger transformation and gain central importance.

In the value chain considered here, reduced to the essentials, the situation of the classic economy is depicted.

- The role of the producer is, as already indicated, clearly defined in its goals: The producer wants to market a product and offer it to the consumer. Despite the strong simplification in this representation, the producer's tasks are extensive. They include both the planning of production and the procurement of raw materials, operating resources, and especially production means. The automotive industry can serve as an example here, where the producer designs a car and sets up and operates the production lines for assembly.
- In this still classic view of the value chain, the distributor takes on the tasks of transport and sales. Here, sales are of particular importance, as it establishes communicative contact with the consumer.
- Although the value chain presented would not exist without the consumer, their functional role in this context is the least pronounced. It merely consists of purchasing and utilizing the offer provided by the producer.

A closer look at the communication flow reveals both an advantage and a disadvantage of this simplified chain. The advantage is undoubtedly that the producer can focus on their core competencies and leave all activities that can be broadly assigned to

Fig. 4.2 Simplified value chain. (Own illustration: Peter Hoffmann, Invisible Cow)

distribution to the distributor. However, this handover also immediately results in the disadvantage that there is no direct connection between the consumer and the producer. This means that information about the consumer's expectations, wishes, and behavior either does not reach the producer or only does so if the distributor, in addition to their actual activities, establishes a communication feedback channel between the consumer and the producer. Through this additional task, the distributor becomes an infomediary, communicating both towards the consumer and the producer.

For the real world with exclusively physical products and services that revolve around these physical products, this view is sufficient. The roles presented in this context remain within their clearly defined areas of responsibility and rarely cross these boundaries.

4.2 First Thoughts on Merging: Prosumerism

The reduced value chain of the classic economy introduced in the previous section 4.1 "The Analog Economy of the 'Classic Value Chain'" established itself on the basis of limited communication and the lack of industrial mass production over a long period. Only with the introduction of automated manufacturing methods and a significant increase in the number of units produced could consumers choose from a growing number of producers and their products. At the latest by this time, it became increasingly important for manufacturers to establish a communication feedback channel to the customer. The simple statement by Henry Ford in 1909 regarding his Model T [CRO22]

> "You can have it in any color you want as long as it's black"

was no longer sufficient for successful market activity. Instead, it became increasingly important for producers to understand the needs and expectations of consumers. During the early days of industrial mass production, this feedback channel was still very weak, but with the introduction of electrical and later digital communication means, consumers and producers came communicatively closer together. As a result, the role of the distributor also began to change, as its significance as an infomediary or communication channel between consumers and producers significantly decreased. New, especially digital communication channels enabled almost direct communication between customers and manufacturers (see Fig. 4.3), making the information transfer via the distributor just one of many possible channels.

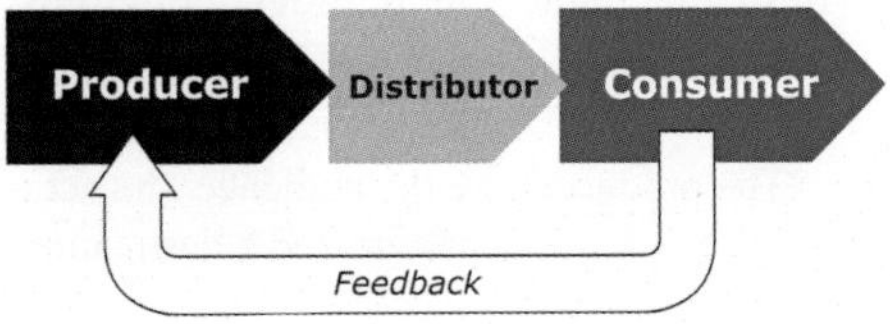

Fig. 4.3 Feedback as an extension of the simplified value chain: prosumption. (Own representation: Peter Hoffmann, Invisible Cow)

The American futurist Alvin Toffler was one of the first to recognize the importance of these developments in economic systems and attributed great potential to them for the future. In his 1980 book "The Third Wave" [TOF80], he predicted the phenomenon known today as Industry 4.0 [PLAoJ]: a continuous, highly communicative networking between consumers, producers, and production machines. These rather technical predictions formed the basis for his work "Power Shift," in which he described in 1991 that the established separation into the aforementioned roles would dissolve due to the close communicative connection between the participants in the value chain: [TOF90]

> "Producer and consumer, separated by the industrial revolution, are reunited in the cycle of wealth creation, with the customer contributing not only money but also market and design information that is crucial for the production process. Buyer and supplier share data, information, and knowledge. One day, customers may also press buttons that activate remote production processes. Consumer and producer merge into a 'prosumer'."

This last aspect, in particular, has been confirmed with the spread of Web 2.0 and the newly emerged possibilities within the framework of Industry 4.0. This development began in the automotive industry, where car manufacturers used the web to give consumers the option to configure the desired model according to their preferences. Initially, consumers had only a few configuration options such as paint, interior color, or rough choices like the engine type. But over time, the level of detail in the configurators increased more and more. Today, it is not only conceivable but also technically possible for all possible characteristics of the future car to be entered by the customer via a web portal or configurator. This information flows directly into production and to the production machines. It is then predicted when the desired vehicle will be finished and ready for the customer to pick up. By pressing the confirmation button, as Toffler predicted, production is then started.

This is not only possible for high-priced and large products like cars. Everyday goods can also be produced and purchased within the framework of this prosumption. An early example of this was presented by Adidas in 2015, which introduced the first web-based configurator for sneakers. This allowed prosumers to design sneakers themselves, have them produced, and then purchase them. [VET15]

From an unbiased external perspective, it indeed appears as if the consumer is taking production into their own hands. However, the original separation, as outlined in the previous Sect. 4.1 in connection with the reduced value chain, still exists. The means of production remain in the hands of the producer, and the consumer's influence on the production machines is only given to the extent that the producer actually allows. Nevertheless, consumer and producer come so close together that a new, albeit abstract, role within the value chain indeed emerges, namely the so-called prosumer. Kevin Kelly described this situation very impressively in Wired magazine in 2005: [KEL05]

> "The producers are the audience, the act of making is the act of watching, and every link is both a point of departure and a destination."

In this scenario, the importance of the distributor may initially seem less relevant and insignificant. When looking solely at the role of the infomediary, this may be true. Nevertheless, this situation also opens up new opportunities for the distributor, as it gives them the chance to take the first step towards a new role, namely that of a platform economist.

To achieve the close communicative bond between consumers and producers for realizing the new abstract role of the prosumer, powerful communication channels are required. The effort to provide such communication channels should not be underestimated, both in terms of hardware infrastructure and software implementation. This effort is usually not borne by the producers, as they generally do not have the necessary competencies to set up and operate such communication channels or platforms. This is where the distributor comes back into play, who can take on the role of the platform operator and offer the channels and tools for communication between consumer and producer.

Technical as well as economic visionaries have recognized for some time now, through ongoing technological developments, the possibility of further advancing Toffler's idea of uniting consumers and producers in the new role of the prosumer. The potentials that 3D printing holds, which is now firmly anchored in industrial manufacturing and increasingly detaching from the industrial context to gain a foothold in the consumer market, seem to actually enable this merging into the prosumer. The consumer can, with the help of 3D printing, advance to become their own producer of physical goods.

4.3 The Merging in the Web Economy: Produsage

When the reality-virtuality continuum is applied not only to digital artifacts but also to the economic environment, the concept of prosumption examined in the previous section 4.2 can be located on the side of 100% reality, as the production of physical products is the goal here. In contrast, on the side of 100% virtuality would be an economy that includes only virtual products and services. In this case, the previously used reduced value chain presents itself completely differently. This can be attributed to the fundamental characteristics of digital objects, which, unlike physical objects, do not need to be individually manufactured with specially designed production machines. Instead, they can simply be copied, with the original and the copy being completely identical. This alone does not yet enable a change in the value chain, because even in the digital world, the targeted development or production of digital goods is required, although this, of course, looks different from the development and production of physical goods.

Through the implementation of Web 2.0 technologies and the associated possibility for users to contribute their own content to the web in the sense of user-generated content, an option for transforming roles and their characteristics along the value chain opens up. The Australian media scholar Axel Bruns outlined the potential for change in 2008 when researching Web 2.0 technologies and their manifestations, for example in blogs, wikis, and the forerunner of the metaverse, Second Life. (see Fig. 4.4) Bruns coined the term "produsage" to describe a then still novel form of collaborative creation and use of content on the internet. Analogous to Toffler, who merged the terms producer and consumer into the new buzzword prosumer, Bruns uses the terms producer and user. He creates the "produser" as a new role in which both aspects merge. [BRU07]

Produsage thus refers to a type of value creation that was only made possible by the widespread dissemination of the internet. More precisely, it is not solely the introduction of the classic internet but especially that of Web 2.0 that is relevant here. For produsage stands for a form of value creation and collaboration in which users, i.e., the users, can not only consume the content but also actively participate in its creation and optimization. Such participation would not have been feasible with the static content of the original web. Through the active involvement of users, added value is created, which often manifests not only in monetary terms but also in aspects of social recognition and individual satisfaction. Bruns' concept of produsage is based on the idea of open access to information on the internet and the collaborative work of users. This type of production and use of content is particularly applicable in the area of Web 2.0 and has contributed to the emergence of numerous successful platforms such as Wikipedia, YouTube, or OpenStreetMap.

The concept of produsage is to be considered as the second significant transformation of the value chain, which goes in the same direction as prosumption. In contrast to the conventional value chain, but also to the value chain changed by prosumers, both of which were still controlled by a limited number of producers, the idea of produsage allows for more comprehensive control over production processes, production machines, and the distribution of digital content and products. As a result, these aspects are distributed among a larger number of participants. Consequently, the traditional value chain is permanently dissolved, and an innovative form of value creation emerges. Here, users do not only take on a passive role, as in mere consumption, but can actively participate themselves.

There are now numerous examples of both non-commercial and commercial applications in the produsage value chain. The best-known example is probably the online encyclopedia Wikipedia. Here, the active user becomes the so-called produser, who can

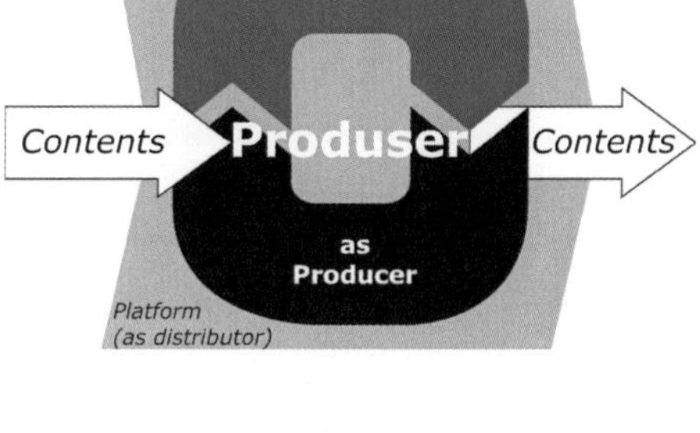

Fig. 4.4 The change in the value chain: Produsage. (Own representation: Peter Hoffmann, Invisible Cow)

continue to consume the encyclopedia entries unchanged as usual. However, the idea behind Wikipedia also allows the produser to create new entries themselves or to edit the entries of other produsers and release them for further use. Wikipedia shows that non-commercial applications, in particular, can benefit from the idea of produsage. The example also illustrates that produsage can only be successful if a sufficiently large community of active produsers forms around the application goal. Only in this way can it be ensured that enough consumable and "produsable" content is created so that the produsers actually become active and enough people are found who actively participate.

As further examples of successful produsage applications, OpenStreetMap and YouTube are often mentioned. However, YouTube does not entirely align with Bruns' ideas in detail. While the content on YouTube and other video platforms is uploaded and provided by users, it is not offered for further processing. A particular problem with produsage is that the content created, uploaded, and offered for further use by produsers must ultimately be free from marketing and licensing considerations. This makes produsage, as described by Bruns, particularly challenging for commercial use. In the context of 3D printing for the consumer market, there have been several attempts to implement produsage. On various web portals related to 3D printing, users could acquire classic licenses for 3D print models. The idea was that users, if they modified these models, would be reimbursed for the use or licensing of the models. [THIoJ, BAI08] However, none of these commercial projects could establish themselves in the long term. The main reason for the failure is not, as often claimed, the only apparent changes made by users. Rather, it turned out that modeling high-quality 3D models is a complex and demanding task that only a limited number of people can master. Here, the relatively small size of the active community seems to stand in the way of success.

The idea of produsage completes Toffler's thoughts on prosumption by merging the previously distributed roles of producer and consumer or user into a new role in one person. The producer and the consumer indeed unite in the new role, rather than just being communicatively close, as with Toffler. In this model, there apparently is no longer a role for the distributor, who played a central intermediary role between producer and consumer in the classic value chain and also had a smaller role in the value chain of prosumption. However, upon closer inspection, it turns out that the value chain of produsage consists of more than one person with two role shares. On the one hand, there is a community necessary to create the content and keep the produsage value chain running. On the other hand, there is also a need for a platform where this community can become active and where the role of the produser can emerge in the first place. The distributor here takes the form and task of a platform provider. Without it, there would be no virtual space for the produsage community. Most examples of produsage have a non-commercial background, but managing a platform now offers the opportunity to develop new business models around this type of value chain. Under the term "platform economy," which has been developed in the field of digital economy and social science since around 2014, this will play a role in the context of the "Digital 49er" presented later.

4.4 The Merged Cross-Economy of the Metaverse: Modusage

To locate the changed value chains in the context of the ideas of prosumption and produsage in the reality-virtuality continuum, they must be situated in the two extremes of real reality and one hundred percent virtuality. Although prosumption according to Toffler only hesitantly leaves the extreme of one hundred percent reality, as this model integrates only a few possibilities of the virtual world, the communication of the consumer with the producer via the internet is an important aspect. Even if the producer directly forwards the information sent by the prosumer to the production means through Industry 4.0 applications, this does not change. Furthermore, the previous strict role separation remains in this model.

In Chap. 2 and especially in Sect. 2.6 it became clear that the metaverse cannot exist in the extreme of real reality and can only be found to a limited extent in the other extreme of one hundred percent virtuality. Instead, the metaverse is located in the flexible area where real and digital artifacts are present in different proportions simultaneously. Neither the classic value chain nor the models of Bruns or Toffler are applicable to this part of the reality-virtuality continuum. Therefore, a renewed change or extension of the value chain for the future metaverse is necessary.

In order to create such a new model of the value chain, as shown experimentally in Fig. 4.5, it is necessary to consider various aspects synchronously. The metaverse typically consists of real-world and virtual components due to its positioning between the two extremes. This requires that participants within this model must be able to handle both real and digital artifacts. Therefore, it would be sensible to expand the idea of separating the real and virtual worlds and to create a bridge between the two worlds. This would then make it possible to create a cross-economy that connects both worlds. This new model incorporates the ideas of the two aforementioned models, connecting and expanding them simultaneously.

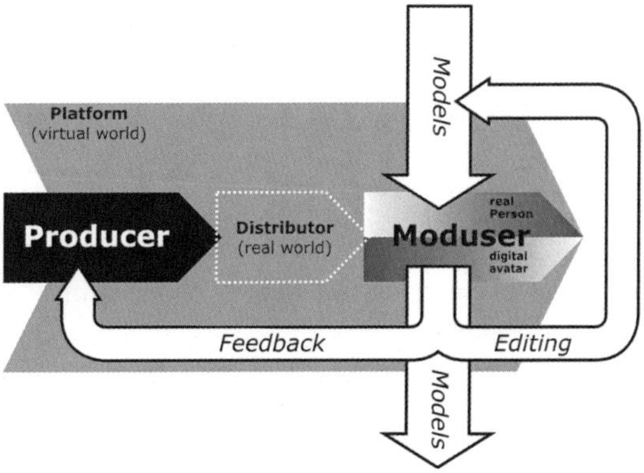

Fig. 4.5 The value chain in the metaverse: Modusage. (Own representation: Peter Hoffmann, Invisible Cow)

- In this new model, the original value chain is not considered, as it is exclusively located in the real world outside the metaverse.
- In the new model, the roles of the producer and the distributor from the classic models are integrated. The producer still provides the means of production, which are used by the new "Moduser" to initiate the individually adapted production of desired artifacts through feedback. The means of production remain in the possession of the producer. Since the produced real-world artifacts need to be delivered to the Moduser, a distributor is required to act as a logistical intermediary between the producer and the Moduser. The question of whether this role is taken on by an independent person or by the "Metaverse" platform can be handled flexibly.
- The idea of produsage also integrates seamlessly into this model. Here, the role of the produser is now replaced by the role of the Moduser. This person accesses existing digital artifacts according to Bruns' idea, uses them, and edits them if necessary, to then return them to the virtual world. This editing can take place within or outside the "Metaverse" platform. Naturally, the creation of new artifacts also counts as editing.
- In the new model, there is also a platform that represents the virtual world of the metaverse and takes on the role of the distributor on the digital side, similar to what is shown in Fig. 4.4 for produsage according to Bruns [BRU07]. The importance of this role is particularly significant here, as the platform provides and assumes all functionalities of the metaverse. This includes not only the usual functionalities of virtual worlds such as personal interaction and the rendering of worlds as a 3D model but also the integration of social interaction possibilities, which enable the formation of communities, as Bruns sees as fundamental for produsage.
- Similar to the consumer in the traditional value chain, the prosumer in Toffler's model, or the produser in Bruns' model, the so-called Moduser stands at the central active core in the new model. The Moduser prosumes on the one hand through feedback with the producer and on the other hand "produses" with the models that are fed into the platform as digital artifacts from the community. In contrast to Bruns' content, which is limited to passive, mostly media content, a significant difference is that the Moduser can also edit complex models and even complex scripts that describe the behavior of digital artifacts in the metaverse platform.
- Internally, the Moduser consists of two sub-roles. As described from various perspectives above, a fundamental characteristic of the metaverse is that digital and real artifacts come together in synchronization. The user is represented in the real world by themselves as a person and in the digital world by their digital twin, the avatar. The person can interact directly with the real environment and through the avatar with the digital environment. At the same time, the avatar also has the ability to communicate with the real world from the digital world, for example through outputs it initiates. For a comprehensive reach of the model, it is important to note that not only the real part of the Moduser but also the digital avatar can send feedback to the producer. Furthermore, the editing of digital models can be carried out by both the real and the digital sub-role of the Moduser. A prerequisite for this concept is that the digital twin,

which takes on the sub-role of the Moduser in the virtual world, has the ability to act independently.

The new role of the Moduser and the connection of its real and digital parts with other actors in the value chain of the metaverse show that the model of Modusage is more than just the merging of Toffler's and Bruns' models. Rather, it becomes clear that in the metaverse, it will be normal for the value chain to switch back and forth between the real and virtual worlds. Thus, a true "cross-economy" emerges between the two worlds, which are economically dependent on each other. This development offers broad opportunities for the emergence of new or at least seemingly new business models, as will be explained in more detail in the following sections.

4.5 The Digital 49ers: New Business Models and Application Fields

Numerous publications about the unforeseen and seemingly limitless opportunities that arise commercially in the metaverse could indicate that a new digital gold rush is imminent. Even when predictions from the more typical marketing sources are discounted, there is still a large amount of serious and independent research that attributes growing significance to the metaverse as an ecosystem for the future. This includes both the roadmap of the German IT industry association Bitkom and internationally renowned think tanks. [BIT22, STO22, WEFoJa, PER22] Almost all such investigations and studies divide the economic development of the metaverse into a nearer and a further time horizon, which suggests that the metaverse is being trusted with a longer-term perspective. These publications assume that numerous new business models that are viable will emerge in the near future. This nearer time horizon extends over the next 5 to 10 years, while generally no further predictions are ventured, as it is always emphasized that it is difficult to impossible to successfully predict business models over a longer period.

However, there seems to be consensus that the metaverse does not merely represent a single business model but will rather host a variety of different business models. These models will emerge from the roles of the various actors in the metaverse. Here, classic business models such as ad-funded or subscription-based financing will continue to exist. At the same time, they will also be further developed to enable better integration into the platform economy environment. In particular, newer technical approaches such as NFTs and similar technologies offer great development potential. One reason for this is, among other things, the comparison with the economic development of the early World Wide Web. For example, Zühlke comments on this: [STO22]

> "Platform economies, in particular, offer themselves as models to become the dominant business models in the metaverse. Global or platform-based currency systems, such as those of the crypto and gaming industries, complement today's platform economies."

The broad spectrum of potential future economic actors in the metaverse is interesting:

- Here, the current and future operators of metaverse platforms must, of course, be mentioned first, as well as
- the large technology providers and manufacturers, with Nvidia certainly being the most visible example. [KER21]
- In addition, there are service providers as "creators and developers" or other professional services for media development.
- The gaming industry must certainly also be included in the "creator and developer" environment, as it can be seen as one of the driving forces in the development of the metaverse and will thus also be economically active.
- In a broader sense, the providers of social media and social media content also fall into the area of media development, as well as, of course,
- the classic marketing and advertising agencies.
- It is interesting that research institutions such as Fraunhofer, MIT, or others are frequently mentioned in the area of business model development.
- Not to be forgotten as participants and also as developers of new business models are the users, who can themselves be economically active in the metaverse as modusers.

It is important that when examining the economic opportunities that the metaverse offers or could offer, not only the pure economic fundamentals and mechanisms are considered. Instead, it is essential to embed these in the technical and technological context. While the Internet or the World Wide Web may be firmly established as technology, the metaverse as the Internet of the future is still in the development phase. Since no precise statement can be made about how the metaverse will be technically designed, future business models depend heavily on which technologies and implementations can be used for various application areas.

In this context, it is helpful to project current examples of business activities from various industries onto the reality-virtuality continuum. A study by Zühlke, which examines five different industries regarding their activities in the metaverse, shows that examples of economic activities are distributed across the entire spectrum of the continuum in almost all industries. [STO22] (see also Fig. 4.6)

- *Fashion:* A frequently cited example of entrepreneurial activities in the metaverse is the fashion industry. This is evident, for instance, in the fact that, similar to the real world, there are now extensive fashion events in the metaverse. The Decentraland Fashion Week is probably the most well-known event in this regard. The aim here is not to take a critical look at this event, as was done in the previously mentioned example of the Decentraland Metaverse Music Festival. Regardless of the size of the participating audience, however, this virtual fashion week illustrates the high number of fashion labels that have already identified the metaverse as a future consumer environment [DEC23, DRA22, METoJa, METoJb]. It is noteworthy that early

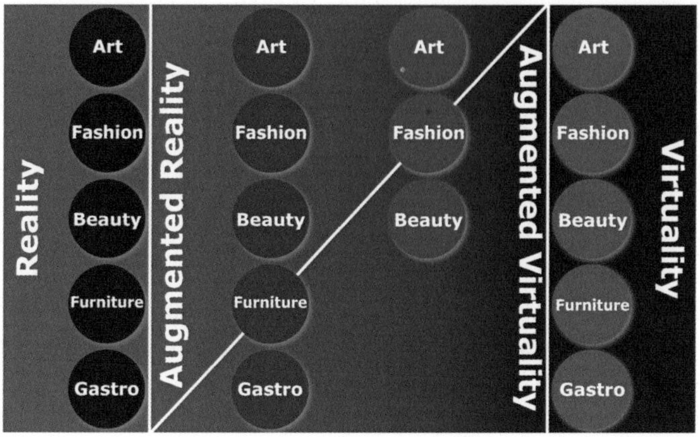

Fig. 4.6 Industry activities in the RVK. (Own representation: Peter Hoffmann, Invisible Cow)

on, opportunities are being explored to connect fashion for the real world with fashion for the virtual world. This seems quite logical, as one of the fundamental ideas for merging the real and virtual worlds is that the user lets an avatar act as their digital twin in the virtual world. This digital twin should, of course, not look like a simple and cheap "digital mass product," but should correspond to the fashion consciousness of the real person and be dressed accordingly. Therefore, it is only consistent that, for example, Gucci offers a handbag as a fashion accessory for the lady in the real world and makes this bag available for the avatar in the virtual world at the same time. The price of nearly $4000 does not seem to be a real obstacle in this context.

- Of course, consumption offers will continue to be made in the real world in the future, because despite the transformation of city centers, it is not to be expected that ordinary department stores or retail shops will completely disappear.
- Nevertheless, some companies are relying on the concept of the digital twin and offering virtual shopping experiences in VR stores on well-known platforms like Roblox or Decentraland. This idea is not new, as even in the precursor of the metaverse, Second Life, not only Adidas but also many other companies from different industries had virtual branches.
- But it is also easy to find numerous applications in this area that connect reality and virtuality. Augmented reality is, as already described in detail above, one of the oldest application examples for technologies that are mentioned today in connection with the metaverse. For example, there is augmented dressing in both a large and a smaller version. The large version can consist of a full-body mirror in the real store, in which digitalized 3D models of clothing items are put on the own reflection, following body posture and movement. This way, an impression of the clothing items can be gained before they are bought or ordered online, without having to actually put them on beforehand. On a smaller scale, this is also

available for shoes, for example. The augmentation here is done via an app on the smartphone, which uses the device's display and camera. Augmented virtuality would also be quite conceivable in this area, although no widely used application for it has been finally shown yet.

- *Beauty and Cosmetics:* An area closely related to the fashion world is beauty and cosmetics. Although there are currently no similarly large-scale events like the Metaverse Fashion Week, there are already many articles in both fashion and business and technology magazines about activities of cosmetic brands aiming to establish themselves in the metaverse. Beauty and cosmetics is an extremely profitable market in the real world, and therefore it makes sense to investigate whether the digital twin can be made even more attractive through virtual cosmetics or can smell better digitally.
  - The consumption of cosmetics in the real world also usually takes place through stationary sales outlets in department stores or specialized retail as well as through online trade. It is expected that this will not change with the establishment of the metaverse.
  - The area of augmenting reality and virtuality seems to be even more interesting for the beauty and cosmetics industry than for the fashion industry across the entire reality-virtuality continuum as a potential field for applications and business models. For example, augmented reality allows the application of virtual makeup, which is only visible in the augmented mirror or on the display of a corresponding smartphone app. This way, the color of cosmetics or accessories like contact lenses can be examined before purchase or application. Interestingly, in this industry example, "augmented virtuality" is also frequently mentioned. A concept mentioned in this context is the so-called "face filter," where the image of the real face is projected onto a made-up avatar in the virtual world. Here, the digital image is overlaid with the appearance of the real person and thus extended.
  - Completely different from the fashion sector, however, is the complete virtuality for the beauty and cosmetics sector. While entire branches and stores are moved to the virtual world in the fashion sector, the beauty sector is still focused on the individual real user, at least for now. At least, no virtual cosmetic stores for avatars in a virtual world are known at the moment. However, on many platforms and with many cross-platform services, such as ReadyPlayerMe, avatars can be changed not only in their fashion appearance but also in their cosmetic appearance. This goes far beyond traditional cosmetics, as the possibilities for designing avatars are not limited to human, humanoid physiognomy. Instead, all conceivable forms can be applied to the avatar, from classic human appearances to cartoon and manga characters to fantasy and furry figures. All this is conceivable and is actually implemented. [WEI20, ORT22]
- *Furniture and Interior Design:*The furniture and interior design industry is another sector with numerous activities related to the metaverse. Even before the term metaverse became common, there was the idea of viewing furniture items virtually before purchasing, delivering, and setting them up. Ultimately, this is also logical, as a

corresponding application can make measuring the apartment and the furniture items, as well as matching the two sizes, unnecessary. The virtual piece of furniture is simply projected into the real space to give the customer an impression of how it fits into the living environment. Although no one can sit on the virtual chair, it can be moved around the room to check if it fits both in size and design with the apartment. A very active player in this industry is Ikea, which has been experimenting with various technologies for several years.

- But not only Ikea, many other furniture stores also offer a variety of AR applications designed to assist customers in selecting furniture and interior items in various ways. [WEI22] The basic idea here is the aforementioned one, namely that a digitized 3D model of the furniture item is integrated into the real living situation to provide a much better impression than a passive image on the screen or the furniture item itself, which is still in the showroom of the furniture store, can offer.
- In the furniture and interior design industry, complete virtuality is used in various ways. The simplest approach is to transfer an entire store into virtual reality, just like in the fashion or other consumer industries. This way, the user can view the furniture items in virtual reality through their digital twin, just like in a real furniture store. The more technically sophisticated scenario at this end of the reality-virtuality continuum for this industry is to transfer the customer's own apartment into virtual reality and insert the digital equivalent of the desired piece of furniture into the living situation. However, for this, a complete 3D model of the apartment must be available, which can either be manually modeled or created from a scan using appropriate technical means. The challenge here, however, is particularly the interior design of the room or apartment if only the architectural dimensions are known. In this case, all the furniture items that exist in the real world and beautify the apartment would also have to be modeled or scanned. Older examples from times before the metaverse should not be forgotten here, such as Second Life or the once very successful social game "The Sims." In both cases, it was quite possible to design one's own apartment in the virtual world, which could also be furnished with pieces of furniture, just like in the real world. How closely these then corresponded to real furniture depended on the modeling willingness and skills of the users.

- *Gaming and Entertainment:*Undeniably, gaming and entertainment are among the most lucrative sectors in computing and the internet. In this area, almost anything is imaginable and is indeed implemented. Although concrete economic goals are pursued here as well, this sector offers a vast experimental space for testing various new technologies and creative ideas that cover the entire spectrum of the reality-virtuality continuum. Some examples have already been mentioned above. It is particularly interesting that there is a high level of customer acceptance, openness, and willingness to experiment for both technology and technical developers as well as for the creators of new business models.

- The playing human, Homo ludens, has existed much longer than all ideas for computers, digital, or electronic media. A look into the game sections of bookstores or toy stores reveals an overwhelming amount and variety of dice, card, and board games. But games are not the only part of the entertainment industry. For at least as long as there have been games, humans have also had the desire to be entertained, for example, through theater or musical performances. Here too, the range of offerings is extraordinarily large, from private campfire concerts to multi-day open-air festivals, almost anything is possible in the real world.
- As already shown above, these activities can be easily implemented in complete virtuality. It is now common to find both games and concert events in virtual reality and on metaverse platforms like Fortnite and Roblox.
- In the area of augmented reality, it is still mainly games that combine and extend both real and virtual elements. Examples of this are Pokémon Go in the field of augmented reality or the already mentioned PacManhattan in the field of augmented virtuality. But augmented reality is also suitable for entertainment events. Here, the examples of Ronnie James Dio, ABBA, and Hatsune Miku should be recalled once again.

• *Art:* The consistent continuation of the ideas presented in the entertainment and gaming sectors consists of applying and transferring them to the field of art. Ultimately, everything that has been and will be said about the entertainment and gaming sector can be directly transferred to art. Art represents an experimental space where everything is feasible and where, as a look into art history shows, everything possible is actually tried out. Therefore, it is not surprising that there are already examples of art along the entire reality-virtuality continuum from times when neither the term "metaverse" nor the terms "virtual" or "augmented reality" were known. However, it is particularly interesting that in connection with the metaverse and Web3 ideas, the economic aspect of managing art in the virtual world is now gaining importance. The currently probably best-known example of this is Bored Ape, an NFT collection based on the Ethereum blockchain. The prices for such a Bored Ape object seem to be almost unlimited. For example, a rare specimen of this collection is said to have already been sold for about one million US dollars. [DRA22]
  - Art in the physical world is ubiquitous and can be found in almost every place. It does not necessarily have to be a museum or a gallery; art can also exist as part of the public space.
  - Even in the area of complete virtuality, the conventional implementation practices that have already been mentioned are recognizable. There are real museums that fully represent themselves with all exhibits and buildings in virtuality, as well as museums and exhibitions that exist exclusively in virtual reality. However, this is also nothing really new, as many museums have already shown presence in Second Life and other early environments. In the area of augmentations, there are also numerous artworks that are partly older than the term "metaverse" itself. Current examples of augmented reality are, for instance, guided tours through a city

where digital artworks are added at selected positions using an app on a mobile device. The ARTour in Basel is a frequently cited example in this area. [BAS22, WEB22] A technology that can actually be considered independent of the idea of the metaverse is currently being used in some examples in the area of augmented virtual reality. The so-called deep fake art allows, for example, embedding one's own real image into famous artworks. In this way, the Mona Lisa can simply take on the viewer's own facial features. [SIR22, BBC19]

- *Gastronomy:* In the context of applications and business models in the metaverse, gastronomy is probably not the first thing that comes to mind. The world of IT, computers, and the internet is primarily visual and, in a few examples, also auditory. While it is technically possible to integrate all other sensory modalities into this world, the technical effort is often very high and the added value low. Nevertheless, there are numerous ideas on how gastronomy could establish itself in the metaverse or make use of it.
  - At this point, it is certainly not necessary to talk about one hundred percent reality, as gastronomy takes place both in inns, hotels, and restaurants as well as in the private environment in the real world.
  - Why should a restaurant be completely virtual? While it may seem sensible for the digital avatar to get a visual impression of a top chef's 5-star restaurant on a metaverse platform to get an insight into the menu and the ambiance, the question arises as to what the avatar could order and actually enjoy there. In gastronomy and hospitality in the metaverse, it is primarily not about providing guests with an experience, but rather about using VR applications to support the training of staff in the real world. Here, spatial arrangements within hotels or workflows can be learned and trained. The business model of the metaverse platforms thus targets professional use rather than the mass or consumer market. Nevertheless, virtual reality will certainly play a role for tourists and guests in the future, for example, by allowing them to view the interior of a cruise ship in virtual reality in advance. In the future, entire destinations could possibly be transferred to virtual reality to experience the flair of cities like Venice without actually having to travel there. This idea could be an interesting alternative for heavily frequented tourist destinations like Venice and is also currently being discussed. [HUG23, SER18] However, there are currently only a few concepts on how such a scenario could be fully implemented.
  - Although gastronomy enables the development of one hundred percent reality and virtuality in the metaverse as a business environment, this is somewhat more difficult in the area of augmentations. There are indeed some mentions of so-called augmented food experiences, but how these are to be implemented technically and sensorily often remains unclear. Here, the question of added value for the user, which still needs to be found, certainly arises. In the area of augmented reality, however, there are already examples such as QR codes that complement menus or beer mats, as shown by Lindenbräu. [NET18]

The presented examples illustrate how intensively and comprehensively new business models and options on a technological level are being explored in connection with the metaverse. In contrast to other hyped topics such as 3D printing or artificial intelligence, not only a few supposed experts predict a promising future for the technologies and ideas of the metaverse, whereby it should be noted at this point that this is now also the case for the field of AI. In the metaverse, it is numerous experts from various fields who share a similar opinion. An example of this is Tim Sweeney, the former game developer and current CEO of Epic Games, who predicted in 2020: [MAR20]

> "Just as every company created a website a few decades ago and then eventually a Facebook page, I believe we are approaching the point where every company will have a real-time 3D live presence."

An analysis of the numerous publications presenting concepts and models for the future economy in the metaverse reveals an overwhelming number of economic options (see also Fig. 4.7), even when only the most relevant tech and business sources are considered. In Fig. 4.7, an attempt is made to present these diverse ideas in a structured manner.

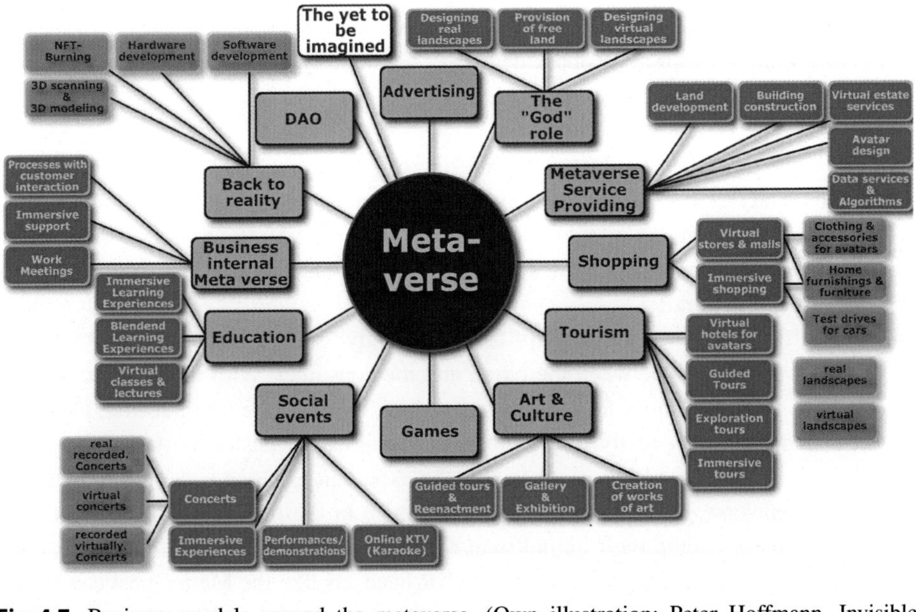

Fig. 4.7 Business models around the metaverse. (Own illustration: Peter Hoffmann, Invisible Cow)

4.5.1 Advertising & Marketing

The intensive blending of the real and virtual world in the metaverse is enhanced by the user's immersion through their avatar or digital twin. This is intended to create a highly individualized experience that seems almost limitless. Although it sounds like typical marketing jargon, it actually reflects the advertising and marketing industry's hope to develop the metaverse into an outstanding platform for marketing activities. This is achieved through the use of immersion, interactivity, and personalization with the goal of increased marketing efficiency. In the meantime, the metaverse has indeed already reached the status of a multi-billion-dollar market, into which not only major brands like Ralph Lauren, Gucci, and Louis Vuitton are investing. These brand pioneers in the metaverse are currently already achieving impressive profits from their investments and are experimenting with new brand management methods that allow users to try and acquire clothing, products, and styles, as described in the previous section 4.5 "The Digital 49ers: New Business Models and Application Fields" about consumption in the reality-virtuality continuum. [BID22, DEW22].

Advertising in the metaverse particularly aims to offer an (inter-) active experience, where potential customers are actively involved in the marketing rather than just being passive spectators. This leads to additional challenges for companies, as the general distrust towards advertising must first be reduced. Successful campaigns, however, emphasize that the key to success lies in collaborating with existing communities rather than fighting against them. For example, some brands have been able to successfully enter into collaborations with the Roblox developer community, which is somewhat comparable to the use of influencers in social media campaigns.

- Within the advertising industry, the offering of interactive events in the virtual worlds of the metaverse has gained significance as a popular marketing tool. It is widespread to integrate advertising into such events and to be present on several of the currently significant platforms like Meta's Horizon Worlds, Decentraland, Sandbox, Fortnite, Roblox, or Minecraft.
- An additional approach is the "try before you buy" strategy, which aims to establish a strong connection between the brand and the consumer. With this method, customers have the opportunity to actively test and get to know the product first, to find out what added value it really offers them. This approach transforms passive marketing into a dynamic experience, emphasizing the experience, which is central to marketing in the metaverse. Such an immersive experience in the metaverse allows customers, for example, to equip their digital twin with new clothing and try it out in the virtual world. [MIRoJ] Additionally, affordable VR headsets like the Meta Quest can be used to simulate a realistic driving experience with the new vehicle the customer is interested in.

- Binding customers through collections and collectibles also seems to be an effective method to draw attention to a brand. Collecting objects and the fascination it exerts on people is a long-known and applied phenomenon even in the purely physical world. Recently, this enthusiasm has also extended to digital collections in the metaverse. Advertising campaigns focusing on digital collectibles aim to create uniqueness and offer exclusivity through the use of NFT and crypto technologies. Virtual goods have gained considerable significance in the metaverse, with a current direct-to-avatar market value of about $30 billion in 2021 and a forecast for the end of 2022 of well over $50 billion. [HAC21] As the above-presented fashion usage model shows, a potential metaverse-to-offline consumption opens up in the future, which will function analogously to the conversion of online-to-offline sales through the internet.
- It is often assumed that the use of the metaverse is inevitably associated with expensive hardware components. However, it is often overlooked that smartphones can already function as metaverse-capable devices suitable for AR applications. Many companies have already recorded significant successes through the use of smartphone-based AR in metaverse advertising. An example of this is the use of AR by Home Depot to demonstrate the effect of different shades from their range in rooms to customers. [CRE20] The renowned company Sephora also offers a product range in the cosmetics sector that many consumers are reluctant to purchase online, as these are very individual products and predicting how a particular product will look on one's skin is difficult. Therefore, many customers prefer to visit Sephora stores in person. However, through the use of augmented reality marketing, Sephora has found a way to meet the needs of its customers. [BAL20c] A technique called "Modiface" is used for this purpose, which enables high-quality facial scans. This allows customers to digitally apply Sephora's makeup to their lips and eyes from the comfort of their homes to get a realistic picture of how it would look on their faces. [ABU21, METoJb]

For companies, advertising and marketing in the metaverse means that new approaches and techniques must be found that have not previously existed in the real world or the World Wide Web. Therefore, many advertising and marketing attempts are currently and likely in the future discovered through trial and error and experimentation.

Even though a smartphone is sufficient for entering the metaverse initially, the costs for metaverse-compatible devices such as VR headsets and powerful computers for the user increase if the immersion of the (advertising) experiences is to be enhanced. This could then lead to only a limited number of users being able to afford access to such advertising campaigns and events in the metaverse, which in turn cannot be in the interest of the advertising companies. Additionally, these companies must also consider new concerns regarding cybersecurity if they want to be successful in the metaverse.

4.5.2 Shopping

Both in 2021 and 2022, online retail recorded a new revenue high, and despite inflation and current crises, a promising situation is emerging in which the metaverse can open up new opportunities for positive development for providers in the shopping sector. To keep pace with the growth of the e-commerce sector, companies must adapt their business practices to the changing consumption habits and use multi-channel distribution approaches. The relevance of social media platforms in the sales context has increased, and many companies are planning to create their own virtual universes in the metaverse.

Companies like Adidas and Netflix have already begun to present their goods and services in the metaverse. The application of virtual fitting rooms and digital replicas of physical store locations is intended to offer consumers an immersive experience and the opportunity to try out products in a realistic way. [FLO22, PAR23]

Other companies and industries are also intensifying their efforts to integrate their businesses and products into the metaverse. In October 2021, Nike filed seven patents with the US Patent Office to sell digital clothing in the metaverse. The company is currently seeking material designers for virtual sports shoes to expand its product development team accordingly. [END21] The fashion industry has also recognized the potential of the metaverse and is experimenting with virtual retail concepts. Gucci is perhaps the most prominent example of this and introduced the online concept store "Vault" in September 2021 as part of its metaverse strategy. Customers can "experience" vintage pieces, limited items, and other articles as well as NFTs selected by the creative director. [NGU22] In June 2022, Gucci Town was launched on the Roblox platform, where users can participate in competitions, create digital artworks, or purchase digital Gucci products. Gucci uses the "Layered Clothing System" to adapt clothing and accessories to the body types of the avatars. [BED22] The US discount retailer Walmart also plans to enter the metaverse and filed applications with the US Patent Office in December 2021 to enable its own cryptocurrency and the sale of virtual goods. The German supermarket chain Kaufland followed Walmart and other discounters into the metaverse with its project "Kaufisland," by acquiring an island in the Nintendo game "Animal Crossing: New Horizon" and setting up a virtual supermarket there. The company does not currently pursue primary profit intentions there but offers users information about food origins and environmentally conscious behavior. Additionally, customers or their avatars can linger in a café or cook in an outdoor kitchen on Kaufisland. [BUS22a, BUS22b] It remains to be seen how companies will actually use the metaverse in the future and what impact the digital world will have on consumers.

A significant advantage that is repeatedly emphasized in this context is the creation of a completely new virtual world in which consumers can immerse themselves and interact. This also opens up a number of more or less new possibilities for shopping:

- *Augmented shopping experiences:*Thanks to augmented reality technology, consumers have the opportunity to try on clothing or accessories virtually without having to access the physical product. In addition to the examples already mentioned above, the app "Sayduck" allows users to virtually position furniture in their own spaces and assess their appearance. [MAR14]
- *Personalization:* Within the metaverse, consumers have the option to create and customize their own avatars. This creates a unique shopping experience where products can be specifically tailored to the avatar, as is the case with the "Layered Clothing System" mentioned above.
- *Interactive shopping experiences:*Brands can intensify their presence and customer loyalty in the metaverse through interactive shopping experiences, including competitions, games, and the collection of digital artworks and artifacts.
- *Virtual payment methods:*Much of the metaverse is designed to use virtual currencies and NFTs for the sale of digital items. [HAM22]
- *Global reach:* Similar to the traditional World Wide Web, companies can reach customers globally in the metaverse without having to open a physical branch in every country. This makes it easier for small and medium-sized enterprises to offer their products worldwide.

In recent years, influencer marketing has seen significant growth and is likely to be further influenced by the metaverse. Companies benefit from using real or virtual influencers by expanding their reach and targeting a specific audience. [METoJb]

Although the metaverse offers many opportunities, challenges such as technical limitations, legal regulatory issues, and uncertainties in an NFT-based economic ecosystem exist. It is important to recognize and address these early to fully leverage the potential of the metaverse for the shopping sector. [BUS22a]

A study by GetApp [PAV23] shows that a considerable number of consumers have expressed interest in the metaverse as a shopping platform. (Fig. 4.8) 48% of survey participants are interested in the possibility of shopping "virtually in 3D" and trying out items. Clothing is the most appealing for 75% of respondents, followed by electronics (57%), household items such as furniture (47%), video games (40%), and music (38%) as preferred product categories. The study also illustrates that the metaverse can help bridge

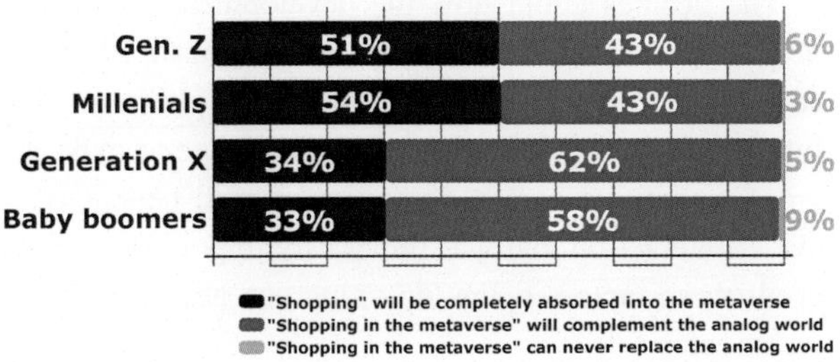

Fig. 4.8 Consumer expectations for the shopping of the future. (Based on [PAV23])

the gap between online shopping and the real in-store shopping experience. After all, 96% of participants interested in metaverse shopping share this view. Although the metaverse offers companies numerous new opportunities for product presentation and monetization, consumer opinions are still divided on whether it will completely replace traditional online shopping. However, the study indicates that consumers consider the convenience of shopping, viewing the latest products without annoying waits, and the option to test items using augmented reality as significant advantages of metaverse shopping.

4.5.3 Gaming & Games

The continuous technological advancement in the field of video games leads to an increasingly realistic depiction of game environments, which enhances players' interest in taking a more active role within the game. The metaverse thus offers a promising opportunity where players can utilize their scope of action and creativity to create their own content and interact with other players. The predicted growing use of the metaverse, however it may ultimately look, will have significant impacts on the video game and film or media industry, as users will not only be able to play games and watch VR movies themselves but also immerse themselves in various virtual worlds and participate in social activities within these worlds. Platforms like "Roblox" already demonstrate that users are capable of creating their own games and content in the metaverse and interacting with each other. Furthermore, the continuous improvement of technologies related to the metaverse is expected to enable the creation of more complex and realistic virtual environments. This development will allow players to also immerse themselves in the world of film and experience it directly. [JAL22]

The pronounced 3D characteristic attributed to the metaverse forms a significant factor for all types of products in the gaming sector and also represents an important economic factor within the metaverse overall. This results strongly from the close cooperation between the "metaverse" sector and the gaming industry. Users can now immerse themselves in the virtual gaming world. This provides them with an immersive experience that goes far beyond what a conventional flat screen can offer, especially when it is also embedded in the player's physical environment. Thus, the metaverse can create worlds in the future where digital education, networking, working, earning money, and even attending concerts can take place entirely digitally.

The debates about how the development of the metaverse will influence the future of gaming are still in their early stages, but it is foreseeable that ongoing research and development as well as new projects and platforms like Decentraland [DEC20] or Axie Infinity [BEL23a] and others will contribute to making this "the next big thing" in gaming. Competitive games, in particular, will benefit from this, as there is now a form of player interaction that was previously impossible and also unthinkable. The combination of all these factors opens up numerous new possibilities for the gaming and entertainment sector:

- The metaverse shows a significant advantage over conventional virtual reality experiences through its social character, where users often act alone and isolated. In the virtual worlds of the metaverse, players have the opportunity to invite multiple friends from the real world, connect with other users worldwide, form relationships, and participate in further social activities. This is somewhat possible in current games, but the intensity of social interaction is still very low.
- Paradigms like "Games-as-a-Platform" enable players to have a more compelling gaming experience characterized by flexibility and expansion possibilities. In the virtual world, users have the opportunity to create their own content and even develop smaller games within a game. By participating in supplementary actions, players can use the game environment as a platform-like space. [BAT23, KIT16]
- The combination of augmented reality and virtual reality in the metaverse offers players a much more natural experience. The mixed AR/VR activities in the metaverse allow users, for example, a seamless transition from an augmented reality group chat to a mixed-reality board game and ultimately into a full virtual reality world.
- Thanks to the intended interoperability structure of the metaverse, the transferability of virtual assets such as weapons, weapon skins, and other items used by players will be facilitated. Assets acquired in one game could thus be transferred to other game environments, provided NFTs and any legislation allow for permanent ownership of these objects.
- An additional special aspect that the metaverse is expected to provide in the future is the opportunity to generate money through gaming. Apart from following a linear (game) storyline, gamers can participate in a variety of more or less lucrative activities, such as selling their assets or those they have acquired in play-to-win games to other users for cryptocurrencies.
- The individually customizable avatars in the virtual world also represent the players and allow them to gather with friends in a virtual environment and play together. Additionally, they can visit virtual worlds created by other gamers, which changes the perception of the entire online gaming communities.
- It is predicted that the metaverse will also have a significant impact on the e-sports sector, which is already extremely popular and excites millions of people worldwide. Through the metaverse, e-sports events can become even more immersive and exciting than before, as players can act in virtual venues while spectators from all over the world can watch and possibly even be passively or actively present in the virtual environment. [ZAV21, SEN22]

4.5.4 Art & Culture

Art has always served as a pioneer for numerous technological and societal developments. Especially in the field of technology, it plays an important role. Many artists experiment specifically with electronic and digital possibilities and can be summarized as "Post-Internet Artists." The experimental nature of art allows for the exploration of societal and technological changes at their fringes. The resulting artworks are already being traded on a virtual market today and purchased by collectors. [STO22] Thus, the metaverse is attributed significant importance for artists and cultural creators in the future. In this world of the metaverse, they can present their works to a global audience and create interactive experiences that would be unthinkable in the physical world. In this context, virtual museums and galleries can emerge, showcasing artworks in digital spaces that do not exist in the physical world. An example of this is "The VR Museum of Fine Art," where visitors can view art from various epochs and different artists. [BEZ19]

The metaverse also opens up opportunities for cultural creators to enable interactive experiences with little effort. An example of this is "The Wave XR," a platform that allows users to participate in joint virtual concerts and experience music in an immersive environment. [WAVoJ] Additionally, as mentioned several times, entire concerts and theater performances can be held virtually, allowing people from all over the world to participate. Besides the already mentioned Ariana Grande, the virtual concert of Travis Scott in 2020 also took place on the "Fortnite" platform and reached over 12 million people. [TIP20] In addition to pure concert events, there is also the possibility of interaction between artists and the audience. Virtual meet-and-greets, where fans can meet their favorite artists, or virtual workshops and courses are examples of this.

Another aspect of the relevance of the metaverse for the art world is also evident in the "Museum of Other Realities" (MOR), a virtual gallery dedicated to the presentation of immersive art. [COA21, MUSoJ, DAM20] Here, artists can exhibit their works while visitors can experience them in an immersive environment independent of the real world. Another example is the "CryptoArt" market, where digital art is traded in the form of NFTs. [CRYoJ, LUC22] Such NFTs can be exhibited and traded in virtual worlds like Decentraland or Somnium Space. It is expected that in the future, the metaverse will play an even more significant role in the art and culture scene than interactive media and immersive worlds do today. The focus will be on developing more advanced technologies and tools for modeling and interaction in virtual environments to further expand the possibilities of the metaverse.

With the predicted increasing popularity of the metaverse, it is expected that opportunities for artists will also evolve and expand in the future:

- *Second Life,* the oldest virtual world in the context of the metaverse, which has existed since 2008 and still has many users, allows users to create their own virtual spaces such as galleries, theaters, or museums and exhibit artworks. Additionally, well-known museums are also present here with their own virtual exhibition spaces.
- Also based on the Ethereum blockchain, *The Sandbox,* a virtual world where users can fully create their own virtual worlds, allows artists to exhibit and sell their artworks by creating their own worlds or integrating their works into existing worlds. [SPE21]

- *Somnium Space* is an immersive virtual world that specifically offers the opportunity to exhibit and sell artworks in virtual galleries or museums. [SOMoJ]
- *SuperRare,* also specializing in digital art and based on Ethereum, allows artists to sell their artworks as digital collectibles represented by unique tokens. [SUPoJ]
- *Nifty Gateway* is a platform that allows artists to sell their digital artworks in limited editions. Here too, the Ethereum blockchain is used to ensure the authenticity and uniqueness of the artworks. [NIFoJ]
- *Art Planet* (ArtsCloud) is an immersive virtual world where users can create, present, and sell artworks. The platform uses the Unity engine to enable users to easily present their artworks in a 3D environment. [ARToJ]

4.5.5 Social Events

Social events are events aimed at connecting people to share common interests, maintain relationships, or make new acquaintances. Such events can be conducted online or offline and encompass a variety of activities such as concerts, celebrations, conferences, networking events, and much more. The metaverse opens up diverse opportunities for such social events to bring together people from the entire real and virtual world, regardless of their respective geographical location:

- *Virtual concerts:* Musicians can perform in a virtual environment and invite fans worldwide to participate in this event. There are various ways in which such virtual concerts can be designed in the metaverse.
  - For example, artists can perform on a virtual stage that has been set up in a specially developed virtual environment, as described multiple times above with the example of Ariana Grande. Fans can then control their avatars and gather near the stage to enjoy the concert. The music is either played live by the musicians or played back as a recording.
  - An alternative approach for virtual concerts in the metaverse involves the use of motion-capture technology to transfer the movements and actions of the musicians in real-time to an avatar. This makes it possible for the musicians to perform simultaneously on a real stage and in a virtual environment, providing a concert for fans there as well.
  - A time-delayed repetition of the once modeled and programmed concert in the virtual world also opens new ways of monetization.
- The economic significance of virtual concerts in the metaverse is immense. By using this technology, artists and organizers can also significantly expand their reach by addressing fans worldwide who would normally not be able to attend a physical concert. This means that more tickets can be sold and that fans around the world have access to music and artists they otherwise would not be able to hear.

- In addition, virtual concerts in the metaverse represent a cost-effective alternative to hosting concerts overall. The expenses for implementing such a virtual concert can be significantly lower than those incurred when planning a real concert. This means that more artists and organizers, especially emerging and not yet established artists, can benefit from this technology.
- An additional advantage of virtual concerts in the metaverse is the creation of new revenue streams. For example, artists and organizers can offer virtual objects such as digital tickets, virtual merchandise, and much more as NFTs to generate additional income.
- *Virtual parties:* In the metaverse, parties are a form of social interaction where people from all over the world come together in a virtual environment to celebrate, dance, and interact collectively. These events can be held in various virtual worlds developed by companies like Facebook, Roblox, or Fortnite:
  - Virtual parties can take place in a variety of environments, from virtual clubs and bars to virtual beaches and festivals. The environments are usually designed by the organizers and can be very detailed to offer a unique and realistic experience. A debatable but significant example is the aforementioned Decentraland Metaverse Music Festival.
  - Virtual parties allow guests to interact by controlling their virtual avatars and sending emotes or text messages. Some platforms also offer the option of voice chat to make the event even more interactive.
  - Music is an essential part of parties, and this is also true in virtuality. Organizers can often use DJ software or music streaming services to provide the music for the event. Participants can create their own playlists or rely on the music provided by the organizers.
  - Often, attending virtual parties can also be personalized by guests designing their own avatars and outfits specifically for this one event. Participants can also create personalized messages and greetings for the event.
  - As with all events, security aspects must also be considered at virtual parties to ensure a safe feeling for participants both in the virtual and real world. Organizers may also need to monitor compliance with rules and guidelines to ensure that the celebration remains enjoyable for all guests.

  Virtual parties in the metaverse have the potential to gain significant economic importance. Companies can use such parties to promote their offerings or services and reach a larger target audience. Likewise, they can generate revenue through admission or the sale of virtual objects such as avatars or clothing. DJs and musicians have the option to provide virtual performances to expand their audience and potentially attract new followers.

  Furthermore, virtual parties offer an opportunity to bring people together during phases of social distancing and travel restrictions, as they are accessible regardless of the respective spatial location. Overall, virtual parties in the metaverse thus have the potential to play a significant role in future social interaction and entertainment.

- *Networking Events:*Companies have the opportunity to organize virtual events to bring together experts from around the world and create opportunities for networking and cooperation. These events can be designed in various ways. For example, companies can hold virtual conferences and networking events entirely in a virtual environment to gather professionals globally. Such events can take place in real-time or on-demand and offer various tools and features to promote interaction and cooperation among attendees.
  An example of this is the virtual platform "VirBELA," which supports companies in planning virtual conferences and networking events. The platform provides a virtual environment where participants can navigate and interact in a 3D space while communicating with each other. Attendees can communicate in both group and individual conversations and navigate through different rooms and thematic areas. Additionally, they have the opportunity to exchange documents and presentations to promote cooperation and knowledge sharing. [VIRoJ]
  Regarding the economic relevance of networking events in the metaverse, there are various factors that can influence this. On the one hand, such virtual events can help companies expand their reach and address a broader audience. As a result, they may be able to acquire more customers and expand their business. On the other hand, organizing networking events in the metaverse can lead to cost savings. Virtual events can often be realized with lower financial expenditure compared to physical events, as there are no expenses for travel and accommodation for the participants. In the current economic situation, where many companies are striving to reduce their expenses and operate more efficiently, this can be particularly advantageous.
  Additionally, the metaverse opens up new business opportunities for companies. By creating virtual environments and platforms, companies can offer novel products and services specifically designed for these environments. For example, they could provide virtual products or services optimized for use in all virtual manifestations of the metaverse.
- *Virtual Trade Shows and Exhibitions*enable providers to showcase their products and services in a digital environment and communicate with customers from around the world. Such events offer companies an innovative opportunity to present their offerings and interact with potential customers globally. Compared to conventional exhibitions, virtual exhibitions offer a range of advantages:
  - A greater reach is achieved through online availability, allowing companies to address potential customers worldwide without incurring travel and accommodation costs.
  - Generally, virtual exhibitions are more cost-effective than traditional ones, as there are no booth rental, travel, and accommodation costs. However, the management of virtual worlds is also evolving, so it is uncertain how companies will market virtual exhibitions in the future.
  - Virtual trade shows offer better tracking options, as companies can precisely determine who visited their booths and what interactions took place.

  - Interactive features such as live chats, video presentations, and webinars are usually part of the respective virtual environments and can be used by companies to showcase their products and services in an engaging manner.

  There are various ways to design virtual trade shows in the metaverse. One option is to create a virtual exhibition hall or trade center as a virtual exhibition venue for companies. The virtual exhibition hall can have different areas where companies can set up their booths and interactively present their products and services to attract visitors and promote interaction.

  Alternatively, virtual booths can be created on platforms like Roblox, Decentraland, or Second Life. Here, companies have the opportunity to present their products and services at individually designed booths with interactive features such as live chats, webinars, and video presentations.

  A significant advantage of virtual trade shows over real trade shows is that they can take place throughout the year, allowing companies to present their products and services at any time instead of being limited to an annual trade show.

- *Virtual Training:* The possibility of conducting training and workshops in a virtual environment offers companies and educational providers in the metaverse some relatively new options:
  - Training sessions can also take place entirely in a virtual environment and include interactive elements such as 3D models, simulations, and animations. In this way, participants can experience and apply what they have learned in a practical manner, even in virtuality.
  - By additionally using AI and machine learning, virtual training can be personalized to better consider the individual learning style and needs of each participant. For example, certain topics or exercises can be automatically selected based on the individual learning needs of each participant.
  - By integrating voice and video chat options, virtual training can also enable real-time communication. This allows participants to ask questions and receive feedback from trainers and other participants.
  - Virtual training in the metaverse can also promote social learning behavior by dividing participants into interactive groups where they can collaborate and support each other. This fosters collaboration and helps participants better understand and apply what they have learned.

  The importance of virtual training for the economy is expected to be significant:
  - On the one hand, they are often more cost-effective than traditional training, as there is no need for room rental, travel, or accommodation costs.
  - On the other hand, they can be easily scaled to reach a large number of participants regardless of their location.
  - Additionally, virtual training offers better learning outcomes through interactive elements, personalized experiences, and social learning, and can be more flexibly designed by offering recorded sessions or live streams to meet the needs of the participants.

With increasing digitization, the demand for virtual training in the metaverse is expected to continue to rise, leading to a growing market for companies and providers of virtual training.

4.5.6 Tourism

In the short time of the previous hype, the metaverse has also received significant attention from the tourism industry. The use of virtual worlds for marketing travel destinations represents a relatively young concept that is already having an impact on the tourism sector. (see Fig. 4.9).

A high potential of the metaverse for tourism lies in providing virtual immersive experiences for travelers. Within the virtual world, users can explore destinations and attractions in a way that would not be feasible in the real world. For example, virtual exploration of ancient sites allows tourists to visit places like the Colosseum in Rome or the Lighthouse of Alexandria on a virtual level. These virtual tours offer a high degree of flexibility, as they provide the opportunity to discover the sights at one's own pace and focus on individual aspects.

In the future, the metaverse is likely to become even more significant for tourism, as it offers travelers an option to participate in virtual experiences and activities. For example, the metaverse could enable users to participate in virtual activities such as diving, mountain climbing, or skydiving without having to be physically present. Additionally, it could offer travelers the chance to learn about different cultures and traditions by virtually participating in festivals and celebrations without leaving their own homes. Although this may initially seem unusual, there are already individual experiences in such rather atypical environments for VR technology. The Rulantica operated by the aforementioned Mack GmbH, where VR is combined with snorkeling and diving, is an example of such approaches. [STU19].

Tourism in the metaverse represents an industry that is also increasingly attracting interest from German users. According to a Bitkom study [BIT22], 21% of Germans can imagine starting their holiday trips with the help of VR headsets from around 2030 to explore the world in a different way and have experiences that would be unattainable in reality and the physical world. Examples of these new possibilities include virtual excursions into the deep sea or into far-back epochs. The potential for virtual travel destinations is obviously great and can help discover hard-to-reach or entirely unreachable places and also to virtually explore potential holiday destinations in advance. The

Fig. 4.9 Traveling in the future metaverse. (Based on [BIT22b])

example was already mentioned in the context of gastronomy in Sect. 4.5 in this context, and other destinations like Machu Picchu in Peru are also considering such a solution. [MACoJ].

Another Bitkom survey [BIT22b] also shows that 87% of respondents believe that traditional travel will continue to represent an important change from daily life in the future. It is assumed that international online portals will continue to dominate travel reservations, while traditional travel agencies are likely to further disappear or be displaced. Most vacation experiences are also already shared via social media channels and messenger apps, indicating a growing relevance of the digital world in our daily lives. Social media users are also interested in participating in the vacations of their friends and families through vacation photos on social platforms.

Although all this may seem strange, it does not seem far-fetched to take a vacation in the metaverse. In view of technological progress, there is a noteworthy development, the "M Social Decentraland," a hotel in the metaverse. This hotel (see also Fig. 4.10) is located near Genesis Plaza, the main entry area of Decentraland, and stands out with its architecture featuring virtual glass walls, neon pink accents, and a large "M" on each side. In the lobby, guests are greeted by an avatar who guides them through the hotel. According to a press release, some lucky virtual guests can even win real hotel surprises. [TEO22, MUL23]

> "The goal of M Social is to be unique and different,"

said Kwek Leng Beng, the Executive Chairman of Millennium & Copthorne Hotels Limited and also responsible for the virtual project: [MIL22]

> *"To look into the future, we must look beyond the traditional model of hospitality and excite our guests with new immersive experiences. The hotel hopes to redefine hospitality through M Social Decentraland by creating online adventures that integrate into real events."*

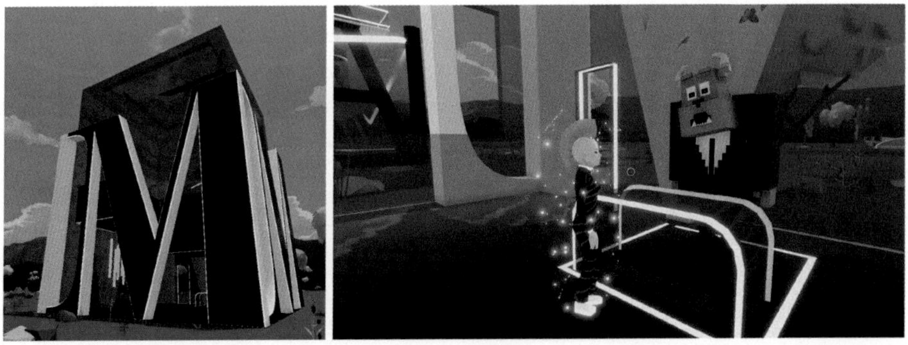

Fig. 4.10 Hotels in the metaverse (here: M Social). ([MUL23, TEO22])

In the future, M Social Decentraland also plans to host special events for holidays and other occasions such as Valentine's Day. Additionally, Millennium Hotels and Resorts plans to hold talks with partners about possible future collaborations on various platforms. Saurabh Prakash, Group Senior Vice President, Commercial, Millennium Hotels and Resorts, told BizBash that the M Social Hotel was launched as a new channel to attract customers and familiarize them with Millennium Hotels and Resorts, particularly the M Social brand. [TEO22]

4.5.7 Education

As already mentioned in Sect. 4.5.6"Tourism," the metaverse also opens up opportunities for educational purposes by creating the possibility of setting up interactive, immersive, and collaborative learning environments that enable learners to gain an improved understanding of ideas, concepts, and entire subject areas.

An example of the application of the metaverse in the school sector is the use of virtual worlds like Second Life or Minecraft. Within such virtual environments, students can implement both individual and collaborative projects, which help to expand their understanding of concepts such as geometry, architecture, and programming. The design of virtual laboratories is also possible in immersive spaces like the metaverse. In these, students can conduct experiments without relying on physical resources. Furthermore, they can try out inaccessible or dangerous experiments that would be unthinkable or too risky in the real world. This allows them to gain a deeper understanding of scientific ideas and improve their skills in data analysis and problem-solving. [RZE20, DAV22, HOW22]

Another example focusing on social education consists of connecting students from different countries and cultures. Through virtual exchange programs, learners from diverse nations and cultures can cooperate in a shared virtual environment and benefit from each other. [RZE20, DAV22, HOW22] In this way, a creative, interactive, and more immersive form of learning is enabled for the students, intensifying their understanding of ideas and topics.

But the metaverse is also gaining increasing acceptance in the academic education sector. It enables students and researchers to present and share their work in innovative ways and promotes collaboration and exchange with like-minded individuals worldwide. Virtual conferences are an example of this. They allow participants from all over the world to attend presentations and poster sessions without physical barriers, exhibit and publish in virtual spaces, and discuss research results and ideas in virtual forums.

Furthermore, virtual laboratories, as already mentioned, offer numerous possibilities for researchers. Experiments that are not possible in the real world due to resource, safety, or ethical constraints could be conducted here. This enables more effective research and the faster acquisition of new insights. [MAC09] Additionally, opportunities for collaboration and exchange between researchers worldwide arise by using virtual workspaces. Regardless of location, they can work together on projects and exchange ideas, which in turn facilitates cooperation between scientists from different countries and promotes international collaboration.

Efforts are also being made to expand learning platforms like Moodle with the help of the metaverse. Moodle is an open-source platform that allows teachers and lecturers to provide and manage learning content online. The metaverse could potentially help make learning platforms like Moodle and similar ones even more efficient and attractive than they already are. [SA23, SAAoJ] One way such platforms can benefit from the metaverse is by integrating into existing virtual environments. Through such a connection, teachers and lecturers can create an interactive and immersive experience for their students. This can be realized, for example, by incorporating virtual learning games or simulations that support and enrich the learning process. By integrating access to the metaverse into Moodle, students can further interact and cooperate to learn together and expand their skills. Moreover, the metaverse opens up great possibilities for the personalization of learning content. By using metadata and machine learning, corresponding learning platforms can better capture and adapt to the learning needs and preferences of students. Thus, options for providing personalized learning content that meets the individual needs and interests of students are available. Overall, the metaverse offers numerous opportunities to optimize teaching/learning platforms like Moodle and others. The integration of virtual worlds, the use as a Moodle extension, and the adaptation of learning materials contribute to making these platforms more efficient and appealing. [HAN23]

Although some critics see the metaverse as a threat to the conventional education system, it actually represents an enrichment and opens up new ways for students to enhance their skills and expand their knowledge. The conventional education system will continue to play an essential role in the education of students, as they still need to acquire basic skills such as reading, writing, and arithmetic, which are taught there. Additionally, the traditional system promotes social skills and the personal development of learners. However, the metaverse can help to expand and optimize the classical education system.

It is, however, essential to ensure that the metaverse is accessible to all students. Especially in Germany, widespread high-quality access to the internet poses a challenge. It would not be surprising if students lacked access to necessary technologies or if students could not afford the necessary devices or had problems learning in a virtual environment. For this reason alone, it is of great importance that the conventional education system is maintained and that students are supported in various ways.

4.5.8 The Metaverse and Medicine

It is to be expected that the idea of the metaverse will also play a significant role in the medical field. One area where this is already the case today is medical education. By setting up virtual environments, medical students can simulate scenarios in a realistic setting and thus improve their practical skills. An example of this is virtual emergency medicine simulators, where students are supposed to learn to react and work quickly and effectively in a stressful environment. [ZIV03, MEDoJ, VIN15] The field of telemedicine is also expected to undergo changes through the metaverse. By using VR, patients and doctors can interact with each other in real-time, regardless of their location. This allows patients to receive a diagnosis or even treatment from doctors who may be far away. [BAL21b, MAR22] This, in turn, could contribute to an improvement in the provision of care, for example, in rural areas.

Furthermore, the metaverse will also be used in medical research to accelerate the development of new drugs and therapies. Virtual environments can be used to simulate the effects of drugs on various human organs and systems or to explore new ways of medical interventions, potentially saving years of research and development. [KAW22]

Clinical treatment and hospitals can also benefit from the metaverse. By integrating virtual reality into hospital operations, they can also increase their efficiency and effectiveness, ultimately achieving better patient outcomes. An example of this is the use of VR for training medical staff. By setting up virtual environments through medical facilities, doctors, nurses, and other staff can be given the option to learn and improve practical skills before applying them in the real world. The hope is that this will help reduce training costs and the time required for training while simultaneously improving the quality of education. Additionally, VR technology allows hospitals to offer a broader range of services and, for example, reach patients from remote locations. This can help reduce waiting times for appointments and improve access to high-quality healthcare. The virtual environments also help improve the accuracy of diagnoses and treatment plans. By generating individual virtual models of the patient, doctors and other medical professionals can obtain an accurate representation of the patient's body and make more informed decisions. Moreover, virtual environments can also help improve the planning of surgical procedures and minimize risks. [WAN22, WU23]

There are also many opportunities in the care sector to benefit from the integration of virtual reality into the metaverse. The technology can help improve the quality of care, increase the efficiency of workflows, and make life easier for those in need of care. One area where the metaverse can be particularly advantageous in the care sector is the training of caregivers. Just like in hospitals, virtual environments can be used to train caregivers in various situations and improve their skills without putting patients at risk. This ultimately increases the quality of care and the safety of patients. [WAN22]

Another area where the metaverse can be beneficial in the care sector is improving communication between caregivers and patients. Virtual environments can be used to better understand the needs and wishes of those in need of care and provide them with better care and support. Additionally, virtual environments have been shown to help reduce social isolation among the elderly by facilitating access to social contacts and activities. [WAN22, MOZ23] Both in care and inpatient treatment in hospitals, the metaverse can help increase efficiency. There is potential to improve logistics and workflow planning by using automated systems or virtual assistants optimized on their digital or real twins. This can help save time and resources and increase the quality of care. [ADI23, Kal22]

Ultimately, health insurance companies also hope to benefit from the metaverse. An example here is the improvement of patient education. By creating virtual environments, health insurance companies can offer interactive training and information that help patients better understand their health and better prepare for their treatment. This, in turn, can help improve adherence to treatment plans and ultimately improve patient health. But business processes such as billing are also expected to benefit from the metaverse by increasing the degree of automation and digitization. Additionally, health insurance companies could set up and use their own virtual environments to accelerate the development of treatment plans and therapies. By simulating diseases and treatment plans, health insurance companies can better understand which treatments are most effective and what risks are associated with them. This can further help reduce overall healthcare costs by avoiding unnecessary treatments and selecting more effective therapies. [SOS22, ADI23, KAL22]

The mentioned possibilities that the metaverse opens up in the medical field also pose a challenge for the traditional medical care system. It offers new opportunities for the provision of health services and collaboration between patients, providers, and health insurance companies, enabling access to medical services in real-time and from anywhere in the world without patients having to physically go to a doctor or medical facility. However, this can lead to traditional "on-site" medical care systems losing significance. Another challenge is that the metaverse gives patients greater control over their healthcare. Patients can access information and resources to manage their own health instead of relying on the help of doctors or other medical professionals. This too can lead to the role of doctors and other medical professionals in healthcare diminishing. [ADI23] The ethical role of "Dr. Google" is deliberately not discussed here.

Ultimately, the metaverse can help improve access to health services, especially for people living in rural areas or regions with limited access to medical care. By using virtual environments, patients and medical professionals can communicate with each other regardless of their location and select any possible medical services and utilize them even more than with or through the WWW.

4.5.9 The Business Internal Metaverse

The term "Business Internal Metaverse" or "Intraverse" [MAL22] refers to virtual environments specifically developed for use within a company or organization. It is an extension of the intranet into a kind of closed virtual ecosystem that is only accessible to employees, executives, and other authorized persons of the company. Such a business internal metaverse allows users to meet, communicate, collaborate, and complete tasks in a virtual environment, just like any other "public" metaverse. However, this virtual world integrates applications and tools specifically tailored to the needs of the company, such as virtual conference rooms, digital workspaces, training modules, and simulation programs, etc. At the same time, this virtual world limits access to company-related information and communication to the corporate context.

The concept of the business internal metaverse is still relatively new, but there are already a number of companies using virtual work environments to better connect their employees and integrate them more optimally into internal processes. An example of this is Spatial, which has developed a virtual work platform that allows users to collaborate in a shared virtual environment, no matter where they are physically located. [CAR23]

However, the future of this form of the metaverse seems to lie particularly in establishing processes that also involve customer interaction. Some examples of such processes could be: [MAL22, ROE22, CAR23]

- Companies can set up virtual conference rooms to hold customer meetings. Customers can simply log in via a virtual platform and participate in a virtual meeting without having to be physically present.
- Companies can also set up customer support. Customers can use such a virtual customer support platform to ask their questions or report problems. The customer support representative or their digital twin can then respond via a virtual platform and provide solutions. This representative can be either a real employee or an autonomously acting support assistant or chatbot.
- Companies can also conduct virtual product presentations. Customers can log in and be virtually guided through the company's products. The advantage here is that customers can see and try out the products in an interactive 3D environment without having to be physically present.
- Companies can offer virtual training for customers in the business internal metaverse. Customers can register for virtual training and then meet in a virtual classroom with other participants. The training can be conducted by either a real employee or a virtual trainer who guides the participants through the training.
- Companies can also host any other type of virtual events in the business internal metaverse. For example, they can set up a virtual, immersive customer forum where customers can discuss ideas and suggestions with each other or with support and provide feedback. Virtual product launch events are also conceivable, where customers have the opportunity to try out the company's newly introduced products in an interactive environment.

A particularly significant area for the implementation of a business internal metaverse is support. "Immersive support" refers to a form of technical support or customer service where support staff meet customers in an immersive, virtual environment to solve problems or answer questions. Unlike traditional customer support, where customers are usually assisted by phone or email, immersive support allows for more intensive and personal interaction between customers and support staff. For example, support staff could show the customer in a virtual but realistic environment how to use a product specifically or how to independently fix a technical problem. This can not only increase customer satisfaction but also improve the efficiency of customer support by solving problems faster and more effectively. [MON22, MAL22]

In the manufacturing industry, virtual reality technology (VR) is already being used to create simulations of factories and production processes. VR technology can also be used in this area for employee training, to prepare them for specific work situations and to improve their skills. However, it gains greater significance through the digital replicas of plants and entire manufacturing and production parts. For example, virtual factories are created in which various production processes can be simulated. [GEY23]

A topic now considered old is the so-called Industry 4.0. It aims to create an intelligent factory where production, logistics, technology, and workforce are interconnected to enable more efficient and flexible production processes. By networking machines, plants, and systems in real-time, autonomous decisions are to be made to optimize production processes. [PLAoJ] At first glance, the idea of Industry 4.0 and that of the metaverse do not have much in common, but there are still some possible connections:

- Both Industry 4.0 and the metaverse are visionary concepts that represent a future of digital optimization and digital coexistence.
- Both concepts use technologies such as artificial intelligence, virtual and augmented reality, the Internet of Things, blockchain, etc. Technology is the key to digitizing and optimizing reality.
- Industry 4.0 strives for seamless networking of production facilities, machines, systems, and people to increase efficiency and improve decision-making. The metaverse is such an extended form of networking, where people can interact in virtual worlds.
- Both concepts involve personalization. In Industry 4.0, products and services are tailored to the individual needs of customers. In the metaverse, users can customize their virtual identity and create their own worlds, and in the future, also influence the formation and processes of procedures.
- Industry 4.0 collects and analyzes large amounts of data to make better decisions and increase efficiency. In the metaverse, a lot of data is also generated, which can be used for personalization and improving the user experience.

The connection between Industry 4.0 and the metaverse could thus lead to production processes being simulated in a virtual world to improve the efficiency and flexibility of the real factory. In such a virtual world, autonomous decisions could be made to optimize production while simultaneously simulating the interaction between employees and facilities. By integrating metaverse technologies into Industry 4.0 solutions, new forms of collaboration and employee training could be enabled.

The ideas usually mentioned for the area of maintenance and repair with the help of the metaverse do not necessarily sound new:

- By using VR and AR, the metaverse can help train and educate employees. For example, maintenance and repair technicians can train in a virtual environment that resembles the real environment in which they will work.
- In the metaverse, sensors and other devices can be monitored in real-time. This allows maintenance technicians to diagnose and fix problems remotely before downtime occurs.
- The metaverse offers a platform for collaboration between maintenance technicians, engineers, and other professionals. For example, they can work together on a virtual model of a machine to solve problems and make improvements.
- With the metaverse, maintenance technicians and engineers can visualize and analyze complex information. For example, they can create 3D models of machines and facilities and access various data in real-time to quickly identify and solve problems.
- By analyzing data in real-time, maintenance technicians and engineers can recognize and predict (error) patterns and when maintenance work will be needed. This allows for preventive maintenance measures to be taken to minimize downtime and extend the lifespan of machines.

4.5.10 Metaverse Service Providing

Not only "the inside" of the metaverse is suitable for being managed. The term "Metaverse Service Providing" refers to the idea of providing services within, but also outside of, the metaverse. Metaverse platforms are virtual environments where users can interact, create and share content, as well as conduct communicative and business transactions. Individual users in private settings, as well as companies, can use these platforms to communicate and interact, but also to present their own products and services and reach their target audiences. A wide variety of services are needed for this:

- Development and design of content and applications in and for the platform
- Hosting and management of servers
- Provision of cloud-based storage and processing services
- Security services and identity management within the metaverse and its platforms
- AI and machine learning services to improve interaction and user experience
- Payment processing and management within the metaverse.

Companies that specialize in services in the field of Metaverse Service Providing offer these services and work closely with platform operators and customers to ensure that the mutual needs are met. Such companies are usually already specialized in the specific requirements of the internet and therefore have sufficient experience to provide services for the new Metaverse environment. This area includes services such as "land development" and building construction, which make an important contribution to the development of virtual worlds in the Metaverse by helping developers and users design virtual worlds and buildings:

- Land developers can, for example, design and create virtual landscapes and environments that can then be used by users for their own purposes. They model the topography, vegetation, and other features of virtual worlds and adapt them to optimize immersion and user experiences.
- Another important role is played by building construction or modeling. Here, the special and individual wishes of the clients are incorporated so that the virtual buildings can be used as virtual offices, shops, apartments, parks, or for other purposes. Companies like VRJAM [VRJoJ] and Sine Wave Entertainment [SINoJ] offer tools and technologies for creating such virtual buildings and environments, which can then be integrated as seamlessly as possible into the Metaverse platforms.
- Both land development and building construction contribute significantly to creating the most immersive and appealing virtual environment possible.
- Companies like Decentraland, Somnium Space, and many others offer virtual plots for purchase. Decentraland has even further developed this and now offers the possibility to lease or rent acquired virtual land. Besides the actual development and modeling of virtual "land," there is an opportunity to establish virtual real estate development as an offered service in the future. Such "Virtual Estate Services" focus on the purchase, sale, and management of virtual plots and properties in the Metaverse. Examples of this can currently be found mainly among platform providers: [STO22]
  - As mentioned above, Decentraland allows users to buy, sell, and manage virtual plots. The company also offers tools and services for developing content and applications on their platform.
  - Somnium Space is another immersive and decentralized virtual world where users can buy, build, and manage plots. This platform also offers users a variety of tools and services to design their virtual worlds. [SOMoJ, SOM22]
  - The Sandbox offers users the option to create their own virtual worlds and share them with other users. Additionally, users have the opportunity to buy, sell, and trade virtual plots. [THEoJ, THE20]
  - A different approach to the concept of "land" is chosen by the platform Upland. The virtual land offered here is based on the real world. Users can also buy, sell, and trade virtual plots here, but these are digital twins of real locations in the real world. [UPLOJ, CHA22]
- Larger goals are pursued by virtual urban planning with the concept of Building Information Modeling (BIM). This approach focuses specifically on the construction sector and enables the creation of detailed digital models of individual buildings or entire urban infrastructures. It includes information on geometry, materials, costs, schedules, and other relevant data. BIM is typically used by architects, engineers, construction companies, and other construction professionals to manage the

entire lifecycle of buildings and urban infrastructures. By combining BIM and the Metaverse, virtual environments are created where buildings and infrastructures can be visualized and manipulated. This opens up new possibilities for collaboration, simulation, and optimization of buildings and infrastructures in the virtual environment. [BOR15]
- Companies like Matterport offer technologies for surveying real conditions and the resulting 3D modeling of buildings and environments, which can then be integrated into the Metaverse using the aforementioned BIM, for example. [JAV21]
- The "Metaverse Service Provider" category also includes the design of avatars, fashion, and accessories. Since avatars represent the digital twins of users, the design of avatars and accessories for them is an important aspect of metaverse service providing, as this increases the possibilities for personalization of the user experience and thus enhances user acceptance and engagement with the platform. A multitude of companies have already established themselves in this area: [STO22]
  - Daz 3D specializes in creating 3D models, characters, and accessories for various applications, including the metaverse.
  - Morph 3D offers a toolkit for creating and customizing avatars for the metaverse.
  - IMVU is a social media platform that specializes in creating and customizing avatars and offers a variety of accessories that users can purchase.
  - Second Life is the oldest virtual world that has demonstrated what monetization and management of services in the metaverse mean. Here, you can find examples of tools offered to users to create their own avatars and accessories, as well as management tools for the real estate market. How powerful these tools can be for trading virtual real estate was shown by a user in 2006, who became the first millionaire in the metaverse as a real estate agent. [RIX22, GOL21]

4.5.11 Back into the real world

The examples of "Metaverse Service Providing" listed in the previous section mainly referred to services within the metaverse. However, a variety of services are also necessary for the development and support of individual users, as well as entire platforms, which are based in the real world and, so to speak, keep the metaverse "running" from the outside. This includes both software and hardware services in the real world:

- Cloud-based services enable users and platform providers to host and operate their own virtual environments and applications in the metaverse.
- Companies that develop VR headsets and other hardware for immersive applications can easily adapt and offer their products for the metaverse as well.
- 3D modeling software can be provided by companies to facilitate the creation of content and entire environments in the metaverse for users and operators.

- The development of haptic feedback systems allows users to experience the virtual world of the metaverse through tactile sensations and feedback.
- This idea can be further developed by considering additional human sensory modalities towards barrier-free access to metaverses. This will gain increased importance in the future, among other things, through the European Accessibility Act [AMT19] and the German Accessibility Strengthening Act. [BMA21]
- Companies can also offer AI-based services that provide users in the metaverse with personalized experiences and recommendations.
- Finally, special devices and apps can also be developed for mobile use, allowing users to flexibly access the metaverse on the go.

4.5.12 The "God Role"

The idea of a "God Role" in the metaverse refers to the fact that users, companies, as well as service providers and platform operators can have "god-like" power and control over the design and development of virtual land, environments, and avatars. In many virtual worlds and platforms based on the concept of the metaverse, it is common for there to be a central authority or a group of individuals responsible for providing virtual land and controlling the design of landscapes and avatars. These individuals, in a way, assume a "God Role" as they have the ability to shape and control the virtual world according to their vision. They alone can decide which types of buildings and objects are allowed in the virtual world and which are not, and they can also decide who has access to certain areas of the virtual world and who is denied entry. From their respective perspectives, they pursue the best goals for "their" worlds.

However, this "God Role" can also be criticized as it ultimately creates an imbalance of power and may take away freedom from the users of the metaverse, i.e., the visitors and participants of the worlds, thus restricting them from making their own experiences and freely designing worlds. Some virtual platforms and worlds have therefore begun to give users more control over the design and development of their own virtual environments to balance this distribution of power.

The evaluation of this role can thus be both positive and negative, depending on how it is exercised and also depending on the values and beliefs of the individuals who assume this role. Abuse of centralized control is possible in virtuality just as it is in reality. Not only can the freedom and creativity of users be restricted in this way. Users can also be discriminated against, for example, by being excluded from the virtual world through the choice of avatar or even without any reason, or by being denied access to certain parts of the platform and the use of certain services.

Indeed, there have already been reports of abuse in the metaverse in some cases. [EHL20, LE22] It therefore seems significant that the operators of virtual platforms and worlds find ways to ensure that, on the one hand, power is distributed more evenly and that, on the other hand, the interests and needs of users are placed at the center. This can be achieved, for example, through the implementation of democratic structures, transparent decision-making, and the creation of an open and inclusive community.

The formation of closed groups, similar to sects and secret societies, could also occur in the context of a "God Role" in the metaverse [END22, MOR22] If a person or a group of people who exercise control over a part of the virtual land or platform exercise their power in an authoritarian or undemocratic manner, this could lead to certain users banding together and forming a kind of cult or secret society to defend their own interests or to resist the ruling authority. Individuals who assume the "God Role" at this point can play an important role in creating a safe and protected environment by, for example, enforcing policies to combat hate speech or cyberbullying. They can also help prevent fraud or abuse by monitoring users and reporting suspicious activities. Here, too, the analogy to the internet can certainly be useful to highlight the significance of these development potentials. Even if it does not necessarily have to be a "Dark Metaverse," platforms like 4chan or 8chan and others can be used as examples for countermeasures. [DAL15, OHL19]

Of course, not every form of group formation in the metaverse must have negative effects. It is quite possible for users to come together in a positive way to work on projects, exchange ideas, or simply form a community of like-minded individuals. The key is to ensure that the role in question is exercised in a way that respects and promotes the freedom and creativity of users and that an open and inclusive community is created based on mutual respect and collaboration.

A centralized control of a virtual world or platform can also have a positive effect by helping to maintain the quality of the virtual world at a high level, as the operators can set the standards and rules that all users must adhere to. This can ensure a uniform appearance and a consistent user experience, which in turn can increase user engagement and promote community growth. Ultimately, individuals in the "God Role" can also act as creative catalysts, promoting the development of new ideas and concepts and inspiring the community to make their own contributions. When this role is used positively, it can help maximize the potential of the metaverse as a virtual world that offers new opportunities for interaction, creativity, and collaboration.

4.5.13 DAOs and the Metaverse

DAO stands for Decentralized Autonomous Organization. These are organizations that are based on a decentralized network such as blockchain technology, where financial and other transactions as well as the rules of the organization are recorded. Unlike traditional companies or organizations that are led by a central authority, a DAO is a self-organized and autonomous structure that is jointly controlled by its members. As a relatively new form of organization, the exact legal status of DAOs is still generally unclear. [CHO17]

In the metaverse, DAOs can be used as tools for community management and project coordination. Furthermore, they can also be used for project financing, decision-making, and resource distribution. DAOs enable users to create a democratic and transparent organization that operates without human intermediaries and is based on consensus. By using smart contracts, a DAO can ensure that decisions and transactions are carried out in a transparent and trustworthy manner without the need for a central authority or intermediaries. This can help foster trust and collaboration within the community, as all members are equally involved and can participate in decisions. Additionally, DAOs can also provide a way to distribute revenues and profits from projects in a fair and transparent manner, creating an incentive for users to participate in the development and growth of the metaverse. [LIU22, MOR20]

An example of a DAO in the metaverse is "The Sandbox." On this platform, players can create their own assets, and these assets can be sold as NFTs on Ethereum. The governance of the game is managed by a DAO called "The Sandbox DAO," which is controlled by the token holders. The DAO decides on the direction of the game, new features and upgrades, and the allocation of resources. [SPE21]

In the future, DAOs in the metaverse could play an even more important role, as they could be used as tools for creating decentralized companies and autonomous organizations. DAOs could also be used to regulate emerging future markets in the metaverse by making transparent decisions and representing the interests of the community. Conversely, existing DAOs from the metaverse could also benefit in the real world by using the metaverse as a tool for creating decentralized organizations and companies. In the real world, DAOs can be used to minimize the risk of fraud and corruption, for example, by making transparent decisions and reducing the influence of human intermediaries:

- An example is "MolochDAO," which is designed as a decentralized investment platform for funding blockchain startups. This DAO consists of members who deposit ETH tokens into the DAO and jointly decide on investments. MolochDAO is managed by a smart contract and is decentralized, meaning that decisions are made by the community and not by a central authority. It should be noted here that MolochDAO is the further development of a DAO that was created in response to a hacker attack on the predecessor DAO. [DUN19]
- Another example is "MakerDAO," also a decentralized platform, but with the goal of issuing stable coins on Ethereum. The DAO members hold MKR tokens, which give them voting rights in decisions regarding the management of the platform. [SMAoJ]

In the future, DAOs in the metaverse could also be used to connect physical and virtual assets. For example, DAOs could be used to enable the tokenization of real estate in the real world, which can then be traded as virtual assets in the metaverse. Additionally, DAOs could also be used to decentralize the governance of open-source software projects by having decisions made by a community rather than a central authority.

DAOs offer a way to create democratic and transparent organizations based on consensus and decentralized governance in both the metaverse and the real world. However, there are currently few political DAOs that explicitly focus on the metaverse. Only a few political organizations are currently explicitly dealing with, for example, blockchain technology and the possibilities for DAOs:

- An example of such political efforts is the party "DEMOCRACY IN MOTION" in Germany, which sees itself as a citizens' movement and wants to use blockchain technology to promote direct democracy. The party is working on developing its own DAO system that allows members to participate in the decision-making and political agenda of the party. [DEMoJ]
- Another example is the "Taipei City Government," which has implemented a blockchain system called "TIPAS" (Taipei Smart City Public Affairs System) in Taiwan. TIPAS aims to improve the transparency and efficiency of the government by giving citizens access to government information and decisions. The platform also uses DAO-like structures to make decisions and perform governance functions. [TAIoJ]

Political DAOs and their use in the metaverse seem to be in a rather early stage of development. It remains to be seen how the underlying technologies and concepts will be used by political organizations in the future.

4.5.14 The yet to be imagined

The technical-technological development not only in the metaverse, but especially there, is diverse and also of high speed. "The yet to be imagined" should therefore refer to future experiences and technologies in the context of the metaverse that are currently not conceivable or even possible. It refers to the idea that the metaverse can and will be a space where new types of experiences will be possible and will emerge, which are currently not really imaginable. While this may sound like science fiction on the one hand, on the other hand, a look at the history of almost every technology shows that there have always been developments and application ideas that were not addressed at the beginning and were not conceivable. Human creativity is always an essential driver of developments and the discovery of new areas of application.

It is foreseeable that the integration of additional human sensory and action modalities, beyond those that have been standardly addressed so far, for the interaction of the human user with IT systems and the internet, will receive a significant boost through the metaverse:

For example, gustatory experiences could be developed in the metaverse for virtual restaurants or shops, so that the enjoyment and consequently the sale of food and beverages would also be possible in virtuality. In this process, smells and tastes can be virtually reproduced to offer a more immersive experience. This could even go so far that food is produced with the help of 3D printers, which can be eaten directly on-site in the metaverse. [BLU23, SNI23] The screen that enables a taste experience by licking already exists for this purpose. [KLA22]

Olfactory experiences can also be simulated in the metaverse. For example, perfumes and scents can be created in the virtual world using special devices. These devices can release specific scent molecules to simulate a particular smell. In the real world, there are already some, though rarely encountered, devices for this purpose. [SCH23a, LIU23]

Brain-Interfaces (BCI, Brain Computing Interface), which are being researched and developed in numerous institutions, can also contribute in the future to making the metaverse even more immersive. Such a brain-interface allows users to interact with the metaverse by using their brainwaves directly and without other interaction devices such as a keyboard, mouse, or even voice input. By wearing a special headset, the user's brain can be recorded and analyzed to control actions in the metaverse. This technology could also be used to create "new senses" that allow the user to gather additional information and experience the world in a new way. [RAB15, BON21]

Not only sensory channels but also actuation modalities can be included in the development of the metaverse. The use of prostheses and implants is also being discussed in the context of the metaverse [BON22]. People with physical limitations can use prostheses and implants to expand their abilities in the metaverse and have new experiences. For example, a person with an arm prosthesis can use a BCI system to grasp and move objects.

The mentioned examples bring to mind the merging of technical devices with the human body. The metaverse and transhumanism are thus closely connected, as both concepts are based on this merging of humans and technology. Transhumanism is at its core a philosophical movement that advocates the use of technology to enhance human abilities and experiences. [BOS14, HUB20] It refers to the idea that humans will be able to improve their physical and cognitive abilities through the use of technology and scientific advances. The metaverse, on the other hand, offers a virtual environment where technology and reality can merge to create an immersive experience that allows the user to move in a different reality. The metaverse can therefore certainly be seen as part of this movement, as it allows the user to expand their experiential worlds and redefine their identity. In this metaverse, the user can, for example, expand their cognitive abilities by interacting with intelligent virtual assistants or by learning new skills in the virtual world. At the same time, the user can also improve their physical abilities by walking through virtual worlds or by interacting with and using robots and artificial limbs in the virtual world. These are all aspects associated with transhumanism, where technological improvements are used to expand and enhance human abilities.

There are already a number of technologies that are associated with both the metaverse and transhumanism, such as the aforementioned examples of brain-computer interfaces, prostheses and implants, and also new artificial senses. A good example of this connection between the metaverse and transhumanism is Neil Harbisson, who was already introduced in Sect. 3.1"Sensory Fusion". He is an artist and activist who was born with the rare condition of monochromatism, which causes a limitation in color vision. However, Harbisson initiated the development of an implant called "Eyeborg," which allows him to "hear" colors and thus perceive an extended color spectrum.

[BAN12, THO13, DON17] He can also use this ability in the metaverse to experience the world in a new way.

Harbisson has clearly spoken out in favor of using such technologies in the context of the metaverse. He believes that the metaverse offers an opportunity to redefine and expand human identities and experiences. By sharing his experiences and technologies with others, he hopes to expand people's imaginations and create new possibilities to further develop the human species. [MAA22] However, how the metaverse and transhumanism as a vision of the future will ultimately look cannot—and should not—be predicted at this point.

4.6 And how is that Supposed to Work?

Another strand of the further development of the internet is seen in the aforementioned Web3. In contrast to Web 2.0, where centralized platforms like Google, Facebook, or Amazon control the majority of user activities, Web3 is designed for the use of decentralized protocols and technologies. In this Web3, data, applications, and assets are no longer stored on central servers but on distributed networks of computers, the so-called Distributed Ledger Technology. The idea of this distribution is largely based on blockchain technology, but also on other technologies and protocols such as the Inter-Planetary File System (IPFS). [SCH19a, IPFoJ, LUN16]

In contrast to Web 2.0, Web3 is designed for the use of decentralized protocols and technologies. This results in differences between Web 2.0 and Web3 in various aspects:

- *Control:* Web 2.0 platforms control the data and activities of users on their platforms. Since Web3, on the other hand, is designed to be decentralized, users are supposed to retain control over their data and their interactions on the web.
- *Security:* In Web 2.0, data and applications are stored on centralized servers. Thus, they offer a large attack surface for hacker attacks and data losses. Since Web3 is supposed to be organized in a decentralized manner, other protocols and technologies such as blockchain are used, which are supposed to increase the security and integrity of data and applications.
- *Transparency:* In Web 2.0, the business models of the platforms are often opaque, which can be at the expense of user privacy. In Web3, on the other hand, the business models are supposed to be more transparent and traceable, which is supposed to open up more opportunities for users to protect their privacy.
- *Innovation:* Likewise, in Web 2.0, innovations are often controlled by the big "GAFA" players. This leads to little room for new ideas and developments. In Web3, on the other hand, there is supposed to be more freedom for developers and users, which is supposed to provide more space for innovations.

Such and other frequently mentioned differences show that the idea of Web3 represents a fundamental change in the way the internet is supposed to be used and can be used. In particular, the decentralized and more transparent infrastructure is supposed to contribute to giving users back control over their data and interactions. The use of new decentralized technologies enables Web3 to bypass many of the centralized control mechanisms of Web 2.0. [NAB23] From this decentralization, a number of advantages are supposed to arise in Web3 in the future:

- *Security:* By storing data and applications on many different computers in the network, it is more difficult to attack, hack, or manipulate them. The use of cryptographic methods and algorithms also ensures the integrity of data and applications.
- *Transparency:* The decentralized approach also offers higher transparency, as every participant has access to the same information. This also means that it is more difficult to spread false or misleading information.
- *Independence:* Furthermore, it also enables users and developers to act independently and without being dependent on centralized platforms. This opens up greater freedom and flexibility in the development and use of applications and services in Web3.
- *Interoperability:* By using open standards and protocols, the decentralized infrastructure of Web3 can enable better interoperability between different applications and services. This, in turn, can lead to improved user-friendliness and smoother information exchange.

The ultimate goal of Web3 is based on the hope of building a truly open and democratic internet that can be used by everyone. A goal that was intended for both the original web and Web 2.0, but which neither achieved—or could achieve. It is therefore actually astonishing that despite this high idealistic goal, many economic and commercial aspects are simultaneously being discussed in the context of Web3. These include the currently hotly debated Non-Fungible Tokens, Smart Contracts, and of course cryptocurrencies.

Cryptocurrencies are digital currencies that are secured and managed through cryptographic methods. In the metaverse, these currencies can play an important role as they offer a secure and transparent way to transfer and store financial values within the virtual ecosystem. In addition to the cryptocurrencies known outside the metaverse, such as Bitcoin and ETHER, numerous platforms also manage their own currencies. An example of this is ROBUX, the currency within Roblox. ROBUX, like other currencies such as SAND on the Sandbox platform or MANA in Decentraland, is used to buy and sell digital goods and services within the game. As with their "big brothers" Bitcoin and ETHER, cryptographic methods are also applied here to ensure the security and integrity of the currency. However, the platforms' own currencies certainly have the goal, in addition to commercial and financial objectives, of binding users to the platform, as the virtual assets such as land or virtual artworks are located on the respective platform. Switching to another platform is associated with high effort. Nevertheless, numerous platforms increasingly rely on the well-known Bitcoin and even more on ETHER, which could at least simplify a switch from one platform to another.

Another way to use cryptocurrencies in the metaverse is the integration of decentralized financial services, known as DeFi. Such applications enable users to access a variety of financial services, such as borrowing or lending money, trading assets, or earning interest on deposits. By using cryptocurrencies, these services can be offered in a decentralized and transparent manner, which means more freedom and autonomy for users. It is likely to be expected that in the future, more and more virtual currencies and financial services will emerge in the metaverse, based on the principles of cryptocurrencies and decentralization. [ZET20]

Decentralization also benefits marketplaces in Web3 and the metaverse by opening up the possibility for users to trade directly with each other as peer-to-peer platforms, without the need for a central intermediary as an infomediary. Traditional marketplaces like eBay or Amazon rely on central systems where the marketplace operator controls pricing, payment processing, and fraud protection. In contrast, decentralized marketplaces enable users to trade directly with each other by using smart contracts, NFTs, and thus blockchain technology to facilitate and secure the trade. A well-known example of such a decentralized marketplace is OpenSea, which claims to be the largest marketplace for NFTs currently. [OPEoJ] OpenSea allows users to trade NFTs directly with each other without an intermediary such as a gallery owner or auction platform. Transactions are processed through smart contracts that ensure the seller transfers the NFT upon receipt of payment and that the buyer actually receives the NFT.

Through such decentralized marketplaces in the metaverse, users gain more control over the trade of virtual goods and services, which they have modeled in the sense of the above-postulated usage model and now want to manage themselves, leading to increased transparency and efficiency of trade transactions. Buyers also benefit from such marketplaces, as they can help reduce buyer and seller fees since there is no longer a central intermediary.

In addition to the commercial aspects, it is also important from the users' perspective to have control not only over the "modeled" and acquired artifacts in the metaverse but even more so to be sure of their own identity. This not only means protection against the "loss" of one's own avatar but also the management and control of personal data. Protecting one's privacy and knowing that personal data is secure should contribute to a safer and more trustworthy virtual experience in the metaverse. In Web3, identity management is seen as an important tool for this purpose. Two decentralized approaches in Web3 and another in the metaverse are usually mentioned for the goal of identity management: [ALZ20, SED21]

- *Decentralized Identifiers* (DIDs) are a concept that allows users to manage their identity across different services and platforms. A DID consists of a unique identifier stored on a blockchain and controlled by the user. This allows the user to manage their identity without being dependent on a central entity that stores and manages personal data.

- *Verifiable Credentials* (VCs) are digital certificates that allow users to prove their identity and the accuracy of their personal data. VCs can be issued by various services and platforms and contain encrypted information controlled by the user. Users can use these certificates to verify their identity and/or gain access to certain services or platforms.
- In addition, identity management in the metaverse is also achieved through the use of *avatars*. These can be linked to various identity solutions to ensure that the user's identity is protected and verified.

These properties of Web3 are also of crucial importance for the implementation of the metaverse. The metaverse requires a decentralized infrastructure, as it is a digital ecosystem consisting of numerous different applications and content that are used by many users simultaneously. The metaverse, therefore, cannot be controlled by a single centralized platform, as this would lead to restrictions on freedom, security, and innovation. For the realization of the idea of the metaverse, Web3 is thus an important foundation, as it prepares the decentralized infrastructure that makes it possible to build an open and free digital ecosystem. By using decentralized technologies, developers and users of the metaverse can act independently while ensuring the security and integrity of the platform.

The metaverse and its foundations, together with Web3, represent promising technologies that seem ready for use. The building blocks mentioned so far, as well as others, have already been able to provc their functionality. However, these proofs have mostly been delivered individually and, moreover, usually only on a small scale. Therefore, there is still a not insignificant number of limitations and challenges that need to be overcome, the most important of which are the following:

- *Scalability:* The metaverse requires an enormous amount of computing power and storage space to process the virtual world and user interactions. How large this will be in detail is unpredictable. But the mere idea that in the future as many and more users will immerse themselves in the metaverse as use the internet today stretches the imagination regarding the required computing power and storage needs. The current infrastructure of Web3 is nowhere near sufficient to meet these requirements. Some scaling solutions that are currently available seem promising but still need to be further developed to meet the demands of the metaverse.
- *Interoperability:* The various platforms and services in the metaverse must be able to communicate with each other to create a seamless and complete experience for users. This requires higher interoperability between the different technologies and platforms in Web3.
- *Privacy and Security:* Since the identity and personal data of users play an important role in the metaverse, appropriate privacy and security measures must be implemented

to ensure that this data remains safe and protected. Whether the approaches mentioned above are sufficient still needs to be examined in detail.
- *Accessibility:* To fully exploit the potential of the metaverse, users must have access to appropriate hardware and infrastructure. Currently, access to this technology is limited, and it is unclear how quickly the affordability and availability of hardware and infrastructure can be improved.

4.7 A Success Story?

According to many forecasts, the metaverse will achieve higher economic and social relevance than all previous technologies in the foreseeable future. It is expected that by the year 2028, the metaverse will reach a market size of more than 800 billion US dollars, while some analysts, such as Morgan Stanley, even predict a market volume of more than eight trillion US dollars. [KAN21, CHI22] Tim Sweeney, the founder of the video game company Epic Games and developer of Fortnite, describes the metaverse as a "multi-trillion-dollar opportunity." As early as 2016, he said: [TAK16]

> "This Metaverse is going to be far more pervasive and powerful than anything else. If one central company gains control of this, they will become more powerful than any government and be a god on Earth."

However, there are also some more cautious voices. For example, Evelyn R. Miralles, the Chief Principal Engineer at NASA's Lyndon B. Johnson Space Center, says: [BAL22]

> "At the moment metaverse is in the path to the 'peak of inflated expectations' phase."

and thus indirectly refers to the annually presented Hype Cycle by Gartner, which shows which technologies could be disruptive in the short and long term and with which technologies large companies should work to open up new markets and opportunities. The Hype Cycle shows the typical reception of a disruptive technology in the form of a curve:

- After a technology is discovered (Innovation Trigger), interest rises and …
- … expectations are inflated (Peak of Inflated Expectations).
- Then follows a phase of disappointment, as the technology cannot meet the expectations (Trough of Disillusionment).
- Subsequently, the technology develops and finds its true use cases (Slope of Enlightenment), …
- … until it finally becomes useful and widespread (Plateau of Productivity).

Gartner also examined the context of the metaverse and introduced a corresponding hype cycle in 2022. In this, some of the technologies that are of interest for immersive realities were examined more closely. For this purpose, Gartner examined more than 2000 technologies and selected 25 of them, which are defined as "must-know innovations to drive competitive differentiation and efficiency." These 25 technologies were included in the hype cycle. These technologies include, among others, Web3, NFT, and "digital humans." According to Gartner, these technologies are of great interest for the next 5 to 10 years. Additionally, Gartner identifies three so-called "macro themes" in this study:

- the expansion of immersive experiences,
- the acceleration of automation through artificial intelligence (AI), and
- the optimization of technology delivery to the market.

Some of the technologies listed in this hype cycle had been considered by Gartner in their analyses since at least 2017, thereby recognizing the technological potential that these are likely to exhibit in the future, as shown in Fig. 4.11. [PER22]

Tech companies, especially Facebook, also see the potential that is presumably in the metaverse and see a strategic future in this virtual world. Despite the positive perception by business consultants and analysts, however, the other possibility remains: [MAT22]

> "The hype around the metaverse will lead to billions of euros being spent on nonsense. A lot of dumb money will flow into virtual real estate and digital trinkets."

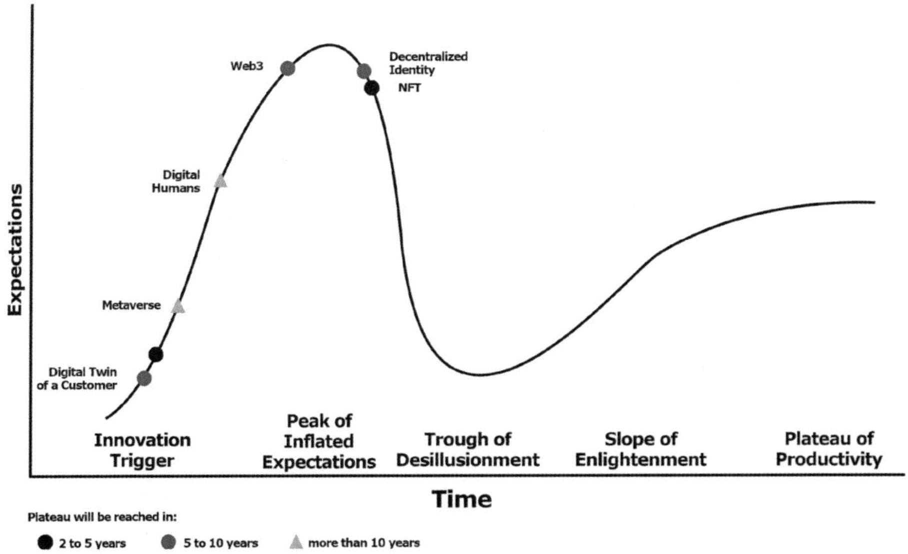

Fig. 4.11 The metaverse and relevant technologies for it. (Based on the Gartner Hype Cycle [PER22])

On the positive side, many companies are already working on "serious" applications in and around the metaverse:

- For example, digital twins of cities and factories are being developed to manage and maintain them remotely using VR technologies.
- Digital twins of humans help doctors prepare for surgeries by allowing the virtual body of the patient to be rotated and enlarged before an operation to better understand where the scalpel needs to be applied later.
- Similarly, digital twins of human organs can help the pharmaceutical industry create better medications and test them more intensively in the virtual space than would be possible in reality.

In addition, investments are being made in powerful infrastructures that can benefit other application areas in the future. However, the multitude of possible applications also shows that it is rather unlikely that a single, complete, and unified virtual world called the "metaverse" will emerge. Instead, many independent small platforms are likely to emerge, which, in the best case, will allow for easy switching between them.

Not least due to the quite impressive speed of development and spread of VR and AR in recent years, the concept of the metaverse has increasingly come into focus. As mentioned several times above, this goes so far that the metaverse is seen as the next major evolutionary stage of the internet. However, one aspect should be considered here that is easily overlooked.

In the development of the WWW, a particular mentality has developed on the part of users, which is likely to change only slowly and thus could stand in the way of a (rapid) success of the metaverse: [BAL21]

> "Metaverse users don't spend money."

Most internet users expect that access to services and information they use on the internet is available for free. Indeed, many social media platforms, search engines, and other online services are initially accessible for free. Their financing is done indirectly through advertising.

However, this expectation can be an obstacle to the success of the metaverse. Operating the metaverse requires a large amount of resources, including advanced technology and human labor, to keep it running. The costs for developing and operating such a platform are immense and cannot be fully financed through advertising. This means, conversely, that other ways of financing must be found. One such way is that users have to pay for access to the metaverse.

However, many users who are accustomed to free services do not have the understanding or willingness to do so. This makes life particularly difficult for high-quality journalistic content or media content such as music and film in today's WWW. This could then lead to insufficient revenue being generated on and through the platforms and services in the metaverse to finance and maintain operations.

To solve this problem, users need to develop a new understanding of the value of the metaverse and the resources needed for its development and operation. Incentives must be created for users who are willing to pay for access to the metaverse and for virtual items or experiences. Companies should also work on creative ways to generate revenue that does not rely solely on advertising.

4.8 (Not only) Economic Concerns: Metaverse-Hopping!

Metaverse-hopping means that users switch from one metaverse platform to another to explore different virtual worlds, gain new experiences, or conduct business. From a technical perspective, this could mean that users need to access various tools, technologies, and programming interfaces provided by the different platforms. To facilitate such a switch, the platforms would need to be interoperable, as Ball [BAL22] and Parisi [PAR21] consider necessary. Such interoperability means that the platforms must offer the ability for data and applications to be exchanged seamlessly. In addition to established data exchange formats like XML, JSON, or IFC, further standards such as OpenXR and WebXR could be used, which attempt to provide a unified interface for the development of XR applications. [W3CocJ, BUIoJ, JSOo.J., KHR19, W3CoJd]

Furthermore, a corresponding platform could support the integration of applications and content from other metaverse platforms to create a truly seamless experience without something similar to a media break for users. However, such integration would foreseeably bring a variety of technical challenges, such as handling the most diverse data formats for the most diverse application areas and ensuring the security and integrity of data exchanged between the different platforms and applications.

As already mentioned in the previous Chap. 3, it is currently unclear how the metaverse will ultimately be structurally built. On the one hand, there is the possibility of a unified metaverse, where there is a single central platform that all users use and in which all digital worlds are integrated. Such a metaverse would have the advantage that each user would only have a single, unified digital identity to maintain and care for. This would certainly also contribute to the social interaction of users benefiting, as "people know and recognize each other," no matter on which platform the users meet.

On the other hand, there is also the greater likelihood that the metaverse will consist of many parallel platforms that differ in structure, functions, and application focus. Each platform could specialize in certain application areas or target groups, thus offering a greater variety of specialized usage possibilities. Furthermore, it is conceivable that competition between different platforms could lead to more innovation and higher quality of offerings.

Which of these possibilities will become reality depends on many factors, such as fundamental technological developments on the one hand and the acceptance and use by users and the decisions of companies operating in the industry on the other hand. It is therefore likely that in the future there will be a mix of different platforms tailored to the different needs and interests of users, some of which, just like today on the WWW, will be so large that they can be considered the de facto standard of the metaverse.

4.8.1 A Unified Metaverse?

A unified metaverse offers a number of advantages not only to users but also to companies, some of which overlap, but some of which also differ. The following aspects could be mentioned as advantages for users:

- *Interoperability:* A unified metaverse would allow users to navigate between different virtual worlds without losing their identity or virtual possessions. Users could thus easily switch between different metaverse platforms and take their virtual goods and identities with them.
- *Community experience:* A unified metaverse would allow users to easily and effortlessly connect with people from all over the world and participate together in various activities such as games, sports, education, or culture. A larger number of users would also enable a broader variety of activities and experiences.
- *Efficiency:* A unified metaverse would allow users to do things like shopping, communication, and education on one platform. This would save time and increase efficiency.

The main advantages for companies, on the other hand, are:

- *Larger target audience:* A single metaverse platform would allow companies to present their products and services to a larger target audience without the need for porting. A larger number of users would also mean a larger number of potential customers.
- *Efficiency:* A unified metaverse would allow companies to manage and offer their products and services more efficiently. A company would not need a separate metaverse platform, thus saving time and money.
- *Collaboration:* A unified metaverse would allow companies to collaborate more easily and form economic partnerships. A single metaverse platform would allow companies to integrate their products and services, thus creating a more unified experience for users.

Although the number of advantages of a unified metaverse is not small, there are also a number of disadvantages that apply to both users and companies and need to be considered in detail. The following aspects could be mentioned as disadvantages for users in particular:

- *Monopoly position:* A largely unified metaverse platform could possibly take a monopolistic position in the market, leading to a lack of competition. This, in turn, could result in users facing higher prices and fewer choices, as seen in the real world or in some areas of the internet, particularly the WWW.
- *Less innovation:* The lack of competition with only a single metaverse platform could possibly lead to fewer innovations and new ideas being developed or, even more fatally, to design and technology decisions being made that lead to a dead end in development in the future.
- *Centralized control:* A unified metaverse could also mean a simple centralized possibility of control, raising concerns about privacy and surveillance practices.

	Advantages	Disadvantages
Users	1. Easy navigation and interoperability 2. Ability to combine different metaverse experiences 3. Better integration of content and data between differentservices and applications 4. Easier access to social interactions and communities	1. Limitation of choice and experiences to one platform 2. Possible lack of competition and innovation 3. Potentially higher prices and fees 4. Potentially higher dependence on a single platform
Companies	1. Larger user base and market opportunities 2. Better integration of services and applications 3. Ability to build and promote brand identity 4. Easier development and publication of content	1. Possible restrictions and regulations by a singleplatform 2. Potentially higher fees and higher dependence on a singleplatform 3. Possible lack of competition and innovation 4. Potentially higher risks if the platform fails or ishacked

The main disadvantages for companies, on the other hand, are:

- *Loss of autonomy:* A single unified metaverse platform could lead to companies losing their autonomy and control over their products and services, as well as being forced to comply with certain rules and regulations that contradict their actual corporate or organizational culture.
- *Limited access to user data:*A single metaverse platform could make it more difficult for companies to access user data, as all data is stored in a central database.
- *Risk of market disruptions:*A unified metaverse could possibly lead to market disruptions, as changes to the platform or unforeseen problems could have a greater impact on the companies operating on the platform and their business models.

4.8.2 Diverse Metaverses?

Diversity in the multitude of platforms could therefore prove to be quite advantageous. From the user's perspective, there are different advantages than for companies. A look at the potential advantages for users shows:

- *More choices:* With many parallel metaverse platforms, users would have more choices and could choose the platform that best suits their needs and preferences.
- *Competition promotes innovation:*The existence of many parallel metaverses promotes competition between platforms, which could lead to more innovation and new ideas. This would provide users with more decision-making freedom and better experiences in the future.
- *Privacy protection:*Multiple parallel metaverses could help better protect users' privacy, as there is less centralized control and fewer central databases.

The main advantages for companies, on the other hand, are:

- *More opportunities for market participation:* The existence of many parallel platforms offers companies more opportunities to enter the market, thus increasing competition among providers.
- *Better control over products and services:* Companies have more control over their products and services when there are multiple parallel platforms. They can specifically choose the platform that best fits their products and services.
- *Better analysis and marketing opportunities:* Companies can access more user data as they can engage on multiple parallel platforms. This offers them better analysis and marketing opportunities to improve their products and services.

However, there are also some noticeable disadvantages for users:

- *Fragmentation:* Many parallel platforms could mean that the user base is split across different platforms. This fragmentation of the user base could further lead to fewer interactions and experiences within the individual platforms.
- *Compatibility issues:* The existence of many parallel platforms can lead to compatibility issues, as certain content and applications may not be available or functional on all platforms.
- *Difficulties with interoperability:*Users might have difficulties switching between different parallel metaverses and interacting or transferring content from one platform to another. This arises especially when development strategies such as different interaction paradigms or forms compete.

In addition to the disadvantages for users, disadvantages for companies must also be mentioned:

- *Challenges in target group analysis:*With the existence of many parallel platforms, it can become more difficult for companies to conduct their target group analysis, which means that more resources must be spent on marketing and advertising.
- *Difficulties in application development:* The existence of many parallel platforms poses a challenge for companies in developing applications, as they may need to be developed and maintained on multiple platforms.
- *Higher costs:* Companies could incur higher costs for developing applications and content on many parallel platforms, as they need more resources and experts to manage and maintain their products on multiple platforms.

It is hard to say whether the advantages of a single metaverse will ultimately outweigh the advantages of many parallel metaverse platforms. The real development will depend on which factors will be economically important in the future and what kind of experience users seek and companies offer. It does not seem unlikely that a hybrid solution will emerge in the future, where different metaverse platforms can interact with each other but also retain their individual identities and controls.

The development of a unified metaverse appears to be a greater technical challenge, raising many complex questions, compared to the development of many individual solutions:

- *Scalability:* A unified metaverse must be able to manage a very large number of users and simultaneously a very large number of active applications and dynamic content. High scalability is necessary to maintain performance and user experience.
- *Interoperability:* A unified metaverse must also be able to integrate and connect different types of applications and content from various providers. This requires the development of standardized interfaces and protocols that can be used by all developers.
- *Security:* A unified metaverse must be secure to ensure the privacy and security of users. This requires the development of robust security protocols and protection mechanisms to prevent access to sensitive data and applications.
- *Scriptability:* A unified metaverse must also be able to support a variety of scripting languages and environments to enable a wide range of applications and content.
- *Infrastructure:* A unified metaverse also requires a solid infrastructure to efficiently manage and deliver all applications and content. This requires the development of powerful cloud computing systems, networks, and storage solutions.
- *Virtual economy:* A unified metaverse must be able to support a virtual economy where users can buy and sell applications, services, and digital currencies. This requires the development of secure payment and trading mechanisms.

- *Immersive technology:*Ultimately, a unified metaverse must also be able to support immersive technologies such as AR and VR to achieve high user acceptance in the first place.

These challenges are faced by other challenges in the development of many parallel platforms:

- *Interoperability:* With the existence of many parallel platforms, it will become difficult to exchange applications and content between them. Developers need to create interfaces and protocols that enable the integration and connection of applications and content across different platforms.
- *Scalability:* Each parallel platform must be able to manage a large number of users and applications to ensure good usability and user experience. Scalability is therefore one, if not the most important technical challenge, when there are many parallel platforms.
- *Standardization:* The standardization of interfaces and protocols touched upon in interoperability means a high degree of coordination between the developers and operators of the platforms.
- *Compatibility:* Each parallel platform can be based on a different technology platform, which further complicates compatibility. Developers must therefore ensure that their applications and content run on as many platforms as possible and are compatible between them. This is a problem whose immense scope is already apparent when looking at the few operating systems for mobile computing or smartphones.
- *Security:* Each parallel platform must be secure enough to ensure the privacy and security of users. This requires the development of robust security protocols and protection mechanisms to prevent access to sensitive data and applications.
- *Competition:* If there are many parallel platforms, this can lead to intense competition between them. Developers would need to ensure that their metaverses are attractive to users and businesses to successfully compete against other metaverses.

The thought that the development of many parallel platforms can also promote the emergence of new business models, which are based, for example, on the integration of multiple platforms, such as for the migration of content and applications between different platforms, appears interesting.

4.9 The Extended Economic Environment

With Computer Aided Manufacturing (CAM), software and computer systems were introduced into industrial manufacturing processes with the aim of controlling, automating, and optimizing them. The origin of CAM lies in the 1940s and 1950s when the first attempts were made to develop numerical control (NC) systems for machine tools. The first commercially successful NC systems were introduced in the 1960s. However, the real revolution in computer-aided manufacturing began in the 1970s when the first CAM systems came onto the market. These systems utilized advances in computer technology to automate and optimize manufacturing processes. Since then, CAM systems have continuously evolved and have become an integral part of modern production facilities. CAM systems enable engineers and technicians to transfer design data directly from Computer Aided Design (CAD) software to machine controls and production facilities. This process improves the efficiency, accuracy, and speed of production. CAM systems are used in a variety of industries, including the automotive, aerospace, electronics, and medical industries. [SCH03, LAN94]

The development of Computer-Aided Manufacturing (CAM) has contributed in recent years to optimizing production processes and increasing their efficiency. By connecting Industry 4.0 and Cyber-Physical Systems, an attempt was made to further improve such processes by networking and further automating them. The idea of the metaverse now opens up the possibility of a next, even more far-reaching step, namely the creation of virtual worlds in which the physical and digital worlds merge. This connection of CAM, Industry 4.0, and the metaverse is then intended to further optimize production processes, reduce costs, and at the same time open up new business fields: [GLU23, BMBoJ]

- The integration of computer-aided manufacturing in the form of CAM and the metaverse enables the development of virtual production lines, which help companies optimize and simulate their production processes before they are implemented in the real world. With the help of AR or VR, employees can interactively examine these virtual production lines and optimize the processes.
- By linking Industry 4.0 and the metaverse, digital twins of machines and systems can be generated from the mentioned simulations. This will enable companies to monitor the condition of the systems in real-time during operation, plan maintenance work more efficiently, and detect potential disruptions early.
- Furthermore, the combination of CAM and the metaverse offers interesting possibilities for training and education, by training employees in virtual environments to better understand and learn processes and procedures. By using AR or VR, employees can even be trained in dangerous situations without actually being exposed to risk.
- The combination of Cyber-Physical Systems and the metaverse also allows for the supplementation of monitoring and control of production facilities in the real world with real-time visualizations in virtual environments.

The advantages of this combination of CAM, Industry 4.0, and the metaverse are manifold:

- Companies can optimize and make their production processes more efficient by using virtual production lines and digital twins. Early detection and resolution of disruptions lead to increased productivity and reduced downtime.
- Employees benefit from realistic virtual environments for training and education, enabled by AR or VR. Better training increases employee qualifications and generally contributes to improved product quality.
- By connecting cyber-physical systems and the metaverse, companies can respond more quickly to changes and adapt their production processes more swiftly. Digital twins of real production lines are easier to modify than physical facilities, making it simpler and more cost-effective to test the impacts of changed production processes in simulations first and only adjust the real facility upon successful simulation.
- Early detection of disruptions and optimal maintenance planning enable cost savings in maintenance. This helps to reduce overall production costs, prevent potential equipment damage, and thus consume less material and energy while reducing waste.

However, such a combination of CAM, Industry 4.0, and the metaverse is not limited to industrial production processes but also affects the world of work itself. With advancing automation and digitalization, existing professions are changing, and new job profiles are emerging. In this context, changes in existing and new professions must also be considered, which are brought about by the connection of the classical, physical world and the metaverse. This will undoubtedly bring many changes to the world of work. Some of the most affected professions are those directly related to technology and virtual environments. But even professions that have so far been considered rather distant from technology could be affected by the impacts:

- *Designers* of virtual environments will be increasingly in demand in the future, as they play an important role in designing user interfaces, models, and avatars used in the metaverse. They must have a deep understanding of the possibilities of the metaverse to ensure an optimal user experience.
- *Software developers* will continue to play an important role in the metaverse, as they are responsible for creating the programs and applications used in the metaverse. They must be able to develop robust applications that are fast and reliable, meet security standards, and consider the requirements from both the real and virtual worlds.
- Likewise, the field of *social work*can be affected by the idea and implementation of the metaverse. More and more people will meet and interact in virtual environments in the future. It does not seem far-fetched that social workers will also be needed to understand the potential psychological impacts of the metaverse on society and to offer comprehensive support and counseling for individual users or user groups of the metaverse.
- As mentioned several times above, the *business world* will also not be spared from the impacts of the metaverse. There is great hope that trade and the management of virtual goods such as clothing and accessories for avatars, gadgets for games, or

entire apartments and furnishings will also be possible in the virtual worlds of the metaverse. Sales and marketing must learn how to advertise effectively in virtual, immersive worlds to attract customers and increase sales.

The examples presented here will in all likelihood only be the tip of the iceberg of professions that will be affected by the changes brought about by the metaverse. It is not yet really foreseeable which other professions will be influenced by the metaverse or will develop as a result. The emerging dynamics will be further intensified by the intensive use of services based on artificial intelligence in the metaverse, which is becoming increasingly apparent. AI can help make virtual environments more realistic and interactive on the one hand and implement new forms of assistance and interaction on the other. Even the professions mentioned as examples could experience significantly further changes through AI:

- AI-powered tools can be used to create or optimize designs automatically. Designers can use these tools to make their work more efficient and possibly also to enhance their creativity.
- AI can be used in the development of software and (data) models to shorten development times and reduce errors. This allows developers to focus on more complex tasks and thus achieve higher productivity.
- The assessment and evaluation of the psychological impacts of the metaverse on society and the development of interventions and prevention systems can support social work. However, social workers must be able to understand the limitations of AI's capabilities and consider that human interactions are indispensable in some cases.
- AI-based marketing tools can create personalized advertising campaigns and optimize the analysis of customer behavior. In sales and marketing, these tools can be useful for creating more effective advertising campaigns and ultimately increasing sales.

In addition to the already mentioned examples of the influence on the professional world, numerous other examples can easily be found that address and cover specific tasks in immersive environments in the metaverse:

- Architects who design and "build" virtual buildings and spaces in the virtual world.
- Event organizers who plan and organize virtual events on the platforms of the metaverse.
- Virtual personal coaches who offer fitness courses and training in the virtual worlds.
- Lawyers who provide legal advice regarding virtual matters, such as disputes over intellectual property or data protection.
- Sales representatives who sell and market virtual products or services in the virtual world.
- Real estate agents who buy, sell, or rent virtual properties in the virtual world.

- Social media managers who specifically manage the social media presence of a person or company on the platforms of the virtual world.
- Psychologists or therapists who offer psychological counseling or therapy in the virtual world under the special conditions there.
- Content creators and modelers who create digital content such as videos, photos, or music in the virtual world.
- Teachers or tutors who offer lessons or tutoring in the virtual world.

The requirements and skills of such professions with the special background of the "metaverse" naturally vary greatly. However, some important competencies overlap.

In considering the professional world in the metaverse, it is noticeable that an understanding of the underlying technologies is of crucial importance in almost all professions. This includes knowledge in the areas of 3D modeling, programming, as well as a basic understanding of the technical nature of virtual reality. Furthermore, many professions in the metaverse are characterized by the necessity of creative thinking, where the ability to develop and implement original ideas may be more demanded than in the physical world. In this context, it is important to emphasize that communication skills in a virtual world, where interactions with other people no longer primarily take place through text or speech but increasingly through visual communication such as the form and behavior of avatars, are of crucial importance. Additionally, many professions in the metaverse require a high degree of cooperation with other people and in virtual teams. The dynamic nature of the metaverse, which will not only be current but also constantly changing in the future, driven by rapid technological progress, requires professionals to quickly adapt to new technologies and trends. In some professions, such as the virtual sales representative or content creator, the ability to analyze data to identify trends and make informed decisions is of great importance. Furthermore, some professions, such as the virtual personal trainer or the virtual teacher, have a pronounced customer orientation, which requires a comprehensive ability to understand and respond to customer needs even in the virtual environment.

The change in job profiles and the development of entirely new professions have an immediate impact on the working world. On the one hand, there will be effects on the classic relationship between employee and employer, as not only the professions themselves will undergo a change, but also the working methods in the professions will be different from the classic job profiles with the background of the physical world. Additionally, these new professions also result in new requirements for vocational training and further education, which must also be adapted to the new circumstances.

The metaverse will undoubtedly have significant impacts on the working world, affecting both employees and employers. Among the advantages for employees is the ability to easily access jobs and opportunities from around the world. This offers them greater flexibility and freedom in choosing their workplace. Additionally, the metaverse will promote the creation of new professions and career opportunities, especially in the field of virtual world and game development. As it is a new technology, there will also be an increased demand for training and further education, allowing employees to enhance their skills. However, challenges for employees are also to be expected. They must acquire new skills and, above all, be willing to acquire them, such as knowledge in virtual world and game development, handling virtual tools and platforms, and interacting with virtual customers and colleagues. Additionally, employees who primarily work in the metaverse may feel isolated and have difficulty building relationships and contacts. Since the metaverse is a new technology, there are currently no regulations or laws to protect employees from abuse or violations of their labor rights.

However, there are also advantages for employers, such as access to a larger pool of workers worldwide, increasing the chance of finding and attracting the best talents for the company. The use of virtual tools and platforms can also increase the efficiency of business processes and thus increase productivity. Furthermore, employers can save costs for office rent and travel expenses by using virtual workplaces and tools. These advantages are also accompanied by challenges for employers. They must invest in the necessary technology and infrastructure to support virtual workplaces and tools. Additionally, they must invest in the training and further education of their workforce to ensure that they have the necessary skills and competencies to work effectively in the metaverse. Finally, employers must ensure that virtual workplaces and tools are secure and comply with data protection regulations to protect the safety of employees and the company.

The emergence of new professions and tasks in the metaverse, however, also requires an adjustment of vocational education and training as well as the entire education system. To meet the specific requirements and competencies of professions in the metaverse, special training and qualification programs may be necessary. This may imply that existing training programs or education systems need to be modified to cover the new requirements.

An example of this is the imparting of technical skills and knowledge, which are essential for many professions in the metaverse. Educational institutions such as schools, universities, and other institutions will need to adjust their curricula and training programs to specifically prepare learners for the requirements of these professions. Additionally, the creation of new professions and tasks could lead to the development of new training and qualification programs that are tailored to these specific requirements. This may require collaboration between educational institutions and companies or organizations to adapt the training to the needs of the industry.

The emergence of new professions in the metaverse will inevitably also require adjustments in the education system itself to ensure that people are prepared for the demands of these professions. To achieve this, certain competencies and skills need to be promoted. Some of the most important competencies that could be of particular importance in the metaverse are technical competence, creativity, adaptability, and communication skills. Furthermore, other competencies related to the virtual environment of the metaverse could also gain importance, such as handling digital tools, virtual communication and collaboration, data protection and security, organization and time management, as well as intercultural understanding.

Schools, universities, and other educational institutions can promote these competencies to prepare people for the demands of professions in the metaverse. Likewise, companies can contribute by providing training and further education to ensure that their employees acquire and develop the required competencies.

References

[ABU21] Abukhadra, Salwa (05.12.2021). Sephora Leading The Way With Augmented Reality. In: Medium, Marketing in the Age of Digital. Online: https://medium.com/marketing-in-the-age-of-digital/sephora-leading-the-way-with-augmented-reality-c117eed0faa0 (accessed on: 28.05.2023).

[ADI23] Adigozel, Ozgur; Mérey, Tibor; Mathews, Madeline (19.01.2023). The Health Care Metaverse Is More Than a Virtual Reality. In: Boston Consulting Group: Health Care Payers, Providers, Systems & Services/Article. Online: https://www.bcg.com/publications/2023/reaping-the-benefits-of-the-healthcare-metaverse (accessed on: 28.05.2023).

[ALZ20] Alzahrani, Bander (2020). An Information-Centric Networking Based Registry for Decentralized Identifiers and Verifiable Credentials. In: IEEE Access, vol. 8, pp. 137198–137208, 2020, https://doi.org/10.1109/ACCESS.2020.3011656.

[AMT19] Amtsblatt der Europäischen Union: RICHTLINIE (EU) 2019/882 DES EUROPÄISCHEN PARLAMENTS UND DES RATES vom 17. April 2019 über die Barrierefreiheitsanforderungen für Produkte und Dienstleistungen. Online: https://eur-lex.europa.eu/legal-content/DE/TXT/HTML/%3Furi%3DCELEX%3A32019L0882 (accessed on: 17.05.2023).

[ARToJ] Artscloud (o. J.). Art Planet – Oasis of Inspiration. In: Artscloud. Online: https://artscloud.net/artplanet (accessed on: 28.05.2023).

[BAI08] Baichtal, John (20.11.2008). Thingiverse.com Launches A Library of Printable Objects. In: Wired. Online: https://www.wired.com/2008/11/thingiversecom/ (accessed on am: 23.05.2023).

[BAL20] Ball, Matthew (13.01.2020). What It Is, Where to Find it, and Who Will Build It. Online: https://www.matthewball.vc/all/themetaverse (accessed on: 17.05.2023).

[BAL20c] Balcazar, Cristina (29.11. 2020). How Augmented Reality lets Sephora „try on" something different. In: Medium, Marketing in the Age of Digital. Online: https://medium.com/marketing-in-the-age-of-digital/how-augmented-reality-lets-sephora-try-on-something-different-23b4446fd5c1 (accessed on: 28.05.2023).

[BAL21] Ball, Matthew (29.06.2021). Virtual Platforms and the Metaverse. In: matthewball.vc. Online: https://www.matthewball.vc/all/virtualplatformsmetaverse (accessed on: 17.05.2023).

[BAL21b] Ball, Matthew (28.06.2021). Evolving User + Business Behaviors and the Metaverse. In: The Metaverse Primer. Online: https://www.matthewball.vc/all/userbehaviors-metaverse (accessed on: 17.05.2023).

[BAL22] Ball, Matthew; Furness, Thomas; Inbar, Ori; Kalinowski, Caitlin; Lange, Danny; Lebaredian, Rev; Mann, Steve; Miralles, Evelyn; Rosedale, Philip; Trevett, Neil; Yuan, Yu (14.06.2022): Metaverse decoded by top experts. In: Versemaker: Metaverse Lands-cape & Outlook Series. Online: https://versemaker.org/download (accessed on: 10.05.2023).

[BAN12] Bannister, Matthew (23.01.2012). Outlook. In: bbc.co.uk. BBC World Service. p. 16m41s. (accessed on: 17.05.2023).

[BAS22] BaselLive (16.05.2022) ARTour – Digitale Kunst in einer neuen Dimension. Online: https://basellive.ch/blog/artour-digitale-kunst-in-einer-neuen-dimension-entdecken/wf6w (accessed on: 10.05.2023).

[BAT23] Batchelor, James (10.05.2023). EA investing in building „games as a platform". In: Gamesindustry.biz. Online: https://www.gamesindustry.biz/ea-investing-in-building-games-as-a-platform (accessed on: 28.05.2023).

[BBC19] BBC (24.05.2019). Mona Lisa ‚brought to life' with deepfake AI. In: BBC Tech. Online: https://www.bbc.com/news/technology-48395521 (accessed on: 10.05.2023).

[BED22] Bedingfield, Will (04.04.2022). Roblox's ‚Layered Clothing' Is Here – but Don't Call It an NFT. In: Wired Culture. Online: https://www.wired.co.uk/article/roblox-layered-clothing (accessed on: 28.05.2023).

[BEL23a] Belocerkov, Andreas (10.02.2023). Blockchain-Gaming – Mehr als nur der Traum vom Spielen um Geld. In: Wirtschaftsinformatik & Management. https://doi.org/10.1365/s35764-023-00451-9.

[BER89] Berners-Lee, Tim (1989). Information Management: A Proposal. In: CERN, W2C. Online: https://www.w3.org/History/1989/proposal.html (accessed on: 23.05.2023).

[BEZ19] Bezmalinovic, Tomislav (29.09.2019). Virtual Reality und Kunst: Die besten Apps und Erfahrungen für Kunstliebhaber. In: Mixed VR und Kunst. Online: https://mixed.de/virtual-reality-und-kunst-die-zehn-besten-apps-und-erfahrungen-fuer-kunstliebhaber/ (accessed on: 28.05.2023).

[BID22] Business Insider Deutschland (03.012022). Ralph Lauren verkauft digitale Kleidung im Metaverse – Analysten glauben, es ist der Beginn eines Milliardengeschäfts. In: Business Insider Deutschland. Online: https://www.businessinsider.de/wirtschaft/ralph-lauren-verkauft-digitale-kleidung-im-metaverse/ (accessed on: 17.05.2023).

[BIT22] bitkom (2022). Wegweiser in das Metaversum – Technologische und rechtliche Grundlagen, geschäftliche Potenziale, gesellschaftliche Bedeutung. In: Bitkom e. V., AG Metaverse Forum, Projektleitung: Dr. Sebastian Klöß. Online: https://www.bitkom.org/Bitkom/Publikationen/Wegweiser-Metaverse (accessed on: 10.05.2023).

[BIT22b] Bitkom Presseinformation (05.06.2022). Ein Fünftel der Deutschen möchte im Metaverse Urlaub machen https://www.bitkom.org/Presse/Presseinformation/Digitaler-Tourismus-2022 (accessed on: 10.05.2023).

[BLU23] Blutinger, Jonathan; Cooper, Christen; Karthik, Shravan; Tsai, Alissa; Samarelli, Noa; Storvick, Erika; Seymour, Gabriel; Liu, Elise; Meijers, Yorán; Lipson, Hod. (2023). The future of software-controlled cooking. npj Science of Food. 7. https://doi.org/10.1038/s41538-023-00182-6.

[BMA21] BMAS (22.07.2021): Barrierefreiheitsstärkungsgesetz. Gesetz zur Umsetzung der Richtlinie (EU) 2019/882 des Europäischen Parlaments und des Rates über die Barrierefreiheitsanforderungen für Produkte und Dienstleistungen (BFSG). https://www.bmas.de/DE/Service/Gesetze-und-Gesetzesvorhaben/barrierefreiheitsstaerkungsgesetz.html (accessed on: 17.05.2023).

[BMBoJ] BMBf (o.J.). Was ist Industrie 4.0? In: Bundesministerium für Bildung und Forschung. Online: https://www.plattform-i40.de/IP/Navigation/DE/Industrie40/WasIndustrie40/was-ist-industrie-40.html (accessed on: 22.5.2023).

[BON21] Bonci, Andrea; Fiori, Simone; Higashi, Hiroshi; Tanaka, Toshihisa; Verdini, Federica (2021). An introductory tutorial on brain–computer interfaces and their applications. In: Electronics, 10(5), 560.

[BON22] Bonifacic, Igor (23.05.2022). Meta's 'MyoSuite' AI platform could help doctors develop better prosthetics. In: engadget.com. https://www.engadget.com/meta-myo-suite-annoucemed-183850677.html (accessed on: 17.05.2023).

[BOR15] Borrmann, André; König, Markus; Koch, Christian; Beet,Jakob (2015). Building Information Modeling. Technologische Grundlagen und industrielle Praxis. Springer Vieweg, Wiesbaden 2015, ISBN 978-3-658-05605-6.

[BOS14] Bostrom, Nick (2014). Introduction – The Transhumanist FAQ: A General Introduction. In: Mercer, C., Maher, D.F. (eds) Transhumanism and the Body. In: Palgrave Studies in the Future of Humanity and Its Successors. Palgrave Macmillan, New York. https://doi.org/10.1057/9781137342768_1.

[BRU07] Bruns, Axel (2007): Produsage: Towards a Broader Framework for User-Led Content Creation. In Proceedings Creativity & Cognition. Washington, DC. 6.

[BUIoJ] Building Smart (o.J.). IFC Specifications Database. In: Building Smart International. Online: https://technical.buildingsmart.org/standards/ifc/ifc-schema-specifications/ (accessed on: 22.5.2023).

[BUS22a] Business Insider Deutschland (22.02.2022).„Kauf Island“ und „Phil Leita“: Wie Kaufland mit einer eigenen Insel ins Metaverse startet. In: Business Insider. Online: https://www.businessinsider.de/wirtschaft/kauf-island-und-phil-leitawie-kaufland-mit-einer-eigenen-insel-ins-metaverse-startet-a/ (accessed on: 10.05.2023).

[BUS22b] Business Punk Redaktion (21.01.2022). Kaufland eröffnet eigenen Store im Animal-Crossing-Universum. In: Business Punk. Online: https://www.business-punk.com/2022/01/kaufland-eroeffnet-eigenen-store-im-animal-crossing-universum/ (accessed on: 10.05.2023).

[BUS45] Bush, Vannevar (1945). As We May Think. Atlantic Monthly 176 (July 1945) pp. 101–108.

[CAR23] Carter, Rebekah (27.03.2023). Introducing Spatial AR Collaboration – Turn any room into an augmented workspace. In: UCToday Collaboration. Online: https://www.uctoday.com/collaboration/introducing-spatial-ar-collaboration/ (accessed on: 28.05.2023).

[CHA22] Chang, Olivia (18.03.2022). Ein Stück Metaverse. In: Forbes. Online: https://www.forbes.at/artikel/ein-stueck-metaverse.html (accessed on: 17.05.2023).

[CHI22] Chittum, Morgan (01.02.2022): Morgan Stanley Sees $8 Trillion Metaverse Market – In China Alone. In: Blockworks. Online: https://blockworks.co/news/morgan-stanley-sees-8-trillion-metaverse-market-eventually (accessed on: 17.05.2023).

[CHO17] Chohan, Usman. (2017). The Decentralized Autonomous Organization and Governance Issues. SSRN Electronic Journal. https://doi.org/10.2139/ssrn.3082055.

[COA21] Coates, Charlotte (31.07.2021). Virtual Reality is a big trend in museums, but what are the best examples of museums using VR? In: MuseumNext. Online: https://www.museumnext.com/article/how-museums-are-using-virtual-reality/ (accessed on: 17.05.2023).

[CRE20] Crets, Stephanie (22.10.2020). Augmented reality boosts conversion for Home Depot. In: Digital Commerce 360. Online: https://www.digitalcommerce360.com/2020/10/22/augmented-reality-boosts-conversion-for-home-depot/ (accessed on: 28.05.2023).

[CRO22] Crowther, Samuel; Ford, Henry (1922). My Life and Work.(Garden City, N.Y., Doubleday, Page & company, 1922.

[CRYoJ] CryptoArt (o.J.). Online: https://cryptoart.io (accessed on: 17.05.2023).

[DAL15] Dale, Brady (14.08.2015). 8Chan Kicked Out of Google Search Results. In: Observer Business. Online: https://observer.com/2015/08/google-blocks-8chan-from-search/ (accessed on: 20.05.2023).

[DAM20] Damiani, Jesse (26.02.2020): The Museum Of Other Realities Officially Opens Its Virtual Doors To The Public. In: Forbes. Online: https://www.forbes.com/sites/jessedamiani/2020/02/26/the-museum-of-other-realities-officially-opens-its-virtual-doors-to-the-public/ (accessed on: 17.05.2023).

[DAV22] Davis, Lakisha (11.01.2022). How the Metaverse Is Shaping the Future of Education. In: metapress. Online: https://metapress.com/how-the-metaverse-isshaping-the-future-of-education/ (accessed on: 23. 07. 2022).

[DEC20] Decentraland (20.02.2020). The gates to Decentraland have opened!. In: Decentraland Blog. Online: https://decentraland.org/blog/announcements/decentraland-launch/ (accessed on: 17.05.2023).

[DEC23] Decentraland (27.02.203). Tradition and Innovation Collide: Decentraland Metaverse Fashion Week 2023. In: Announcements. Online: https://decentraland.org/blog/announcements/tradition-and-innovation-collide-decentraland-metaverse-fashion-week-2023 (accessed on: 17.05.2023).

[DEMoJ] Demokratie in Bewegung (o. J.). Demokratie in Bewegung. Online: https://dib.de/ (accessed on: 17.05.2023).

[DEC23] Decentraland (27.02.203). Tradition and Innovation Collide: Decentraland Metaverse Fashion Week 2023. In: Announcements. Online: https://decentraland.org/blog/announcements/tradition-and-innovation-collide-decentraland-metaverse-fashion-week-2023 (accessed on: 17.05.2023).

DEW22] Dewerne, Yvonne (24.01.2022). Gucci, Louis Vuitton, Balenciaga: Diese Luxusunternehmen sind schon längst im Metaverse. In: Esquire. Online: https://www.esquire.de/style/smart-fashion/nft-metaverse-modebrands-louis-vuitton-gucci-nike-balenciaga (accessed on: 17.05.2023).

[DON17] Donahue, Michelle Z. (09.11.2017). Ein farbenblinder Künstler wurde zum ersten Cyborg der Welt. In: National Geographic. Online: https://www.nationalgeographic.de/wissenschaft/2017/04/ein-farbenblinder-kuenstler-wurde-zum-ersten-cyborg-der-welt (accessed on: 21.05.2023).

[DRA22] Draht, Moritz (24.11.2022). „Danke für den guten Deal" Bored Ape für fast eine Million US-Dollar verkauft. In: BTC-Echo. Online: https://www.btc-echo.de/schlagzeilen/nft-dauerbrenner-bored-ape-fuer-fast-eine-million-dollar-verkauft-155084/ (accessed on: 17.05.2023).

[DUN19] Duncan, James (12.05.2019). MolochDAO: a primitive solution. In: Medium, MetaCartel DAO. Online: https://medium.com/metacartel/molochdao-a-primitive-solution-d11cc522b18e (accessed on: 20.05.2023).

[DUS23] Dusold, Julia (04.06.2022). Nächste Ebene der Digitalisierung: Metaverse für die Industrie: Siemens und Nvidia gehen es an. In: Produktion. Online: https://www.produktion.de/technik/zukunftstechnologien/metaverse-fuer-die-industrie-siemens-und-nvidia-gehen-es-an-308.html (accessed on: 20.05.2023).

[EHL20] Ehlert, Cindy; Rüdiger, Thomas-Gabriel (2020). Defensible Digital Space: Die Übertragbarkeit der Defensible Space Theory auf den digitalen Raum. In: Cyberkriminologie: Kriminologie für das digitale Zeitalter (2020): 151–171.

[END21] Enderes, Felicia (03.11.2021). Nike meldet Marken für virtuelle Nutzung an. In: Fashion Network. Online: https://de.fashionnetwork.com/news/Nike-meldet-marken-fur-virtuelle-nutzung-an,1349436.html (accessed on: 29.11.2023).

[END22] Enderle, Rob (08.08.2022). The Metaverse Future: Are You Ready To Become a God? In: TechNewsWorld. Online: https://www.technewsworld.com/story/the-metaverse-future-are-you-ready-to-become-a-god-176974.html (accessed on: 17.05.2023).

[FLO22] Flohr, Nicholas (29.08.2022). Für „The Gray Man" kooperiert Netflix mit dem Metaverse Decentraland. In: Finanzen.net. Online: https://www.finanzen.net/nachricht/devisen/metaverse-erlebnis-fuer-34-the-gray-man-34-kooperiert-netflix-mit-dem-metaverse-decentraland-11655915 (accessed on: 28.05.2023).

[GEY23] Geyer, Mike (21.03.2023). BMW Group Starts Global Rollout of NVIDIA Omniverse. In: Nvidia Blog. Online: https://blogs.nvidia.com/blog/2023/03/21/bmw-group-nvidia-omniverse/ (accessed on: 20.05.2023).

[GLU23] Glushkova, Todorka (2023). Modeling in Cyber-Physical Systems. In: Povdiv University Press, ISBN 978–619–7663–49–5.

[GOL21] Golden, Jessica (02.11.2021). Nike is quietly preparing for the meta-verse. In: CNBC. Online: https://www.cnbc.com/2021/11/02/nike-is-quietly-preparing-for-themetaverse-.html (accessed on: 17.05.2023).

[HAC21] Hackl, Cathy (29.01.2021). How Brands Can Thrive In The Direct To Avatar Economy. In: Forbes. Online: https://www.forbes.com/sites/cathyhackl/2021/01/29/how-brands-can-thrive-in-the-direct-to-avatar-economy/ (accessed on: 28.05.2023).

[HAM22] Hammer, Peter (19.04.2022). Walmart: an der Schwelle des Metaversums. In: W&V. Online: https://www.wuv.de/Themen/Markenstrategie/Walmart-an-der-Schwelle-des-Metaversums (accessed on: 10.05.2023).

[HAN23] Han, Jining; Geping Liu; Yuxin Gao (2023). Learners in the Metaverse: A Systematic Review on the Use of Roblox in Learning. In: Education Sciences 13, no. 3: 296. https://doi.org/10.3390/educsci13030296.

[HOW22] Howell, Jame (10.02.2022).Metaverse For Education – How Will The Metaverse Change Education?. In: 101 Blockchain. Online: https://101blockchains.com/metaverse-for-education/ (accessed on: 23. 07. 2022).

[HRZoJ] HRZ Justus Liebig Universität Giessen (o.J.). Historie. Online: https://www.uni-giessen.de/de/fbz/svc/hrz/org/mitarb/abt/3/zms/schulung/webtechniken/internet/historie (accessed on: 17.05.2023).

[HUB20] Huberman, Jenny (2020). Introduction: Thinking through Transhumanism. In Transhumanism: From Ancestors to Avatars. In: New Departures in Anthropology, pp. 1–20). Cambridge: Cambridge University Press. https://doi.org/10.1017/9781108869577.001.

[HUG23] Hughes, Rebecca Ann (15.02.2023). Do You Have To Pay To Visit Venice? Here's What To Know About The Entry Fee. In: Forbes. Online: https://www.forbes.com/sites/rebeccahughes/2023/02/15/do-you-have-to-pay-to-visit-venice-heres-what-to-know-about-the-entry-fee/ (accessed on: 10.05.2023).

[IPFoJ] IPFS (o.J.). IPFS powers the Distributed Web. Online: https://ipfs.tech/ (accessed on: 28.05.2023).

[JAL22] Jalalow, Damir (11.11.2022). Wie treibt Metaverse den Gaming-Sektor voran? In: Metaverse Post. Online: https://mpost.io/de/how-does-metaverse-drive-the-gaming-sector/ (accessed on: 17.05.2023).

[JAV21] Javaid, Mohd; Haleem, Abid; Singh, Ravi Pratap; Suman, Rajiv (2021). Industrial perspectives of 3D scanning: Features, roles and it's analytical applications. In: Sensors International, Volume 2, 2021, 100114, ISSN 2666–3511, https://doi.org/10.1016/j.sintl.2021.100114.

[JSOo.J.] JSON Schema (o. J.). JSON Schema. In: JSON Schema. Online: https://json-schema.org/ (accessed on: 22.5.2023).

[KAL22] Kalis, Brian; McHugh, Jenica; Safavi, Kaveh T.; Truscott, Andrew (05.09.2022). Accenture Digital Health Technology Vision 2022. In: Accenture: Digital Health. Online: https://www.accenture.com/de-de/insights/health/digital-health-technology-vision (accessed on: 28.05.2023).

[KAN21] Kanterman, Matthew; Naidu, Nathan (01.12.2021). Metaverse may be $800 billion market, next tech platform. In: Bloomberg Intelligence. Online: https://www.bloomberg.com/professional/blog/metaverse-may-be-800-billion-market-next-tech-platform/ (accessed on: 17.05.2023).

[KAW22] Kawarase, Mrudul A; Anjankar, Anish (08.11.2022). Dynamics of Metaverse and Medicine: A Review Article. In: Cureus 14(11): e31232. https://doi.org/10.7759/cureus.31232.

[KEL05] Kelly, Kevin (01.08.2005). We Are the Web. In: Wired. Online: https://www.wired.com/2005/08/tech/ (accessed on: 17.05.2023).

[KER21] Kerris, Richard (Juni 2021). The Metaverse Begins: NVIDIA Omniverse and a Future of Shared Worlds. Von: Nvidia. Online: https://www.nvidia.com/en-us/on-demand/session/computex2021-com2104/ (accessed on: 17.05.2023).

[KHR19] Khronos (18.03.2019). Khronos Releases OpenXR 0.90 Provisional Specification for High-performance Access to AR and VR Platforms and Devices. In: Khronos Press Release. Online: https://www.khronos.org/news/press/khronos-releases-openxr-0.90-provisional-specification-for-high-performance-access-ar-vr-platforms-and-devices (accessed on: 22.5.2023).

[KIT16] Kitatus (1507.2016). Games-As-A-Platform – The Future of Games or an Inconvenience?. In: Medium. Online: https://medium.com/@Kitatus/games-as-aplatform-the-future-of-games-or-an-inconvenience-505e719a2cdf (accessed on: 28.05.2023).

[KLA22] Klatt, Robert (01.01.2022): Taste the TV Display mit leckbarem Geschmack entwickelt. In: Forschung und Wissen. Online: https://www.forschung-und-wissen.de/nachrichten/technik/display-mit-leckbarem-geschmack-entwickelt-13375683 (accessed on: 29.11.2023).

[LAN94] Lange, Rüdiger und Günter Watzlawik (1994). Lexikon der CA-Anwendungen : CAD. CAM/CAE/CAI/CIM. In: VDE-Verlag, 1994. ISBN 10: 3800719207 ISBN 13: 9783800719204.

[LAY07] Layton, Julia (26.01.2007): Can I make my living in Second Life? In: howstuffworks. https://computer.howstuffworks.com/internet/social-networking/networks/second-life.htm (accessed on: 10.05.2023).

[LE22] Le, Trang (22.07.2022). Sexual assault in the metaverse is part of a bigger problem that technology alone won't solve. Von: (Monash University) . Online: https://lens.monash.edu/@politics-society/2022/07/22/1384871/sexual-assault-in-the-metaverse-theres-nothing-virtual-about-it (accessed on: 17.05.2023).

[LEWoJ] Lewis, Irene (o. J.). Augmented Reality in the Furniture Industry: 5 Benefits of Using AR for Shopping Apps. In: CGIFURNITURE. Online: https://cgifurniture.com/augmented-reality-in-furniture-industry/ (accessed on: 10.05.2023).

[LIU22] Liu, Lu; Zhou, Sicong; Huang, Huawei; Zheng, Zibin (2021). From Technology to Society: An Overview of Blockchain-Based DAO. In: IEEE Open Journal of the Computer Society, vol. 2, pp. 204–215, 2021, https://doi.org/10.1109/OJCS.2021.3072661.

[LIU23] Liu, Yiming; Yiu, Chun, Zhao, Zhao; Park, Wooyoung; Shi, Rui; Huang, Xingcan; Zeng, Yuyang; Wang, Kuan; Wong, Tsz; Jia, Shengxin; Zhou, Jingkun; Gao, Zhan; Zhao, Ling; Yao, Kuanming; Li, Jian; Sha, Chuanlu; Gao, Yuyu; Zhao, Guangyao; Huang, Ya; Yu, Xinge (2023). Soft, miniaturized, wireless olfactory interface for virtual reality. Nature Communications. 14. https://doi.org/10.1038/s41467-023-37678-4.

[LUC22] Luck-Hille, Esmay (02.11.2022). NFTs and CryptoArt: a revolution. In: University of Oxford: Oxford Talks. https://talks.ox.ac.uk/talks/id/d8dff615-efa4-4008-bd83-fadfe9d9fc8f/ (accessed on: 17.05.2023).

[LUN16] Lundkvist, Christian; Lilic, John (17.02.2016). An Introduction to IPFS. In: Medium, ConsenSys. Online: https://medium.com/@ConsenSys/an-introduction-to-ipfs-9bba4860abd0 (accessed on: 28.05.2023).

[MAA22] Maas, Hartwin (2022). Der Cyborg in der Industrie 5.0. In: Wissensmanagement Wissenplus. Online: https://www.wissensmanagement.net/themen/artikel/artikel/der_cyborg_in_der_industrie_50.html?no_cache=1&cHash=ccceebb6c6361250801a6ea32472b88f (accessed on: 17.05.2023).

[MACoJ] MachuPicchu360 (o.J.). Machu Picchu Virtual Tour. Online: https://www.machupicchu360.com (accessed on: 29.11.2023).

[MAC09] Maciuszek, Dennis; Martens, Alke. (2009). Virtuelle Labore als Simulationsspiele. INFORMATIK 2009 – Im Focus das Leben, Beitrage der 39. Jahrestagung der Gesellschaft fur Informatik e.V. (GI). 1965–1979.

[MAL22] Mallis, Athina (14.09.2022). Meet the intraverse, the metaverse's office-based cousin. In: Digital Nation News Web3. Online: https://www.digitalnationaus.com.au/news/meet-the-intraverse-the-metaverses-office-based-cousin-585182 (accessed on: 28.05.2023).

[MAR14] Martikainen, Mikko (07.04.2014). Mikko Martikainen, CEO, Sayduck, Finland. In: The Sin Off Stories. Online: https://www.the-spin-off.com/news/stories/Mikko-Martikainen-CEO-Sayduck-Finland-8141 (accessed on: 28.05.2023).

[MAR20] Martens, Todd (13.05.2020). Epic's Tim Sweeney reveals a more connected, 'Fortnite'-driven, game-unified world. In: Los Angeles Times, Entertainment & Arts. Online: https://www.latimes.com/entertainment-arts/story/2020-05-13/epicgames-outlines-a-fortnite-driven-more-connected-future (accessed on: 10.05.2023).

[MAR22] Marr, Bernhard (23.02.2022). The Amazing Possibilities Of Healthcare In The Metaverse. In: Forbes. Online: https://www.forbes.com/sites/bernardmarr/2022/02/23/the-amazing-possibilities-of-healthcare-in-the-metaverse/%3Fsh%3D59f2f2109e5c (accessed on: 23. 07. 2022).

[MAT22] Matthes, Sebastian (14.02.2022). Der Hype um das Metaverse wird dazu führen, dass Milliarden Euro für Unsinn ausgegeben werden. In: Handelsblatt. Online: https://www.handelsblatt.com/meinung/editorial-der-hype-um-das-metaverse-wird-dazu-fuehren-dass-milliarden-euro-fuer-unsinn-ausgegeben-werden/28058770.html (accessed on: 17.05.2023).

[MEDoJ] Medinstrukt (o. J.). Simulation in der Notfallmedizin. Online: https://www.medinstrukt.de/notfallschulungen/simulation-in-der-notfallmedizin/ (accessed on: 17.05.2023).

[METoJa] Metamandrill (o. J.). Metaverse Werbung; Arten von Metaverse Marketing & Beispiele. In: metamandrill metaverse information. Online: https://metamandrill.com/de/metaverse-werbung-2/ (accessed on: 17.05.2023).

[METoJb] Metamandrill (o.J.). AR-Marketing; Top-Beispiele für Augmented-Reality-Marketing. In: metamandrill information. Online: https://metamandrill.com/de/ar-marketing/#great-examples-of-ar-marketing (accessed on: 17.05.2023).

[MIL22] Millennium (27.04.2022): Millennium Hotels and Resorts Launches M Social Decentraland. In: jospitalitynet. https://www.hospitalitynet.org/news/4110172.html (accessed on: 10.05.2023).

[MIRoJ] Mirrorworld (o.J.). Try Before You Buy with AR. In: Mirrorworld. Online: https://www.mirrorworld.media/try-before-you-buy/ (accessed on: 28.05.2023).

[MON22] Monsanto, Charlton; Embry, Alexandre; Shankavaram, Darshan; Smith-Bingham, Alex; Zhang, Jiani ; Rolley, Carina; Huestegge, Nica; Denaro, Andrea; Buvat, Jerome (2022). Total Immersion: How Immersive Experiences And The Metaverse Benefit

Customer Experience And Operations. In: Capgemini Insights. Online: https://www.capgemini.com/us-en/insights/research-library/total-immersion-how-immersive-experiences-and-the-metaverse-benefit-customer-experience-and-operations/ (accessed on: 28.05.2023).

[MOR20] Morrison, Robbie; Mazey, Natasha C. H. L.; Wingreen, Stephen C. (27.05.2020). The DAO Controversy: The Case for a New Species of Corporate Governance? In: Frontiers in Blockchain, Vol. 3, 2020. https://doi.org/10.3389/fbloc.2020.00025 ISSN=2624-7852. Online: https://www.frontiersin.org/articles/10.3389/fbloc.2020.00025 (accessed on: 20.05.2023).

[MOR22] Morrison, Ryan (24.02.2022). Metaverse users will be granted god-like powers to create their own virtual world just by speaking things into existence, Zuckerberg reveals. In: Dailymail.Com. Online: https://www.dailymail.co.uk/sciencetech/article-10547361/Metaverse-users-granted-god-like-powers-create-virtual-world.html (accessed on: 17.05.2023).

[MOZ23] Mozumder, Md Ariful Islam; Armand, Tagne Poupi Theodore; Uddin, Shah Muhammad Imtiyaj; Athar, Ali; Sumon, Rashedul Islam; Hussain, Ali; Cheol Kim, Hee (2023). Metaverse for Digital Anti-Aging Healthcare: An Overview of Potential Use Cases Based on Artificial Intelligence, Blockchain, IoT Technologies, Its Challenges, and Future Directions. In: Applied Sciences 13, no. 8: 5127. https://doi.org/10.3390/app13085127.

[MUL23] Mullenlowe Group (22.02.2023). Metaverse Builders. In: Web In Travel. Online: https://www.mullenlowegroup.com/news/metaverse-builders/ (accessed on: 10.05.2023).

[MUSoJ] Museum of Other Realities (o. J.). https://www.museumor.com/ (accessed on: 17.05.2023).

[NAB23] Nabben, Kelsia (2023). Web3 as 'self-infrastructuring': The challenge is how. In: Big Data & Society, 10(1). https://doi.org/10.1177/20539517231159002.

[NET18] netzreich GmbH (16.04.2018): Augmented Bier - Die neue Version ist online. Online: https://www.youtube.com/watch?v=EpPaQ9Qfci4 (accessed on: 10.05.2023).

[NGU22] Nguyen, Hai Son (07.02.2022). Metaverse: Marketing in einer neuen Ära. In: pwc Online Consulting. Online: https://digital.pwc.at/2022/02/07/metaverse/ (accessed on: 29.11.2023).

[NIFoJ] Nifty (o. J.). Nifty Gateway. In: Nifty. Online: https://niftygateway.com (accessed on: 28.05.2023).

[OHL19] Ohlheiser, Abby (05.08.2019). Will taking down 8chan stop the worst people on the Internet? In: The Washington Post, Technology, Internet Culture. Online: https://www.washingtonpost.com/technology/2019/08/05/will-taking-down-chan-stop-worst-people-internet/ (accessed on: 20.05.2023).

[OPEoJ] OpenSea (o.J.). OpenSea. Online: https://opensea.io/about (accessed on: 28.05.2023).

[ORT22] Ortiz, Laura (2022). Risks of the Metaverse: A VRChat Study Case. In: The Journal of Intelligence, Conflict, and Warfare. 5. 53–128. https://doi.org/10.21810/jicw.v5i2.5041.

[PAR21] Parisi, Tony (22.10.2021). The Seven Rules oft he Metaverse – A framework for the coming immersive reality. In: Medium. Online: https://medium.com/meta-verses/the-seven-rules-of-the-metaverse-7d4e06fa864c (accessed on: 22.5.2023).

[PAR23] Parashar, Radhika (13.04.2023). Adidas Expands 'Into The Metaverse' Web3 Initiative with Chapter 1 of ALTS Dynamic NFTs. In: Gadgets360. Online: https://www.gadgets360.com/cryptocurrency/news/adidas-metaverse-web3-initiative-chapter-1-alts-dynamic-nft-series-3945006 (accessed on: 28.05.2023).

[PAV23] Pavlakoudis, Rosalia (31.01.2023). Wird das Metaverse Shopping grundlegend verändern? Verbrauchermeinungen sind gemischt. In: GetApp. Online: https://www.getapp.de/blog/3415/wird-das-metaverse-shopping-entscheidend-veraendern#Jeder-Zweite-ist-am-Metaverse-Shopping-interessiert (accessed on: 17.05.2023).

[PER22] Perri, Lori (10.08.2022). What's New in the 2022 Gartner Hype Cycle for Emerging Technologies. In: Gartner Insights. https://www.gartner.com/en/articles/what-s-new-in-the-2022-gartner-hype-cycle-for-emerging-technologies (accessed on: 17.05.2023).

[PLAoJ] Plattform Industrie 4.0 (o.J.). Was ist Industrie 4.0? Von: BMBF, BMWK. Online: https://www.plattform-i40.de/IP/Navigation/DE/Industrie40/WasIndustrie40/was-ist-industrie-40.html (accessed on: 17.05.2023).

[RAB15] Rabie,Ramadan; Samah, Refat; Marwa, Elshahed; , Rasha, Ali (2015). Basics of Brain Computer Interface. In: Intelligent Systems Reference Library. 74. 31-50. https://doi.org/10.1007/978-3-319-10978-7_2.

[REDoJ] Redaktion ComputerWeekly.de, TechTarget (2015). Definition ARPANET/DARPANET. Online: https://www.computerweekly.com/de/definition/ARPANET-DARPANET (accessed on: 17.05.2023).

[RIX22] Rixecker, Kim (23.02.2022): Metaverse-Selbstversuch: Wir waren da – und schwer gelangweilt. In: t3n. Online: https://t3n.de/news/metaverse-selbstversuch-decentraland-1451407/ (accessed on: 17.05.2023).

[ROE22] Roe, David (20.01.2022). Where the Metaverse and Digital Workplace Meet. In: Reworked. Online: https://www.reworked.co/digital-workplace/where-the-metaverse-and-digital-workplace-meet/ (accessed on: 28.05.2023).

[RZE20] Rzeszewski, Michał; Evans, Leighton (2020). Virtual Place During Quarantine – a Curious Case of VRChat. In: Rozwój Regionalny I Polityka Regio-nalna, no. 51 (November), 57 – 75.

[SA23] Sá Maria José; Serpa Sandro (2023). Metaverse as a Learning Environment: Some Considerations. In: Sustainability. 2023; 15(3):2186. https://doi.org/10.3390/su15032186.

[SAAoJ] SaaSHub (o. J.). Moodle VS Metaverse – Compare Moodle VS Metaverse and see what are their differences. In: SaaSHub. Online: https://www.saashub.com/compare-moodle-vs-metaverse (accessed on: 28.05.2023).

[SAM22] Samuels, Mark (24.10.2022). Metaverse and immersive experiences: How one company is getting started on the journey. In: ZDNet Tech/Werables/AR+VR. Online: https://www.zdnet.com/article/metaverse-and-immersive-experiences-how-one-company-is-getting-started-on-the-journey/ (accessed on: 28.05.2023).

[SCH03] Schoonmaker, Stephen J. (2003). The CAD guidebook : a basic manual for understanding and improving computer-aided design. In: Marcel Dekker, New York. ISBN 0-8247-0871-7. OCLC 50868192.

[SCH19a] Schüffel, Patrick; Groeneweg, Nikolaj; Baldegger, Rico (2019). The Crypto Encyclopedia: Coins, Tokens and Digital Assets from A to Z. In: Hochschule für Wirtschaft Fribourg/Growth Publisher, Bern. Bern/Fribourg August 2019.

[SCH22] Schulz, Madelein (27.10.2022. Gucci Vault opens metaverse world in The Sandbox with games and vintage fashion. In: Vogue Business. Online: https://www.voguebusiness.com/technology/gucci-vault-opens-metaverse-world-in-the-sandbox-with-games-and-vintage-fashion (accessed on: 28.05.2023).

[SCH23a] Schlott, Karin (10.05.2023). Wenn die Computerblume duftet. In: Spektrum.de. Online: https://www.spektrum.de/news/virtuelle-realitaet-wenn-die-computerblume-duftet/2137641 (accessed on: 17.05.2023).

[SCHm21a] Schmidt, Cord (2021): Wie das Internet zum Metaverse wird. In: hy – the Axel Springer Consulting Group. Online: https://hy.co/2021/12/01/into-the-metaverse-oder-die-naechste-aera-des-internets/#1 (accessed on: 10.05.2023).

[SEC19] Second Life (2019). Guide to Jobs in Second Life (Version 27.07.2019). In: Second Life Wiki. Online: https://wiki.secondlife.com/wiki/Guide_to_Jobs_in_Second_Life (accessed on: 10.05.2023).

[SED21] Sedlmeir, Johannes; Smethurst, Reilly; Rieger, Alexander; Fridgen, Gilbert (2021). Digital Identities and Verifiable Credentials. In: Business & Information Systems Engineering 63, 603–613 (2021). https://doi.org/10.1007/s12599-021-00722-y.

[SEN22] Sensorium (16.11.2022). Esports And The Metaverse. In: Sensorium Blog Gaming. Online: https://sensoriumxr.com/articles/esports-and-the-metaverse (accessed on: 28.05.2023).

[SER18] Seraphin, Hugues; Sheeran, Paul; Pilato, Manuela. (2018). Over-tourism and the fall of Venice as a destination. Journal of Destination Marketing & Management. 9. https://doi.org/10.1016/j.jdmm.2018.01.011 (accessed on: 10.05.2023).

[SINoJ] Sine Wave Entertainment (o. J.): https://sinewaveentertainment.com (accessed on: 17.05.2023).

[SIR22] Sirisha (29.07.2022). You Can Be Monalisa in Seconds, Thanks to this Deepfake Tech. In: Analytics Insight. Online: https://www.analyticsinsight.net/you-can-be-monalisa-in-seconds-thanks-to-this-deepfake-tech/ (accessed on: 10.05.2023).

[SMAoJ] Smart Valor (o. J.). Maker (MKR). In: Smart Valor Digitale Asset Börse. Online: https://smartvalor.com/de/maker (accessed on: 20.05.2023).

[SNI23] Snider, Mike (21.03.2023). Is 3D printing the future of food? Well, if you like cheesecake things are already cooking. In: USA Today. Online: https://eu.usatoday.com/story/news/nation/2023/03/21/food-future-3-d-printed-cheesecake-dessert/11514028002/ (accessed on: 17.05.2023).

[SOM22] Somnium Space (on Medium.com) (Sep 12, 2022): Somnium Space partners with Prusa Research and Vrgineers to further develop its open source „Somnium VR ONE" headset. Online: https://somniumspace.medium.com/somnium-space-partners-with-prusa-research-and-vrgineers-to-further-develop-its-open-source-8d1dca74dae2 (accessed on: 17.05.2023).

[SOMoJ] Somnium Space (o. J.). Somnium Space. Online: https://somniumspace.com (accessed on: 17.05.2023).

[SOS22] Sosa [2022]. Metaverse, insurance, and mental health. The new new thing. In: SOSY Blog. Online: https://www.sosa.co/blog/metaverse-insurance-mental-health (accessed on: 28.05.2023).

[SPE21] Speakman, Jay (22.11.2021). Was ist The Sandbox? – Das Metaversum. In: Blockzeit.com. Online: https://blockzeit.com/de/was-ist-sandbox-das-metaversum/ (accessed on: 17.05.2023).

[STO22] Stoyanov, Nadine; Moser, Christian; Kwiatkowski, Marta (2022). Extended Retail – Die Zukunft des Handels ist grenzenlos. Zühlke und GDI/Studie zu «Extended Retail». Von: – Zühlke Engineering AG. Online: https://www.zuehlke.com/de/extended-retail-die-zukunft-des-handels-ist-grenzenlos (accessed on: 17.05.2023).

[STU19] Stuttgarter Nachrichten (28.11.2019). Europa-Park Rust: Rulantica jetzt für alle offen. In: stuttgarter-nachrichten.de. In: Stuttgarter Nachrichten. Online: https://www.stuttgarter-nachrichten.de/inhalt.europa-park-rust-es-ist-angebadet.9b719233-02e7-4628-bee7-32e18fa91acd.html (accessed on: 28.05.2023).

[SUPoJ] SuperRare (o.J.). SuperRare. In: SuperRare. Online: https://niftygateway.com (accessed on: 28.05.2023).

[TAIoJ] Taipei City Government (o.J.). Taipei City Government. Online: https://www.gov.taipei/ (accessed on: 17.05.2023).

[TAK16] Takahashi, Dean (09.12.2016). The DeanBeat: Epic graphics guru Tim Sweeney foretells how we can create the open Metaverse. In: Venture Beat. Online: https://venturebeat.com/games/the-deanbeat-epic-boss-tim-sweeney-makes-the-case-for-the-open-metaverse/ (accessed on: 17.05.2023).

[TEO22] Teo, Cheryl (09.05.2022). M Social stamps its 'M' in the metaverse. In: Travel Weekly Asia. Online: https://www.travelweekly-asia.com/Travel-News/Travel-Technology/Millennium-Hotels-and-Resorts-launches-world-s-first-hotel-in-the-metaverse (accessed on: 10.05.2023).

[THE20] The Sandbox (30.06.2020): What Is The Sandbox? In: Medium.com. Online: https://medium.com/sandbox-game/what-is-the-sandbox-850de68d893e (accessed on: 17.05.2023).

[THEoJ] The Sandbox (o.J.). The Sandbox. Online: https://www.sandbox.game (accessed on: 17.05.2023).

[THIoJ] Thingiverse (o.J.). About. In: Thingiverse. Online: https://www.thingiverse.com/about (accessed on: 23.05.2023).

[THO13] Thoma, Jörg (08.05.2013). Wie klingt ein Sonnenuntergang? In: golem.de. Online: https://www.golem.de/news/eyeborg-wie-klingt-ein-sonnenuntergang-1305-99161.html (accessed on: 17.05.2023).

[TIP20] Tip (24.04.2020). Rapper Travis Scott sorgt für „Fortnite"-Rekord. In: Soiegel.de Netzwelt. Online: https://www.spiegel.de/netzwelt/web/fortnite-konzert-von-rapper-travis-scott-sorgt-fuer-nutzerrekord-a-b377df69-74d2-4103-bbaa-98b40392afaf (accessed on: 28.05.2023).

[TOF80] Toffler, Alvin (1980). The Third Wave. Bantam Books, London.

[TOF90] Toffler, Alvin (1990). Powershift: Knowledge, Wealth and Violence at the Edge of the 21st Century (1990) Bantam Books, London.

[VET15] Vetter, Philipp (18.08.2015). Das Adidas-Experiment mit dem personalisierten Schuh. In: Welt. Online: https://www.welt.de/wirtschaft/article145329973/Das-Adidas-Experiment-mit-dem-personalisierten-Schuh.html (accessed on: 17.05.2023).

[VIN15] Vincent, M. A.; Sheriff, S.; Mellott, S. (2015). The efficacy of high-fidelity simulation on psychomotor clinical performance improvement of undergraduate nursing students. In: Computers, Informatics, Nursing : CIN. 2015 Feb;33(2):78–84. DOI: https://doi.org/10.1097/cin.0000000000000136. PMID: 25636043.

[VIRoJ] Virbela (o. J.). Virbela: A Virtual World for Work, Education & Events. In: Virbela. Online: https://www.virbela.com (accessed on: 28.05.2023).

[VRJoJ] VRJAM The Multiverse Plattform (o.J.). Revolutionising Live Events fort he WEB3 World. Online: https://vrjam.com/ (accessed on: 17.05.2023).

[UPLoJ] Upland (o. J.). Upland. Online: https://www.upland.me/ (accessed on: 17.05.2023).

[WAN22] Wang, Ge; Badal, Andreu; Jia, Xun; Maltz, Jonathan; Mueller, Klaus; Myers, Kyle; Niu, Chuang; Vannier. Michael; Yan, Pingkun; Yu, Zhou; Zeng, Rongping (2022). Development of metaverse for intelligent healthcare. In: Nature Machine Intelligence. 4. 1–8. https://doi.org/10.1038/s42256-022-00549-6.

[WAVoJ] Wave (o. J.). The Show Must Go Beyond. In: Wave XR. Online: https://wavexr.com/about/ (accessed on: 28.05.2023).

[WEB22] Weber, Urs (11.10.2022). ARTour – Kunstspaziergang durch Basel mit Augmented Reality. In: Tourismuspresse, Schweiz Tourismus. https://www.tourismuspresse.at/presseaussendung/TPT_20221011_TPT0004/artour-kunstspaziergang-durch-basel-mit-augmented-reality-bild (accessed on: 10.05.2023).

[WEFoJa] World Economic Forum (o. J.). Defining and Building the Metaverse. In: World Economic Forum. https://initiatives.weforum.org/defining-and-building-the-metaverse/home (accessed on: 21.05.2023).

[WEFoJb] World Economic Forum (o. J.). Agenda Articles, filtered by „The Metaverse“. In: World Economic Forum. https://www.weforum.org/agenda/the-metaverse/ (accessed on: 21.05.2023).

[WEI20] Weiss, Christoph (22.05.2020). Kreatives Chaos in VRChat. In: ORF Radio FM4. Online: https://fm4.orf.at/stories/3002767/ (accessed on: 10.05.2023).

[WEI22] Wei, Hongtao; Tang, Lei; Wang, Wenshuo; Zhang, Jiaming (26.05.2022). Home Environment Augmented Reality System Based on 3D Reconstruction of a Single Furniture Picture. In: Sensors 2022, 22(11), 4020; https://doi.org/10.3390/s22114020.

[Wu23] Wu, Tzu-Chi; Ta, Chien; Ho, Bruce (2023). A scoping review of metaverse in emergency medicine. In: Australasian Emergency Care, Volume 26, Issue 1, 2023, Pages 75–83, ISSN 2588-994X, https://doi.org/10.1016/j.auec.2022.08.002. Online: https://www.sciencedirect.com/science/article/pii/S2588994X22000525 (accessed on: 28.05.2023).

[W3CocJ] W3C (o. J.). Extensible Markup Language (XML). In: W3C. Online: https://www.w3.org/XML/ (accessed on: 22.5.2023).

[W3CoJd] W3C (o. J.). WebXR Device API. In: W3C. Online: https://www.w3.org/TR/webxr/ (accessed on: 22.5.2023).

[ZAV21] Zavian, Ellen M. (07.12.2021). Esports And The Metaverse – Predictions For 2022. In: Forbes Business, Sports Money. Online: https://www.forbes.com/sites/ellenzavian/2021/12/07/esports-and-the-metaversepredictions-for-2022/ (accessed on: 28.05.2023).

[ZET20] Zetzsche, Dirk Andreas; Arner, Douglas W.; Buckley, Ross P. (30.09.2020). Decentralized Finance (DeFi). In: Journal of Financial Regulation, 2020, 6, 172–203. https://doi.org/10.2139/ssrn.3539194. Online: https://ssrn.com/abstract=3539194 (accessed on: 28.05.2023).

[ZIV03] Ziv, Amitai;Wolpe, Paul; Small, Stephen; Glick, Shimon (2003). Simulation-Based Medical Education: An Ethical Imperative. Academic medicine : journal of the Association of American Medical Colleges. 78. 783–8.https://doi.org/10.1097/01.SIH.0000242724.08501.63.

5 What Must Not Be Missing: Criticism

The metaverse, as a virtual world primarily based on advances in VR and AR as well as blockchain technologies, presents both opportunities and risks concerning the physical world. A possible consequence of the increasing spread of the metaverse is the decrease in real social interactions, as people might spend a considerable part of their time in this virtual environment. This could have negative impacts on social relationships and mental health, including the neglect of physical health due to a lack of exercise. [ZUC13]

Furthermore, the metaverse enables the creation of a parallel world characterized by different norms and values than physical reality. This poses the risk that cultural identities and values may be transformed and consequently influence the real world. An increased dependence on technology could also lead to people having difficulties making independent decisions and solving problems. This could be particularly the case if the metaverse becomes the main medium for communication and interaction, which could limit the ability to interact effectively in the physical world. [LES06]

Additionally, privacy concerns related to the metaverse must be considered, as comprehensive monitoring of the virtual world could impair users' privacy. Furthermore, cyberbullying and cybercrime could increase, with potential impacts on the physical world.

The future challenge will therefore lie in understanding the metaverse as a potential parallel world that can influence physical reality. It thus seems essential that the development of the metaverse occurs in alignment with the physical world and recognizes possible mutual impacts. Even though it may sound undesirable today, official regulatory authorities, among others, should ensure that the development of the metaverse takes place responsibly and that privacy and security concerns are adequately addressed to promote the positive aspects of the metaverse without negative consequences.

The future development of the metaverse and its impacts on the real world are currently uncertain. On the one hand, there is the possibility that social parallel societies

P. Hoffmann, *Next Generation Internet*, https://doi.org/10.1007/978-3-658-46424-0_5

may emerge if certain groups of people isolate themselves from the real world and prefer to live in the virtual world. This could lead to further fragmentation of society as a whole, with different identities and communities emerging in the virtual and real worlds. On the other hand, the metaverse can also play a positive role in promoting global collaboration and cohesion, depending on how it is developed and used. [RHE00]

There are various risks that need to be considered in the discussion about the metaverse. A central concern is the danger of addictive behavior, which can lead to the neglect of real responsibilities and negative impacts on individual mental health. Such behaviors and the resulting addiction potential are already known from MMORPGs and will become even more pronounced in the more immersive worlds of the metaverse. Additionally, the metaverse could deepen social divisions by providing privileged groups with access to technology while others remain excluded.

User interaction within a virtual world also entails significant security and privacy risks, such as hacking, data breaches, fraud, identity theft, and cyberbullying. Furthermore, there is concern that dependence on technology could increase due to the metaverse, leading to a loss of autonomy, independence, and social skills. Finally, there is the risk that governments and companies could use the metaverse to manipulate opinions and actions by sending targeted messages to specific user groups. [LAN14, MAY11, NIS09]

5.1 The General Themes of Criticism

The metaverse is a virtual world that is highly dependent on technology. However, with this dependence on technology, privacy concerns that can affect the users of the metaverse also increase.

First of all, the metaverse or the applications on the metaverse platforms can collect an enormous amount of data about its users. Every action a user performs within the virtual world can be recorded and stored. This data can be used to analyze and monetize user behavior within the virtual world. There is also the possibility that this data could be used by third parties such as advertisers or governments. [LAN14, LANoJ, ZUB19]

Another problem is the potential danger of identity theft. Since the metaverse allows virtual identities, it can be difficult to ensure that users are actually who they claim to be. This is already evident in the current internet or WWW. This danger can lead to fraud and other illegal activities. Moreover, the metaverse can be a perfect target for hackers and cybercriminals. Since the metaverse will have to manage a significant amount of financial transactions and sensitive information, a security breach can have substantial impacts. [GIE23]

As already seen in the current internet or WWW, it is even more important to consider in the technologically much more complex environment of the metaverse that users may not fully understand what data is being collected about them and how this data is being used. This can lead to a lack of transparency and result in users being unable to make informed decisions about which data they want to disclose and which they do not. [SAL23, LAN14]

To address these privacy concerns, regulators must ensure that the metaverse is subject to strict privacy policies. The developers of the individual platforms in the metaverse should also ensure transparency regarding the data they collect and how it is used. Users should be able to control their data at any time and decide which data they want to disclose and which they do not. It is also important to implement security measures to protect user data from potential security breaches.

A central part of the idea of the metaverse is the ability to connect people from different parts of the world. However, since the virtual world of the metaverse has no geographical boundaries, it can be difficult to determine which law applies in this virtual world or parts of it. In principle, the applicable law initially depends on where the operator of the respective platform, on which the users are active, is located and which laws apply in that country. For example, if the operator of the metaverse is based in the USA, they are initially subject to the laws of the USA and the respective states. However, users of the metaverse can come from different parts of the world and have different laws and legal systems. It is possible that the metaverse is operated in a country whose laws are contrary to the laws of another country. In this case, users may have different legal claims depending on their nationality and residence.

However, it could happen that some aspects of the metaverse may not be covered by existing laws and regulations. Since the metaverse is a relatively new technology, there are no specific laws or regulations for many situations that specifically address the peculiarities of virtual worlds. In this case, it seems highly relevant that governments and international organizations work together to create appropriate legal frameworks for the metaverse. [DEF18, DEF19, DEA21]

As a vision, it is also conceivable that the metaverse could develop its own legal system in the future. The users of the metaverse could agree on a common code of conduct, given appropriate transparency and agreement, which regulates certain behaviors within the virtual world. Such self-regulation could help resolve conflicts and protect the users of the metaverse. However, it will be a major legal challenge to determine which law applies in an internationally connected, virtual world like the metaverse. Possibly, a combination of national and international laws, regulations, and self-regulatory measures could be the most sensible way to regulate the metaverse.

In such an internationally connected, virtual world like the metaverse, there are a multitude of privacy concerns. Users constantly leave digital traces while interacting in the metaverse, which may result in their personal data being shared with operators, developers, or other users. Therefore, it is important that privacy law in the metaverse is comprehensive and adequate to protect the privacy and rights of users. However, privacy law can vary from country to country, making it difficult to create a unified privacy law for the metaverse. For example, the EU General Data Protection Regulation (GDPR) applies to all companies that process personal data of EU citizens, regardless of where the company is located. This means that operators of the metaverse who process data of EU citizens must comply with the GDPR.

Another problem in the metaverse is that it can also be difficult to determine jurisdiction for privacy violations. For example, if a company is based in the USA and processes personal data of users from Europe, it must first be clarified which data protection authority is responsible for monitoring and enforcing data protection laws. [EURoJ]

To address these challenges, internationally valid standards for data protection and data security in the metaverse should be created as soon as possible. It is also important that operators of the metaverse have clear privacy policies that all users of the metaverse must adhere to. Furthermore, users of the metaverse should have the right to control and delete their personal data.

Another, more technically oriented, way to ensure privacy in the metaverse is the introduction and use of blockchain technologies. This can help ensure the integrity and security of personal data by storing it in a decentralized network that only authorized persons can access.

In addition to the privacy aspects considered so far, another major problem area opens up, in which the metaverse brings a new dimension of tax issues. A central activity of users in the metaverse will foreseeably be, just like in the times of Second Life, that users can buy, own, and trade real estate. In this context, there are a number of questions regarding the taxation of real estate and real estate transactions that are largely unresolved so far. [DEF18, DEF19]

As a continuation of this thought, questions regarding the taxation of income from the ownership of virtual real estate should not be forgotten. When a user buys a plot of land in the metaverse and rents it out or otherwise earns profits from it, the question arises whether taxes must be paid on these earnings and which tax laws and regulations are applicable. The situation becomes even more complex when users come from different countries and have different tax laws and regulations that need to be reconciled. This issue is further exacerbated by the topic of cryptocurrency taxation, which is already frequently used in the metaverse today. Cryptocurrencies are a difficult tax issue due to their decentralized nature and the difficulty of tracking their origin. When users use cryptocurrencies to buy or sell virtual real estate in the metaverse, it is unclear how the profits from these transactions should be taxed. [MOR16, FAI17]

In some countries, governments and authorities have begun to address these questions and develop guidelines for the taxation of virtual real estate in the metaverse. However, most countries have not yet issued specific guidelines, further complicating the international legal situation. To solve such problems, it seems urgent that governments and international organizations collaborate to develop clear guidelines and regulations for tax-relevant transactions. It is important that these regulations are fair and consistent and affect users from different countries equally.

The metaverse is being discussed as a potential future vision where people can interact, do business, learn, and play. These activities require a sophisticated technical infrastructure, which has ecological impacts. Criticism of the ecological impacts of the metaverse mainly focuses on energy consumption and the associated greenhouse gas emissions. Creating and maintaining the infrastructure for such a virtual world requires an enormous amount of energy. The computing power needed for creating 3D graphics, simulations, and AI-based interactions requires a lot of electricity. The energy consumption is also foreseeably going to increase with the rise in the number of users utilizing the metaverse.

Another problem is that many of the companies building and operating the metaverse run their servers in regions with cheap electricity, which are often still powered by coal plants. The use of fossil fuels for electricity generation has been proven to increase greenhouse gas emissions and contribute to global warming. There are indeed companies that are trying to minimize these and other environmental impacts. Some are relying on renewable energy and using technologies like AI to optimize energy consumption. However, it remains to be seen whether these efforts will be sufficient to reduce the environmental impact of the growing metaverse. [BLU19, MON11, ARA21]

"The metaverse", or rather its operators, will have to face this justified criticism of the ecological impacts. As the metaverse continues to grow, the companies operating the platforms and infrastructures must handle their resources more responsibly. Even if it may sound absurd, regulatory authorities will also have to ensure in the virtual world that environmental aspects are considered in the design and use of the metaverse. Only in this way can the metaverse unfold its advantages without having negative impacts on the real environment.

5.2 The Merging of the Political World?

The metaverse is increasingly being seen as a phenomenon with the potential to bring about significant changes in society. These changes affect social, economic, and political aspects and are not limited to individual states but impact both the first and third worlds.

Socially, the metaverse has the potential to enable an extended form of social interaction and change the way people communicate and interact with each other. It can serve as a platform in both the first and third worlds where people can express their creativity, create art, and form virtual identities. It also allows for overcoming physical barriers such as distance or language barriers and promotes global collaboration. However, there is a risk that the metaverse could contribute to increased social isolation and undermine traditional social relationships.

Economically, the metaverse offers numerous opportunities, especially in the area of virtual real estate and virtual commerce. In the first world, companies can offer virtual products and services, while users can use digital currencies to shop in the virtual world. This can, in turn, create jobs and foster innovation. In the third world, the metaverse can contribute to economic development and poverty reduction by opening up access to new markets and opportunities. However, there is a danger that the metaverse could exacerbate existing economic inequalities by providing more opportunities to those who have access to the necessary resources and skills.

Politically, the metaverse could also enable new forms of government participation and serve as a platform for the discussion and dissemination of political ideas. This applies to both the first and third worlds, where the metaverse can help amplify the voices of marginalized groups and provide a platform for political change. Nevertheless, there is a risk that the metaverse could be dominated by authoritarian regimes or corporations, leading to further division in the world. Therefore, the need for regulations and ethical guidelines is increasingly being discussed to ensure that the metaverse does not lead to further social, economic, and political inequalities, especially between the first and third worlds.

5.3 Or Rather the Division of the Political World?

In the previous Sect. 5.2, the merging of the political world as a potential consequence of the implementation of the idea of the metaverse was examined. In contrast, the possibility should also be considered that the realization of the metaverse could rather lead to a division of society or the international community. Such a division could have far-reaching consequences on social, economic, and political levels.

The effects of a division caused by the metaverse could include increased fragmentation and isolation, exacerbating inequality in the creation of wealth and political power, and impairing political stability and cooperation. Therefore, it is crucial to carefully analyze the societal impacts of the metaverse to promote a fairer and more integrated world. In particular, a division between the first and third worlds through the metaverse could further deepen existing inequalities on social, economic, and political levels.

Social impacts of this division could include increased isolation and fragmentation of society. Individuals with access to the metaverse could distance themselves from the physical world and weaken their social bonds, while people without access to the metaverse could feel isolated and cut off. This division could lead to strong polarization and radicalization as groups with different access to the metaverse increasingly focus on their virtual identities and social groups.

Economically, such a division could contribute to further inequality by excluding certain regions or population groups from the economic opportunities of the metaverse. Companies and individuals with access to the metaverse could gain competitive advantages over those without access, leading to an imbalance in job creation and economic development. This gap could exacerbate income inequality between countries and further strain the already weak economies of the third world.

The potential division of the world through the metaverse could contribute to deepening political differences between various regions and countries. This is because some countries or governments might try to control or restrict their citizens' access to the metaverse, which in turn could result in additional restrictions on freedom of expression and political participation. In this context, people with access to the metaverse could form virtual political groups and possibly become alienated from the physical world. This phenomenon could create an imbalance in political power and influence and further widen the gap between the first and third worlds. [MOZ11, PIL11, SHI09]

On a political level, the metaverse could cause a division between the first and third worlds, which in turn leads to an exacerbation of political differences and tensions. First-world governments might also strive to control or regulate access to the metaverse to protect their own interests. Similarly, third-world governments might view access to the metaverse as a threat to their sovereignty and accordingly control or limit access. Such a division has the potential to create further imbalances in political power and influence, negatively affecting political stability and cooperation between the involved countries.

Undoubtedly, the metaverse has the potential to deepen the digital divide between the first and third worlds and to amplify the already existing social, economic, and political differences. To prevent such a division, various measures should be taken. Firstly, it is crucial to enable people in the third world to access the metaverse by creating the necessary infrastructure to provide fast and reliable internet. Governments, international organizations, and the private sector will likely need to cooperate more intensively to facilitate access to the metaverse. Furthermore, emphasis should be placed on education and training so that people in the third world can effectively use the metaverse. This helps improve their skills and enables them to fully exploit the opportunities offered by the metaverse. Additionally, it is important to promote cultural sensitivity and ensure that the metaverse is accessible and relevant to all cultures. Developers must be careful to respect cultural differences and not reinforce cultural stereotypes and prejudices. [SUD22, WEF22]

Careful regulation of the metaverse can help ensure fairness and security for all. Regulatory authorities should ensure that the metaverse does not contribute to deepening existing social, economic, and political differences. Finally, cooperation between governments, international organizations, and the private sector should be promoted to achieve common goals and ensure that the metaverse is accessible and beneficial to all.

Governments and international institutions such as the United Nations are crucial in shaping the metaverse to avoid discrepancies between the first and third worlds. Through various measures, including regulation, infrastructure promotion, education and training, international cooperation, and consumer protection, governments can help make the metaverse fair and accessible to all without exacerbating existing regional differences.

On the one hand, governments can play a significant role in regulating the metaverse by establishing specifically oriented regulatory authorities to ensure fairness and security for all users and not to deepen social, economic, and political inequalities. On the other hand, they can promote investments in the necessary infrastructure, such as broadband internet and mobile networks, to enable people in the third world to access the metaverse and benefit from its advantages. Additionally, governments can develop training and education programs to ensure that people in the third world have the necessary skills and knowledge to effectively use the metaverse. This can also include the development of appropriate curricula in schools and universities to prepare young people for the use of the metaverse.

Furthermore, international cooperation is of central importance in developing common standards and regulations that ensure the metaverse does not deepen existing disparities between the first and third worlds. Finally, governments can protect consumers from fraud and abuse in the metaverse by enacting laws and regulations aimed at protecting consumers and preventing fraudulent practices.

The implementation of regulations and ethical guidelines at the political level is a necessary measure to ensure the use of technologies like the metaverse is safe and socially beneficial without causing negative consequences. One of the possible challenges is the emergence of another digital divide between those who have access to the metaverse and those who do not. This aspect can be addressed through regulations and ethical guidelines to ensure accessibility and fairness for all. [LANoJ]

Moreover, abuse and violations of privacy and personal rights can occur in the metaverse. The introduction of regulations and ethical guidelines helps to minimize such risks by setting standards for privacy protection and abuse prevention. At the political level, such regulations and guidelines can also ensure that companies operating in the metaverse act responsibly and align their business practices with social and environmental interests. This also ensures fair treatment of users, who must not be disadvantaged by fraudulent practices or discrimination.

Since the metaverse is still a relatively new phenomenon and its impacts on society are not yet fully understood, this requires the development of regulations and ethical guidelines that are flexible enough to accommodate changes and new developments related to the metaverse. In summary, it is therefore crucial to develop and enforce regulations and ethical guidelines at the political level to shape the use of the metaverse in a way that benefits society as a whole and does not have negative consequences.

5.4 But: A Look from Another Perspective

Unlike in industrialized nations, a significantly higher conviction that the metaverse will influence daily life is evident in so-called developing countries compared to wealthier countries. A survey conducted on behalf of the World Economic Forum (WEF), whose results were published in 2022 by the market research company Ipsos, shows a significantly greater enthusiasm for the metaverse and virtual or augmented reality in developing countries as opposed to high-income countries. [WEF22]

The survey, which included more than 21,000 adult participants from 29 countries, found that 52% had heard of the metaverse and 50% had a positive feeling about its use in everyday life. In countries like China, India, Peru, Saudi Arabia, and Colombia, two-thirds or more of the respondents reported having a positive feeling. In particular, 78% of respondents in China expressed positive feelings, followed by India with 75%.

In contrast, the countries with the highest incomes showed the lowest values, such as Japan (22%), the United Kingdom (26%), Belgium (30%), Canada (30%), France (31%), and Germany (31%), showing less enthusiasm and awareness regarding the metaverse.

The survey results also indicate that "developing countries" like South Africa, China, and India believe that applications of the metaverse, such as virtual learning, entertainment, digital interactions, and remote surgeries, will significantly influence people's lives. In high-income countries like Japan, Belgium, and France, there is a significantly lower conviction regarding such changes.

Additionally, developing countries overall seem to be more enthusiastic about cryptocurrencies and blockchain, as analyses by CB Insights, Deloitte, or the cryptocurrency exchange Gemini from the years 2021 and 2022 illustrate. [CBI21, DEL21, GEM22] These reports show that half of the respondents in India, Brazil, and the Asia-Pacific region acquired their first cryptocurrency in 2021. Inflation and currency devaluation were identified as the main drivers for the acceptance of cryptocurrencies in these regions. In countries experiencing a currency devaluation of 50% or more, the likelihood of planning cryptocurrency purchases is five times higher than in countries with lower inflation.

The discrepancy in the acceptance and enthusiasm for emerging technologies like the metaverse, VR/AR, and cryptocurrencies between developing countries and high-income countries could be due to various factors. One possible explanation is the different willingness to adapt to technology:

- Developing countries might view innovative technologies as an opportunity to bridge economic and social development gaps and make their economies more competitive.
- Furthermore, limited access to traditional financial services in developing countries could increase the attractiveness of cryptocurrencies by offering an inclusive alternative that is accessible regardless of geographic location or socioeconomic status. In countries with high inflation rates and currency devaluations, cryptocurrencies could serve as a hedge against such risks and represent a more stable store of value than the local currency.

The willingness to adopt new technologies could also be related to educational and infrastructural factors. Developing countries with a younger population and better digital infrastructure might be more inclined to adopt technologies like the metaverse and cryptocurrencies. Younger individuals are generally more tech-savvy and adaptable to changes. Cultural differences and attitudes may also play a role in the perception and acceptance of new technologies. In some cultures, there may be a greater willingness to try and adapt to new technologies, while in other cultures, skepticism or reluctance towards changes may prevail. To gain a comprehensive understanding of the underlying causes of these disparities, a detailed analysis of the survey results and additional research would be necessary.

References

[ARA21] Aratani, Lauren (27.02.2021). Electricity Needed to Mine Bitcoin Is More Than Used by ‚Entire Countries.' In: The Guardian. Online: https://www.theguardian.com/technology/2021/feb/27/bitcoin-mining-electricity-use-environmental-impact (accessed on: 20.05.2023).

[BLU19] Blum, Andrew (2012). Tubes: A Journey to the Center of the Internet. Ecco (2012).

[CBI21] CB Insights (01.02.2022). State Of Blockchain 2021 Report. In: CB Insights Research Report. Online: https://www.cbinsights.com/research/report/blockchain-trends-2021/ (accessed on: 28.05.2023).

[DEA21] Deakin, Simon; Markou, Christopher (29.06.2021). Is Law Computable: Critical Perspectives on Law and Artificial Intelligence. Oxford: Hart Publishing.

[DEF18] De Filippi, Primavera; Wright, Aaron (2018). Blockchain and the Law: The Rule of Code. Harvard University Press.

[DEF19] De Filippi, Primavera; Wright, Aaron (04.10.2019). The Rule of Code vs. The Rule of Law. In: Medium: Harvard University Press. Online: https://hup.medium.com/the-rule-of-code-vs-the-rule-of-law-8dfe75631fee (accessed on: 20.05.2023).

[DEL21] Deloitte (2021). Deloitte's 2021 Global Blockchain Survey – A new age of digital assets. In: Deloitte Insights. Online: https://www2.deloitte.com/us/en/insights/topics/understanding-blockchain-potential/global-blockchain-survey.html (accessed on: 28.05.2023).

[EURoJ] Europäische Kommission (o.J.). Für wen gilt die Datenschutz-Grundverordnung? In: Europäische Kommission. Online: https://commission.europa.eu/law/law-topic/data-protection/reform/rules-business-and-organisations/application-regulation/who-does-data-protection-law-apply_de (accessed on: 20.05.2023).

[FAI17] Fairfield, Joshua. (2017). Owned: Property, Privacy, and the New Digital Serfdom. Cambridge University Press. https://doi.org/10.1017/9781316671467.

[GEM22] Gemini (2022). 2022 Global State of Crypto. In: Gemini. Online: https://www.gemini.com/state-of-crypto (accessed on: 28.05.2023).

[GIE23] Giese, Sascha (27.02.2023). Metaversum 2023 – Neues Terrain, alte Gefahren. In: IT-Daily. Online: https://www.it-daily.net/it-sicherheit/cloud-security/metaversum-2023-neues-terrain-alte-gefahren (accessed on: 20.05.2023).

[IPS22a] Ipsos (25.05.2022). Enthusiasm for the metaverse and extended reality is highest in emerging countries. In: Ipsos. Online: https://www.ipsos.com/en-ch/global-advisor-metaverse-extended-reality-may-2022 (accessed on: 20.05.2023).

[IPS22b] Ipsos (2022). How the world seas the metaverse and extended reality – A 29-country Global Advisor survey. In: Ipsos. Online: https://www.ipsos.com/sites/default/files/ct/news/documents/2022-05/Global%20Advisor%20-%20WEF%20-%20Metaverse%20-%20May%202022%20-%20Graphic%20Report.pdf (accessed on: 20.05.2023).

[LAN14] Lanier, Jaron (2014). Who Owns the Future? Simon & Schuster.

[LANoJ] Lanier, Jaroin (o. J.). Who Owns the Future. In: Web Ressources tot he book Who Owns the Future by Jaron Lanier. Online: http://www.jaronlanier.com/futurewebresources.html (accessed on: 20.05.2023).

[LES06] Lessig, Lawrence. (2006). Code Version 2.0. Basic Books.

[MAY11] Mayer-Schönberger, Viktor (2011). Delete: The Virtue of Forgetting in the Digital Age. Princeton University Press.

[MON11] Monserrat, Steven Gonzaleze (27.01.2022). The Cloud Is Material: On the Environmental Impacts of Computation and Data Storage. In: MIT Shcwarzman College of

Computing. Online: https://mit-serc.pubpub.org/pub/the-cloud-is-material/release/1 (accessed on: 20.05.2023).

[MOR16] Morse, Edward A. (2016). Regulation of Online Gambling. In: Research Handbook on Electronic Commerce Law 449 (John A. Rothchild ed).

[MOZ11] Morozov, Evgeny (2011). The Net Delusion: The Dark Side of Internet Freedom. Perseus Book Group, Philadelphia 2011, ISBN 978–1–58648–874–1.

[NIS09] Nissenbaum, Hellen (2009). Privacy in Context: Technology, Policy, and the Integrity of Social. Life. Stanford University Press.

[PIL11] Pilkington, Ed (13.01.2011). Evgeny Morozov: How democracy slipped through the net. In: The Guardian. Online: https://www.theguardian.com/technology/2011/jan/13/evgeny-morozov-the-net-delusion (accessed on: 20.05.2023).

[RHE00] Rheingold, Howard (2000).The Virtual Community: Homesteading on the Electronic Frontier. The MIT Press.

[SAL23] Salvi, Vishal (13.04.2023). Neue Technologien, alte Herausforderungen: Die dunkle Seite der Metaverse Security. In: Security Insider. Online: https://www.security-insider.de/die-dunkle-seite-der-metaverse-security-a-0de3030b47342c6af81dff-534f1e848e/ (accessed on: 20.05.2023).

[SHI09] Shirky, Clay (2009).Here Comes Everybody: The Power of Organizing Without Organizations. Penguin Books.

[SUD22] Sudan, Randeep; Petrov, Oleg; Gupta, Garima (09.03.2022). Can the metaverse offer benefits for developing countries? In: World Bank Blogs. Online: https://blogs.worldbank.org/digital-development/can-metaverse-offer-benefits-developing-countries (accessed on: 20.05.2023).

[TUR11] Turkle, Sherry (2011). Alone together: Why we expect more from technology and less from each other. Basic Books.

[WEF22] World Economic Forum (25.05.2022). How enthusiastic is your country about the rise of the metaverse? In: WeFOrum. Online: https://www.weforum.org/agenda/2022/05/countries-attitudes-metaverse-augmented-virtual-reality-davos22/ (accessed on: 20.05.2023).

[ZUB19] Zuboff, Shoshana (2019). The Age of Surveillance Capitalism: The Fight for a Human Future at the New Frontier of Power. PublicAffairs.

[ZUC13] Zuckerman; Ethan (17. Juni 2013). Rewire: Digital Cosmopolitans in the Age of Connection. Norton & Company; 1. Edition.

6 The True Vision

All discussions that deal with the metaverse, both positively and critically, ultimately exhibit a significant weakness that manifests in two different forms:

- On the one hand, the discussions remain superficial and fundamentally vague because the metaverse is viewed as an all-encompassing and thus unmanageable large future construct.
- On the other hand, many discussions are based on isolated examinations of small and very small niches and use cases that are not placed in any overarching context.

Both perspectives share the same weakness, namely that it is ultimately never precisely known what the metaverse will be, or more specifically formulated: how the metaverse will be technically and functionally structured. Nevertheless, both established national and international organizations and renowned experts from various disciplines attempt to identify potential applications and use cases.

6.1 The Institutional View of the Metaverse

In recent years, the metaverse has received much attention from various national and international organizations interested in the social, economic, technological, and political aspects of this vision:

- The *International Telecommunication Union* (ITU), as an agency of the United Nations, is committed to promoting information and communication technologies worldwide. It is interested in the metaverse because it advocates for the creation of an inclusive, open, and secure digital space.

P. Hoffmann, *Next Generation Internet*, https://doi.org/10.1007/978-3-658-46424-0_6

- The *Institute of Electrical and Electronics Engineers* (IEEE) is an international organization dedicated to research, development, and promotion of technological innovations. It is interested in the metaverse because it attributes the potential to fundamentally change the way people live and work to this technology.
- The *World Wide Web Consortium* (W3C) is the international institution dedicated to standardizing the internet. The W3C is interested in the metaverse because it sees it as the further development of the WWW and aims to create or at least enable an open and accessible digital space.
- The *World Economic Forum* (WEF) is interested in the metaverse because it sees the potential to revolutionize the way people work, learn, and interact. The WEF aims to explore the opportunities and challenges of the metaverse and develop recommendations for its sustainable design.
- In addition, various organizations, such as the *Electronic Frontier Foundation* (EFF) or *Privacy International,* are interested in the metaverse to ensure that it respects users' privacy and civil rights.
- A growing number of *governments* and national organizations are also showing interest in the metaverse because they recognize its potential and its impact on the economy, education, healthcare, and culture. They want to ensure that their countries and citizens benefit from the opportunities the metaverse offers.
- Ultimately, many *technology companies* and industry associations, such as the VR/AR Association VRARA or the Augmented Reality for Enterprise Alliance (AREA), are also participating in the discussion and development of the metaverse because they recognize its potential for creating new business models and revolutionizing existing industries.

The following organizations will be examined in more detail regarding their views on the metaverse: ITU and IEEE, W3C, WEF, and the Metaverse Standards Forum.

6.1.1 ITU and IEEE

The International Telecommunication Union (ITU) and the Institute of Electrical and Electronics Engineers (IEEE) are two high-ranking international organizations that deal with technologies and standards related to the metaverse. Both organizations have different focuses and goals, but both work to advance the development of the metaverse and ensure that it is open, accessible, and secure.

The ITU is a specialized agency of the United Nations that deals with the standardization and development of information and communication technologies (ICT). It is heavily involved in the research and development of the metaverse, focusing on three main aspects: standardization, digital access, and security and privacy. In terms of standardization, the ITU continuously works on developing international standards aimed at ensuring interoperability, compatibility, and accessibility in telecommunications in general and specifically in the metaverse. This process ensures that different metaverse platforms can effectively communicate with each other and that users can easily switch between these platforms, thereby achieving a unified user experience. [ITUoJa, ITUoJb]

Furthermore, the ITU is committed to making the metaverse accessible to all people, regardless of factors such as geographic location, income situation, or educational background. The organization supports a variety of initiatives aimed at bridging the digital divide and facilitating access to the metaverse for disadvantaged communities. These efforts help ensure that the metaverse becomes an inclusive and accessible space for everyone, maximizing its potential benefits and impacts on society.

Finally, the ITU places great emphasis on security and privacy in the metaverse. To achieve this goal, the organization develops policies and best practices aimed at minimizing cybersecurity risks and ensuring the protection of users' privacy in the metaverse. By creating such frameworks, the ITU contributes to creating a secure and trustworthy environment for users in the metaverse, where they can continue their interactions and activities without concerns about the security of their personal data. Overall, the ITU's commitment to standardization, digital access, and security and privacy in the metaverse demonstrates its endeavor to create an open, inclusive, and secure digital space for all.

The IEEE, as a globally operating technological and scientific organization, focuses primarily on technological innovations and standardization as well as knowledge transfer in various fields of electrical engineering, electronics, and computer science. The IEEE's relationship to the metaverse is characterized by its interests in the technological, ethical, and social aspects of metaverse development. Like the ITU and others, the IEEE aims to develop the metaverse into an open, inclusive, and ethically responsible digital space that considers human needs and has the potential to fundamentally change the way we live, work, and interact. [IEEoJa, IEEoJb]

The IEEE is dedicated to developing technology standards and best practices to ensure seamless interoperability and integration of various systems within the metaverse. In this context, the organization engages in working groups and committees focused on creating such standards. The ethical and social issues that arise in connection with technological innovations like the metaverse are of great importance to the IEEE. This is reflected in initiatives such as "Ethically Aligned Design," which has created ethical principles and recommendations for the development and implementation of AI and autonomous systems. In the context of the metaverse, the IEEE advocates for the underlying technologies and systems to consider ethical principles such as fairness, transparency, and privacy.

As a central entity for promoting research and knowledge transfer in the field of the metaverse, the IEEE publishes journals and organizes conferences and workshops. Additionally, it supports research projects and provides educational materials and resources to give its members the opportunity to stay informed about the latest developments and trends in the metaverse and actively participate in them.

Finally, the IEEE strives to connect various stakeholders from industry, academia, and politics to work together on shaping the metaverse. Through its global reach, it promotes collaboration and knowledge exchange to drive innovation and ensure that the metaverse becomes an open, inclusive, and sustainable ecosystem.

Certainly, the current president of the IEEE, Yu Yuan, also deserves credit for the IEEE's strong engagement in this context.

6.1.2 World Wide Web Consortium W3C

The World Wide Web Consortium (W3C) is the international organization that aims to develop web standards to ensure the interoperability and user-friendliness of the internet. [W3CoJa] In relation to the metaverse, the role of the W3C is primarily characterized by its function as a standards organization and its vision of an open, accessible, and secure digital environment.

The development of standards is a central aspect of the W3C's work in connection with the metaverse. Since the metaverse is seen as an extension of the internet, the W3C considers it its task to develop standards and guidelines that ensure the interoperability, user-friendliness, and accessibility of the metaverse. [W3CoJb] This is achieved through the development of standards for interfaces, protocols, and data formats that enable different metaverse platforms and applications to communicate and collaborate smoothly. By providing such standards, the W3C can ensure that the metaverse functions as a coherent digital environment where users can seamlessly switch between different platforms and applications without encountering compatibility issues. [BER19] Furthermore, the W3C's standards contribute to promoting security and privacy in the metaverse by providing clear guidelines for handling sensitive user information. [W3CoJc]

Like others, the W3C views the metaverse as an advanced extension and further development of the internet, in which technologies such as VR, AR, and WebXR will be interconnected to enable an immersive, interactive, and seamless digital experience. The connection of the metaverse with these technologies is seen as a crucial factor for creating an open, accessible, and interoperable digital space.

WebXR is a collection of standards and Application Programming Interfaces (APIs) developed by the W3C to provide VR, AR, and mixed reality content in as many types of web browsers as possible. [W3CoJe] This technology facilitates the development and provision of immersive content on various platforms and devices by enabling developers to create uniform applications that work on different hardware. The W3C sees WebXR as a central building block for the metaverse, as it enables the interoperability and general accessibility of VR and AR content on the web. By developing web standards and APIs that support VR and AR content, the W3C enables developers to create and provide immersive 3D content over the internet. [W3C23a] The integration of VR and AR into the metaverse contributes to creating an immersive, interactive, and continuous user experience that spans multiple platforms and devices.

The W3C is actively committed to realizing a metaverse that is accessible to all users, regardless of their technical abilities, cultural background, or physical limitations.

[W3CoJf] To achieve this goal, the W3C develops guidelines and best practices that promote the accessibility of the metaverse. This includes, for example, considering accessibility in the design of user interfaces or developing technologies that enable people with disabilities to have full access to the metaverse. [W3CoJg] The W3C emphasizes the importance of accessibility and inclusion for the metaverse and supports the development of technologies and standards that enable all users to utilize virtual reality, augmented reality, and WebXR content regardless of their abilities or device limitations. [W3CoJe] This can be achieved by considering accessibility in the design of user interfaces and by developing technologies that enable people with limitations or disabilities to fully experience the metaverse. Furthermore, the W3C values the metaverse as a safe and secure space for its users. To this end, the organization develops standards and guidelines that ensure the protection of privacy, data security, and the confidentiality of communication. The W3C also provides best practices for metaverse development aimed at protecting user security and privacy and reducing vulnerability to cyberattacks or data breaches. [W3CoJh]

The W3C advocates for an open and interoperable metaverse based on open standards and technologies. [W3CoJf] This is intended to enable different platforms and applications to connect and allow users to switch seamlessly between different metaverse environments. Openness and interoperability also promote innovation and competition, as they enable the development of new applications and services built on existing platforms and standards.

Through the development of standards and guidelines as well as collaboration with other organizations, companies, and developers, the W3C aims to help make this vision of the metaverse a reality and develop the metaverse into a positive and inclusive environment for the future version of the internet.

6.1.3 World Economic Forum

The World Economic Forum (WEF), which has set itself the goal of promoting cooperation between businesses, governments, and other stakeholders to address global challenges and foster progress and prosperity, sees the "Metaverse as the next major computing platform." [DAS23, WEFoJa, WEFoJb]

The WEF is interesting in relation to the metaverse because it has launched a number of initiatives and projects to explore and promote the potential of the metaverse. The metaverse is considered a forward-looking technology that could have far-reaching impacts on how we work, play, communicate, and connect.

The WEF has set itself the goal of creating a platform for the exchange of knowledge, ideas, and best practices in the field of the metaverse. To this end, it has already organized a number of events and workshops where experts from various fields come together to discuss the impacts of the metaverse on society. In this way, the World Economic Forum plays a not insignificant role in exploring and promoting the potential of the metaverse. It provides a platform for the exchange of ideas and best practices and helps to raise awareness of the impacts of the metaverse on society.

Furthermore, the WEF has also established a working group on the context of the metaverse, which focuses on exploring the potentials of the metaverse and addresses issues such as privacy, security, and regulation. According to the WEF's idea, this working group is intended to enable experts and interested parties from various fields to exchange information on the latest developments, challenges, and opportunities of the metaverse. The working group is also intended to serve as a platform for communication. An online community is to be formed, allowing members to contribute, engage in discussions, share resources, and participate in virtual events. The community is expected to consist of a wide range of stakeholders, including scientists, technology experts, representatives from governments and businesses, as well as other interest groups.

Additionally, a number of events and workshops are being organized that focus on the metaverse and bring together experts from various related fields to discuss the impacts of the metaverse on the economy and society. These events are intended to help raise awareness of the potentials of the metaverse and provide a platform for the exchange of knowledge and ideas.

Another goal is to identify and share best practices in dealing with the challenges of the metaverse. This includes, for example, discussions on privacy, security, and regulation to ensure that the metaverse is developed in a way that aligns with the interests of the global society. The World Economic Forum has already identified and discussed a number of economic applications of the metaverse that could be implemented in the foreseeable future. One of these applications relates to the possibility that the metaverse could allow companies to sell their products and services within a virtual environment. This could simplify trade processes and increase their efficiency.

Furthermore, the WEF sees the possibility that the metaverse could enable the creation of virtual currencies that can be used within the virtual world. This could reduce transaction costs and facilitate business transactions. Additionally, virtual real estate within the metaverse could be bought, sold, and rented, creating new business models and expanding the real estate market.

The potential ability of the metaverse to enable companies to hire virtual workers who can perform tasks in the virtual world could increase the flexibility and efficiency of the workforce. Moreover, there is the possibility that the metaverse could allow companies to advertise their products and services within the virtual world, creating new advertising opportunities and expanding the advertising market.

Finally, the WEF sees the metaverse as a potential foundation for the establishment of virtual financial services, such as virtual banks and insurance companies. This could expand access to financial services and enlarge the market for financial services. Overall, from the WEF's perspective, the metaverse offers a variety of economic applications that could be realized in the future, contributing to a transformation of the economic landscape.

These potential applications formulated by the WEF are not to be seen as final and complete. Rather, the WEF considers it more than likely that further applications and fields of application will emerge in the future.

6.1.4 Metaverse Standards Forum

The development of an open and inclusive metaverse presents a significant challenge, particularly with regard to the need to develop and adopt standards for interoperability. This requirement has been formulated as a central goal by the Metaverse Standards Forum (MSF). Kevin Collins, Managing Director at Accenture, emphasizes the importance of interoperability: "Regardless of whether you subscribe to a single metaverse or a multiverse model, users need interoperability to realize the value of the metaverse." [SCH23]

Collins further explains that interoperability is necessary for different platforms to interact with each other and for users to seamlessly switch between these platforms while maintaining their identity, assets, and communication. He believes that the efforts of the MSF will help promote and coordinate the development and adoption of the necessary standards to ensure the creation of a connected and consistent metaverse.

To promote the development of open standards for the metaverse and support collaboration across the industry, leading industry organizations and companies have launched the Metaverse Standards Forum. So far, 1,800 members have joined the MSF, including the usual and expected companies Google, Meta, Microsoft, and Nvidia, but also institutions like the Khronos Group and the W3C, and many other hardware and software companies have announced their participation in the MSF. [MSF0J, RAV22]

The MSF was launched with the goal of promoting consensus-based collaboration between various standardization organizations and companies. Specifically, this means defining and aligning requirements and priorities for metaverse standards, accelerating the availability of such standards, and reducing duplication of effort in the industry. Neil Trevett, current chair of the MSF, Vice President of Ecosystem Development at Nvidia, and President of the Khronos Group, described the forum as "a unique place for coordination between standardization organizations and the industry."

To take a pragmatic approach, the forum supports projects such as the development of prototypes, hackathons, plugfests, and open-source tools to accelerate the testing and adoption of metaverse standards. At the same time, it is developing a unified terminology and deployment guidelines. Given the numerous standardization organizations in this area, it may initially seem confusing to establish yet another group. However, IT leaders hope that the new efforts will consolidate existing work and suggest areas for further harmonization.

The MSF emphasizes that it intends to coordinate the requirements and resources of other standardization organizations rather than create new standards. To this end, it collaborates with various standardization organizations in related fields, including the

Khronos Group, the World Wide Web Consortium (W3C), the Open Geospatial Consortium, Open AR Cloud, the Spatial Web Foundation, and many others. Frank Palermo, Executive Vice President and Head of Technology, Media and Telecommunications (TMT) at Virtusa, a digital engineering consulting firm, emphasizes that this coordination will help participants think through the types of standards needed for consumer and business use cases. "It is important to have some cooperating bodies thinking through standards. Otherwise, different companies will build their own variation of the metaverse across a variety of technologies that may not easily work together," said Palermo, and therefore believes that data exchange is one of the most important technical areas that need to be considered for standardization. Virtual worlds can have different ways of representing the size, shape, behavior, sounds, and animations of objects. Standards like the Khronos Group's glTF help ensure the efficient transmission and loading of 3D objects. Other standards are emerging to describe the physical properties of objects, how to assemble objects, and how to animate them. For example, 3D Tiles stream massive 3D datasets in real-time, while Universal Scene Description organizes a collection of objects in such 3D scenes, PhysX brings in the physical properties and behavior characteristics of objects, and MaterialX describes the texture and appearance of objects.

6.2 The Perspective of Professionals and Users

In addition to governmental and economic organizations, the topic of the "Metaverse" has also piqued the interest of many individuals and professionals from various industries, including technology entrepreneurs, game developers, investors, artists, and academics. Some relevant names have already been mentioned at various points up to here, but there is also a growing circle of interested parties:

- *Mark Zuckerberg,* the CEO of Meta, formerly Facebook, is heavily invested in the idea of the Metaverse and believes it will be the next major technological revolution. Meta has heavily invested in projects like Oculus Rift to further develop and make the Metaverse accessible. [HOL21]
- *Tim Sweeney,* CEO of Epic Games, the company behind Fortnite, has also shown great interest in the Metaverse. Sweeney sees the Metaverse as an opportunity to create a shared digital world where people can come together, play, and interact. [WEB23]
- *Philip Rosedale* is a pioneer in the field of virtual worlds and has founded both Second Life and High Fidelity. He is fascinated by the vision of the Metaverse and is working on developing technologies and platforms that enable the realization of the idea. [HAT22]
- *Matthew Ball* is an investor and currently one of the most well-known experts in the field of the Metaverse. He publishes extensively on the Metaverse and shares his ideas on how it could develop and change the world in numerous articles and essays. [BALLoJ]

- The previously introduced *Cathy Hackl*is a futurist and expert in augmented and virtual reality. She is enthusiastic about the vision of the Metaverse and often speaks about how it could change the future of work, education, entertainment, and social interaction. Hackl is also working on developing applications and strategies for the Metaverse and is an important voice in the discussion about its potentials and challenges. [HACoJ]
- *Amy Webb* is a futurist, author, and founder of the Future Today Institute. In her publications on the future of technology and the internet, she has addressed the Metaverse and emphasized the importance of ethics and responsibility in shaping the Metaverse. She particularly warns that without careful planning and regulation, it could lead to a dystopian future. [WEBoJa]
- *Steve Mann* is the pioneer in the field of wearable computing and augmented reality. Although he is not explicitly known as an advocate of the Metaverse vision, his work has had a significant impact on the development of technologies that could enable the Metaverse. Mann has focused on creating interfaces and devices that enhance human perception and enable interaction with digital worlds. These technologies are now considered crucial for the realization of the Metaverse. [MAN13]

The following sections will take a closer look at Matthew Ball, Cathy Hackl, Amy Webb, and Steve Mann and their respective views on the Metaverse.

6.2.1 Matthew Ball

With his professional background in the media and technology industry, Matthew Ball has managed to establish himself as one of the leading voices on the topic of the Metaverse. He sees the Metaverse as a new form of virtual reality that goes far beyond the current internet, as well as today's VR and AR applications, creating an open, persistently connected world where people, businesses, and machines can interact. He was one of the first to describe the Metaverse as a continuation of the development of the internet and predicts that it will become a central platform for a variety of applications and business models. In his contributions, he emphasizes that the Metaverse brings with it great challenges and potentials, including issues of privacy, security, and regulation.

However, he considers it important that the Metaverse must not be controlled by a single company but must be built on an open infrastructure that allows everyone to create and share content and applications. He sees the Metaverse as an opportunity for a new wave of innovations and possibilities in the virtual world, which will be significant for both businesses and consumers.

Tony Parisi, who has significantly contributed to the integration of VR into the WWW through his work on the Virtual Reality Markup Language VRML, formulated seven rules for the Metaverse based on Ball's statements, which form the basis for the work of many others. [PAR21] (Fig. 6.1)

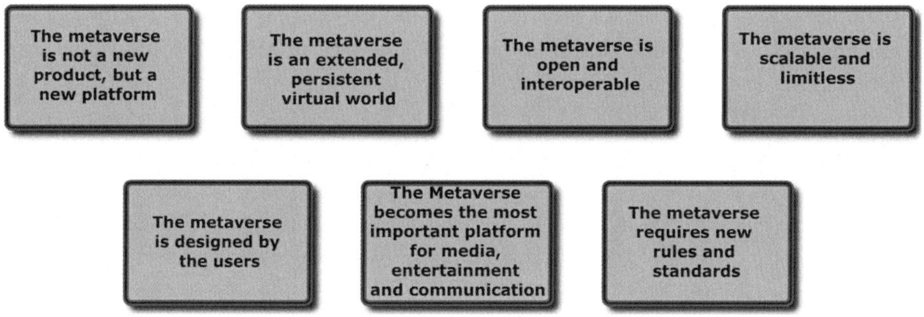

Fig. 6.1 Seven rules for the Metaverse. (According to: Tony Parisi [PAR21])

1. *The Metaverse is not a new product, but a new platform*
   Ball emphasizes that the Metaverse is not simply a new application or technology, but rather a platform where various applications and technologies come together and continuously evolve and grow by integrating different applications and technologies and creating new possibilities for users. Therefore, the Metaverse should not be viewed as a single product or service, but as an open, scalable, persistent, and boundless virtual (application) environment that is utilized by many different applications and is formed by many different technologies. This platform allows users to interact in a variety of different but interconnected environments, including games, social networks, e-commerce, education, and other applications.
   By creating such a platform, the Metaverse becomes an ecosystem where the applications and services existing within it can interact with each other and provide users with a seamless experience. This means that the Metaverse can be used not only for creating new applications and content but also for integrating and interacting with already existing technologies.
2. *The Metaverse is an extended, persistent virtual world*
   Unlike traditional VR applications, which are limited to individual sessions, the Metaverse will be a persistently connected world that will be accessible around the clock. This means that users can access and immerse themselves in the Metaverse at any time, and their interactions and their consequences within the virtual world will be maintained even if they leave the platform or the individual application. This persistence allows users to build lasting relationships with other users, acquire and manage resources and property within the virtual world, and conduct a variety of activities within the virtual world.
   This rule also shows that the Metaverse, as a persistent virtual world, offers a completely new experience that goes beyond traditional VR applications. It offers users the opportunity to deepen their experiences within the virtual world and perform various activities while staying in a constant environment.

3. *The Metaverse is open and interoperable*
   According to Ball, the Metaverse must be open so that everyone can create and share their own content and applications. Additionally, it must be interoperable so that different applications and platforms can communicate with each other. However, this almost inevitably means that the Metaverse is not simply an extension of today's internet, but a completely new type of platform that enables new interactions and experiences.
   While today's internet mainly consists of individual websites and applications displayed in a two-dimensional browser window, the Metaverse will essentially be a three-dimensional world in which users can immerse themselves and interact and communicate in real-time, including games, social networks, e-commerce, and education. This also implies that it will be a new type of platform that enables completely new applications and business models that go beyond traditional online interactions and transactions.
4. *The Metaverse is scalable and boundless*
   The Metaverse must be scalable to meet the demands of millions of users and countless applications and content. Additionally, it must be boundless to enable seamless integration and interaction between different users and applications. Ball formulates this rule such that the Metaverse must be a platform on which other platforms and applications can build. Developers and companies create their own applications and content that function within the virtual world. These applications and content can then be used by other developers and companies in the sense of produsage and modusage to improve and expand their own applications and services. Only in this way will the Metaverse become an open ecosystem where different applications and services can work together seamlessly.
5. *The Metaverse is shaped by its users*
   The Metaverse is to be shaped and developed by the users and not by a few large companies or institutions, as is generally the case with today's internet. This would mean that users have control and influence the development of the platform. It also follows that the Metaverse must be decentralized, as this is the only way to ensure that control over the virtual world does not lie with a single company or organization, but with a collaborative community of users and developers. Ideally, decentralization should help make the Metaverse transparent and fair.
6. *The Metaverse will become the most important platform for media, entertainment, and communication*
   Not only according to Ball but also according to other voices, the Metaverse will become the most important platform for media, entertainment, and communication in the future, as it enables a completely new kind of experiences and interactions. This also includes the importance of user-generated content in the Metaverse. This can include artworks, music, videos, games, virtual objects, and much more.
   The importance of user-generated content in the Metaverse lies in the fact that it offers a way to constantly expand and improve the virtual world. It allows users to

be creative and integrate their own ideas and concepts into the virtual world. Furthermore, user-generated content can help make the Metaverse an open, diverse, and accessible ecosystem. However, it is necessary that the various applications and services within the Metaverse can work together seamlessly, regardless of who created them.

7. *The metaverse requires new rules and standards*
   New rules and standards are therefore of particular importance to ensure the privacy, security, and quality of content for users and their user experience. These rules and standards should be developed jointly by the entire industry. This also includes social interaction as an important part of the human experience, which the metaverse ultimately aims to replicate in the virtual world. This means that the metaverse must be a place where people can meet, communicate, collaborate, play, and much more. To enable this, social interaction opportunities must be provided, such as chat rooms, forums, groups, games, and events. These interaction opportunities should include both formal and informal options to meet the needs of different user groups.
   The importance of social interactions in the metaverse lies in the fact that they offer a way to build human connections and relationships in the virtual world and enable users to share common interests, make friendships, and even find a kind of virtual home.

These seven rules reflect Ball's vision of how the metaverse will look as an open, scalable, boundless, and user-designed platform, and what challenges and potentials it brings. They have now become a much-cited framework that developers and companies should consider when designing and implementing the metaverse. By following these rules, they can ensure that the metaverse is developed in a way that meets the interests and needs of users while also adhering to general ethical and moral standards.

If users feel that the metaverse is open, transparent, and fair and is tailored to their needs, they are more likely to engage in the virtual world and actively participate in it. These rules help to promote user trust and acceptance. They also provide a guide for designing a virtual world that is based on the needs and interests of users while also meeting ethical and moral standards.

However, the rules set by Matthew Ball, like so many others, are subject to different criticisms depending on the perspectives and backgrounds of the critics. Some critics believe that Ball's principles are too idealistic and impractical. They argue that implementing these principles could be extremely complicated or even unattainable given the numerous challenges associated with constructing a virtual world.

Other critics believe that the rules proposed by Ball could impair innovation by imposing excessive restrictions on developers and companies. These critics advocate for allowing innovation and creative ideas to fully exploit the potential of the metaverse. Conversely, another perspective criticizes that Ball's rules may not sufficiently consider the business interests of companies and developers. Here, it is argued that the rules are too focused on the interests of users, thereby neglecting the commercial dimension of the metaverse.

Finally, there is also the view that the rules proposed by Ball are simply not relevant to all user groups in the metaverse. These critics argue that certain user groups have different needs and interests that are inadequately addressed by Ball's rules.

6.2.2 Cathy Hackl

Cathy Hackl is an internationally recognized publicist for Augmented and Virtual Reality and the Metaverse. She is a speaker, consultant, author, and founder of a VR/AR think tank. [HACoJ]

Regarding the Metaverse, she is quite a significant voice in the discussion about the future of this virtual world. She believes that the Metaverse will soon play an important role in our society, as it provides a space where people from all over the world can come together and interact. She has also contributed to raising awareness about the Metaverse by speaking about its potentials and challenges at conferences and in the media. Through her expertise in AR and VR, Cathy Hackl has also emphasized the importance of these technologies for the Metaverse. She believes that AR and VR will enhance the user experience in the Metaverse and enable people to immerse themselves even deeper into the virtual world. Additionally, she emphasizes the importance of data protection and ethical standards not only in general but especially for the Metaverse and calls for an open and transparent discussion about how this virtual world should be designed. She holds the view that it is important to set these standards as early as possible to ensure that the Metaverse becomes and remains a positive and safe environment.

Hackl sees the Metaverse as a virtual world seamlessly integrated with the real world, where people, businesses, and even governments will interact. She believes that the Metaverse will play a major role in the future, as it provides a central space where people from all over the world can come together and interact without being physically present. In her opinion, the Metaverse should represent an immersive, interactive, and personalized experience that allows users to interact with other people, virtual objects, and digital information. Therefore, she sees the implementation consisting of a combination of various technologies such as AR, VR, AI, Blockchain, and others.

In various previous sections, examples of how Cathy Hackl envisions the future Metaverse and the applications it enables have been addressed and presented as illustrative examples. In her contributions to the discussion about the use of the Metaverse, she shows an even broader range of applications, in which the Metaverse is seen as a …

- … platform for virtual conferences and events.
- … opportunity for retailers to open virtual stores where customers can select and purchase products without leaving their homes.

- ... platform for virtual education, where students can attend virtual classrooms and interact with teachers and other students from around the world.
- ... platform for virtual collaboration, where employees can work together on projects in virtual spaces.
- ... opportunity to undertake virtual travels to visit historical sites or fantastic worlds.

Hackl looks in a quite similar direction with her views, as described by Matthew Ball. She also predicts that the digital economy of the Metaverse will be multiple times the size of today's digital economy and emphasizes the enormous economic opportunities that the Metaverse can offer. However, she emphasizes even more clearly than Ball the relevance of ethical standards and data protection regulations and their early definition to ensure that the Metaverse remains a positive and safe environment.

Another topic Cathy Hackl has commented on is Ball's predictions about the speed at which the Metaverse will grow. Matthew Ball believes that the Metaverse will grow faster than the Internet and that it will become an important part of our society within 10 to 20 years. Cathy Hackl fundamentally agrees here as well, but she also emphasizes that the development of the Metaverse is still in its early stages and that there are still many challenges and obstacles to overcome, thus relativizing Ball's statements.

6.2.3 Amy Webb

Amy Webb is a futurist, entrepreneur, and author who specializes in researching technology trends. She is known for her work in the field of future studies and has written several books on technology and innovation. [WEBoJb] Amy Webb is one of the leading experts on technology trends, and her work influences many industries and companies. Her assessments and predictions about the metaverse are therefore taken seriously by many experts and decision-makers in the tech industry.

Regarding the metaverse, Amy Webb has frequently written about it in her publications and given lectures on how the metaverse will influence future life and work. She also views the metaverse as a technological evolution of the internet and believes that it will play an increasingly important role in the coming years.

Despite her recognized expertise, Webb does not provide a final description of how the metaverse will ultimately develop, as she also considers that it is still in its early stages of development and many questions remain open. Nevertheless, Webb attempts to describe possible scenarios of the metaverse. Webb generally sees the metaverse as a future place where people come together virtually to work, play, and interact in a variety of environments. She particularly emphasizes the completely new form of collaboration that arises from the fact that physical boundaries and distances no longer matter. Webb is one of the few who, in her scenarios, sees the option of a developing cross-economy, where people own digital identities and assets that they can also use in the real world. She describes the metaverse as a kind of parallel world where people can shape their lives in new and creative ways, but which is closely intertwined with the real world. Webb also predicts that the metaverse will enable a wide range of applications, from entertainment to education to healthcare and more.

From these general scenarios, Webb develops a series of concrete use cases.

- Virtual workplaces where people from all over the world collaborate by meeting in shared virtual work environments. The platforms of the metaverse will enable a significantly higher level of immersiveness in virtual meetings and collaborative work on documents and projects in the future.
- Virtual conferences and events that take place in virtual environments, eliminating travel and event costs.
- Entertainment, where people immerse themselves in virtual worlds and have interactive experiences that would not be possible in the real world, such as historical events and worlds or virtual experiences like movies.
- Digital identities and virtual assets that people can own and use in the metaverse, but also use in the real world. For example, people could earn a type of cryptocurrency in a virtual environment that they could then spend or manage in the real world.
- In healthcare, Webb sees the possibility of offering virtual treatments and consultations in the metaverse, allowing doctors and patients to meet in a virtual environment and prepare or conduct treatments there if necessary.

6.2.4 Steve Mann

The Canadian researcher and developer Steve Mann is a pioneer in the field of wearable computing and augmented reality. He has been working and researching the paradigm of wearable computing since the 1980s, which he has since further developed into what is now known as Humanistic Intelligence. [MAN02] He has also made a number of significant contributions to the development of AR glasses and systems. Since 1998, he has shaped the concept of "sousveillance" (underwatching, or surveillance from below), where wearable cameras are used to monitor the activities of the powerful. [MAN12, HOF23]

Steve Mann has also made important contributions regarding the metaverse. He developed the concept of "Mediated Reality," where AR technology is used to overlay the physical world with virtual information, creating an augmented reality. This concept forms the basis for many of the AR applications used in the metaverse today and is an evolution of the originally more technologically oriented AR paradigm. This could play an important role in the metaverse in the future, as it allows users to immerse themselves in an augmented reality while continuing to interact with the physical world.

In the context of his own work, Steve Mann has also commented on his vision of the metaverse in the past and believes that such an evolution of the internet will play an important role in the future. He sees the metaverse as a place where people can experience an augmented reality and interact with each other beyond the physical world. In addition to a virtual place with many different applications such as gaming, social interaction, education, and work, he sees it as a place where people can express and share their creativity and ideas, and where the boundaries between the physical and virtual worlds blur.

Regarding the appearance of the metaverse, Mann does not commit himself. Rather, he believes that the appearance of the metaverse will depend heavily on who uses it and for what purposes it is implemented. He assumes that there will be a variety of different metaverses, each tailored to specific target groups and fulfilling a wide range of functions. Some could be very realistic and represent an exact copy of the physical world, while others could be more surreal and fantastic. Nevertheless, Mann also sees the typical use cases of virtual conferences and workplaces, social interaction, education, gaming, as well as art and creativity.

The Wearable Computing defined by Steve Mann refers to computer-based systems that are worn directly on the human body to enable seamless integration and constant interaction with the digital world. In doing so, sensors, actuators, and processing units are used to collect and evaluate data about the environment, the movements, and the physiological states of the wearer. The Metaverse, on the other hand, is a collective virtual space that consists of a variety of digital environments and simulations and is shared by many users.

The connection between Wearable Computing and the Metaverse lies in the way these technologies can interact with and complement each other. Wearable computing devices, such as smart glasses or haptic suits, can make the experience of the Metaverse more immersive and interactive. They allow users to transfer their physical presence into the virtual world and make their interactions with digital objects or other users more realistic. At the same time, the Metaverse can serve as a platform on which wearable computing applications are developed and deployed. For example, users could use special wearables to monitor their health data in the Metaverse or track their fitness goals. Companies could offer virtual work environments where employees are equipped with wearable computing devices to improve their productivity and collaboration.

From the combination of the wearable computing paradigm and the idea of the Metaverse, a deeper and more immersive experience can be created that enriches both the individual and society as a whole. The focus here is on the respective information flow. Within wearable computing, the information flow concerns the exchange of data between the sensors, actuators, and processing units integrated into the body-worn devices. These devices continuously capture data about the environment, the physiological states, and the activities of the wearer. They then process this information to gain useful insights and provide it to the user in real-time. These insights can be used to trigger notifications, make adjustments to the user interface, or even perform physical actions through actuators. Steve Mann illustrates a diagram of the information flows for this context (see Fig. 6.2). In the Metaverse, on the other hand, the information flow consists of communication and interaction between users, digital objects, and environments within

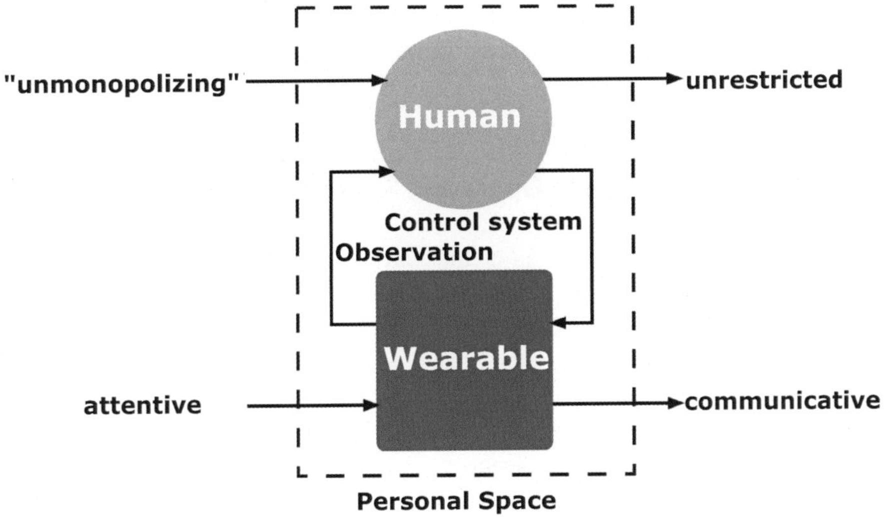

Fig. 6.2 The information flow in the paradigm of wearable computing. (Based on [MAN98])

the virtual space. Information is exchanged in the form of text, audio, video, and other media that users can share and use together in real-time. The platforms on which the Metaverse is built collect and process this data to offer users personalized and context-based experiences. A comparison of the information flows between wearable computing and the Metaverse shows both differences and similarities.

- *Type of data:* Wearable computing focuses mainly on capturing personal and environmental data of the user, while the Metaverse emphasizes interactions and the exchange of information between users and virtual environments.
- *Contextualization:*Wearable computing devices process the captured data to put it into a useful and personal context for the user. In the Metaverse, contextualization occurs through the adaptation of environments, objects, and interactions based on the needs and preferences of the users.
- *Real-time interaction:*Both wearable computing and the Metaverse rely on real-time interaction and communication to enable a seamless and engaging user experience.
- *Data processing:*Wearable computing devices process the data internally and can even make decisions and perform actions without relying on external systems. In the Metaverse, on the other hand, data processing usually takes place on central servers or in the cloud.

In combination, wearable computing and the Metaverse can expand the information flow and create an even more immersive and personalized experience. Wearables can act as an interface between the physical and the virtual world, allowing users to bring information from their environment into the Metaverse or vice versa. This creates a deeper connection between the real world and the virtual world of the Metaverse, resulting in a unique and fascinating user experience.

6.3 The Metaverse—the Operating System of the Future?

From the previous considerations, an architecture of the Metaverse and its anticipated infrastructure can be developed, which is built in layers and integrates into the real world. This architecture and a computer operating system have parallels, especially in terms of the organization and management of resources as well as the interaction between different layers and components. Both systems allow for the organization and control of complex structures and processes at a higher level of abstraction to improve the user experience and increase efficiency.

A computer operating system is responsible for managing a computer's hardware resources and running software applications. Similar to the metaverse architecture, an operating system is divided into multiple layers that cover different functions and aspects of the system. The lowest layer is the hardware on which the operating system runs. Above it lies the system layer, which provides the basic operating system functions, such as file systems, memory management, and process management. The next layer consists of system applications and services that provide additional functions and tools for the user. Finally, the top layer encompasses the user applications that are directly used by the users.

The connection between a possible architecture of the metaverse, as suggested in Fig. 6.3, and an operating system can be seen in the way both systems are based on layers to enable efficient interaction and management. In both cases, the different layers are used to abstract complex processes and structures, thereby enabling a better user experience. In the metaverse architecture, the focus is on the integration of digital and physical worlds, while an operating system is geared towards managing computer resources and running software applications. Despite these differences, both systems can be viewed as platforms that provide an interface between users and the underlying technology. They enable interaction and collaboration in a structured and abstracted environment to make complex processes more efficient and user-friendly. In this context, the metaverse can be considered an extended, immersive, and interconnected environment that goes beyond the capabilities of a traditional operating system. While an operating system provides the basis for interacting with computers and running applications, the metaverse opens up new possibilities for communication, collaboration, and interaction between people, machines, and the physical world.

Metaverse and classic operating systems initially pursue different goals and therefore also set their priorities differently. While classic operating systems are designed to maximize the efficiency and productivity of the user, the metaverse focuses on creating shared experiences and promoting social interactions. However, the aforementioned Matthew

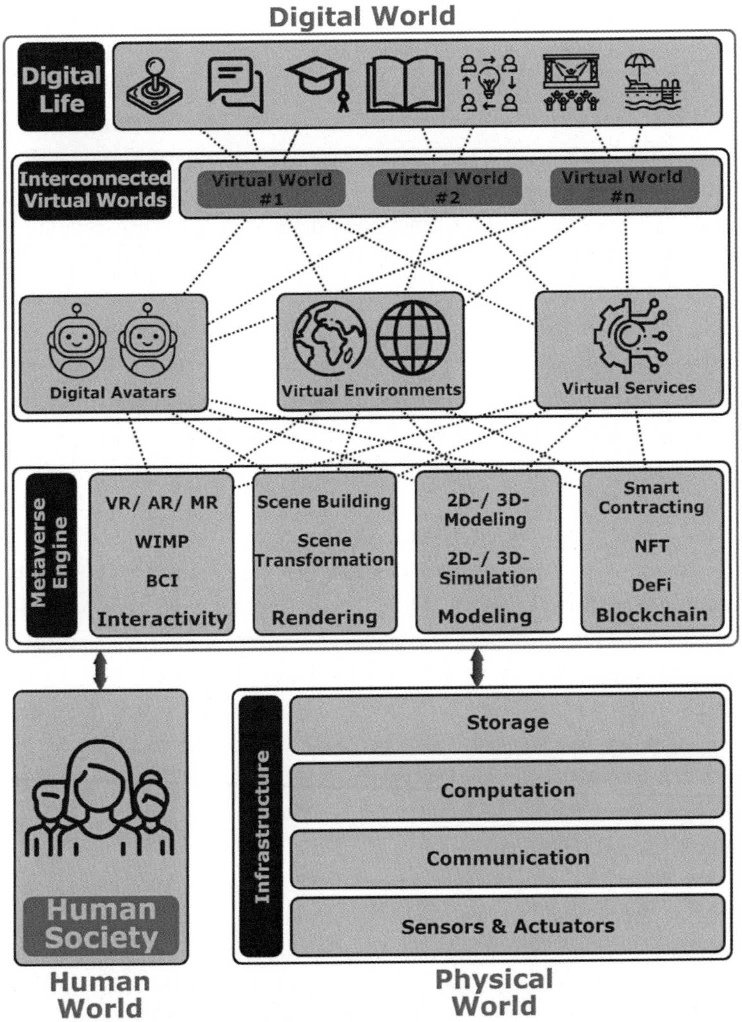

Fig. 6.3 An architectural image for the metaverse. (Based on [JAB22, DED09])

Ball also frequently compares the metaverse directly to a computer operating system. Just as an operating system is the fundamental software that enables a computer to run applications and manage various hardware components, Ball sees the metaverse as the fundamental platform that allows users to execute a variety of applications and activities. The metaverse is essentially a virtual world where users can interact, trade, and play. Similarly to how an operating system supports various applications and programs, the metaverse can also support different types of activities on a higher level, from virtual meetings to gaming and shopping experiences.

Just as an operating system requires various technologies and functions to operate properly, the metaverse requires different technologies such as VR, AR, AI, and blockchain to create, operate, and secure the virtual world. For example, VR technology is used to create a more immersive and realistic virtual environment, while AI systems can help create intelligent NPCs and virtual assistants. Similar to how an operating system requires constant updates for drivers and security functions, the metaverse must also be regularly "updated" to ensure it functions properly and remains secure. One way to achieve this can be the use of blockchain technologies, which enable a transparent and secure transaction history. Finally, as with an operating system, interoperability and compatibility are important factors in the metaverse. Seamless integration of various applications and systems allows users to access and use a variety of services and activities seamlessly. Therefore, the metaverse must be able to support a variety of devices, platforms, and applications to provide users with an optimal experience.

The question of whether the metaverse could be considered the operating system of the future is of considerable importance, as the concept of the metaverse has the potential to change and, ideally, improve human life in many areas.

A key difference between the two systems lies in the metaverse's focus on social interactions and shared experiences, while classic operating systems primarily focus on running applications and services. The metaverse offers users the opportunity to communicate, collaborate, and play in real-time, whereas classic operating systems are primarily designed to optimize the user's productivity and efficiency. Another significant difference is that the metaverse is built on cloud computing technology, while classic operating systems typically run on a single computer or server. This makes the metaverse superior in terms of scalability and flexibility, allowing multiple users to interact in the same virtual world simultaneously.

The convergence of the metaverse and traditional operating systems is an important step in realizing the potential of the metaverse as the operating system of the future. Traditional operating systems like Windows, MacOS, and Linux are designed to control and manage the basic functionality of devices such as computers and smartphones. They provide users with an interface to run applications and programs, store and organize files, use the internet, and much more.

The metaverse, on the other hand, offers a fully immersive experience and allows users to live, work, and play in a virtual environment. It provides opportunities for immersive learning and training experiences, virtual collaboration, e-commerce, and more. When these two concepts are combined, they can create a powerful operating system on a higher level that leverages the best of both worlds.

One way to achieve the convergence of the metaverse and traditional operating systems is to integrate metaverse platforms as applications or programs within traditional operating systems. For example, a user could launch a metaverse platform by opening a corresponding application on their computer or smartphone, similar to how they would with any other program or application. The metaverse platform would be seamlessly integrated into the traditional operating system, and users could switch from one application mode to another. The switch between "classic" office applications, which run and are operated outside the metaverse, and immersive experiences in the metaverse would thus be easily possible.

Another possibility is for traditional operating systems to directly integrate native metaverse functions. For example, operating systems could offer an integrated virtual interface in the form of a VR view, allowing users to access the metaverse directly from their operating system. This would enable users to switch seamlessly and without significant media and interaction breaks from the traditional operating system to the metaverse.

Such convergences of the metaverse and traditional operating systems will be an important step in the development of the metaverse as the "real" operating system of the future. This will improve the integration and interoperability between traditional and virtual environments and make it possible to unlock the metaverse for broader application and use.

References

[BAL20] Ball, Matthew (13.01.2020). What It Is, Where to Find it, and Who Will Build It. Online: https://www.matthewball.vc/all/themetaverse (accessed on: 17.05.2023)

[BALLoJ] Ball, Matthew (o. J.). The Metaverse Primer. In: Mathhewball.vc. Online: https://www.matthewball.vc/the-metaverse-primer (accessed on: 21.05.2023).

[BER19] Berners-Lee, Tim (12.03.2019). 30 years on, what's next #ForTheWeb? In: World Wide Web Foundation. Online: https://webfoundation.org/2019/03/web-birthday-30/ (accessed on: 21.05.2023).

[CNB21] CNBC (15.11.2021). Metaverse similar to rise of internet, Matthew Ball says. In: CNBC, Closing Bell. Online: https://www.cnbc.com/video/2021/11/15/metaverse-similar-to-rise-of-internet-matthew-ball-says.html (accessed on: 28.05.2023).

[DAS23] Das, Basudha (17.01.2023). Davos 2023: WEF launches metaverse platform to tackle crises, challenges; Check details here. In: Business Today. Online: https://www.businesstoday.in/wef-2023/story/davos-2023-wef-launches-metaverse-platform-to-tackle-crises-challenges-check-details-here-360692-2023-01-17 (accessed on: 21.05.2023).

[DED09] Dede, Chris. (2009). Immersive Interfaces for Engagement and Learning. Science (New York, N.Y.). 323.66-9. 10.1126/science.1167311.

[HACoJ] Hackl, Cathy (o. J.). Cathy Hackl. In: Forbes. Online: https://www.forbes.com/sites/cathyhackl/ (accessed on: 21.05.2023).

[HAT22] Hatmaker, Taylor (13.01.2022). Second Life's creator is returning to advise the original metaverse company. In: TechCrunsch. Online: https://techcrunch.com/2022/01/13/second-life-philip-rosedale-returns-linden-lab-high-fidelity/ (accessed on: 21.05.2023).

[HOF23] Hoffman, Jascha (10.12.2003). Sousveillance. In: The New York Times Magazine. Online: https://www.nytimes.com/2006/12/10/magazine/10section3b.t-3.html%3F_r%3D0 (accessed on: 21.05.2023).

[HOL21] Hollister, Sean (22.07.2021). California sues Activision Blizzard over a culture of ‚constant sexual harassment‘. In: The Verge. Online: https://www.theverge.com/2021/7/22/22588215/facebook-mark-zuckerberg-metaverse-interview (accessed on: 21.05.2023).

[IEEoJa] IEEE Metaverse Standards Committee (CTS/MSC) (o. J.). Demystifying, Defining, Developing, and Deploying the Metaverse. In: IEEE. Online: https://sagroups.ieee.org/metaverse-sc/ (accessed on: 28.05.2023).

[IEEoJb] IEEE Metaverse Working Group (CTS/MSC/MWG) (o. J.). IEEE P2048: Standard for Metaverse: Terminology, Definitions, and Taxonomy. In: IEEE. Online: https://sagroups.ieee.org/2048/ (accessed on: 28.05.2023).

[ITUoJa] ITU (o. J.). About International Telecommunication Union (ITU). In: ITU About. Online: https://www.itu.int/en/about/Pages/default.aspx (accessed on: 28.05.2023).

[ITUoJb] ITU FG-MV (o. J.). ITU-T Focus Group on metaverse (FG-MV). In: ITU Focisgroups. Online: https://www.itu.int/en/ITU-T/focusgroups/mv/Pages/default.aspx (accessed on: 28.05.2023).

[JAB22] Jaber, Tanya Abdulsattar (2022). Security risks of the metaverse world. In:International Journal of Interactive Mobile Technologies, Vol. 16 No. 13, 2022. Online: https://online-journals.org/index.php/i-jim/article/view/33187 (accessed on: 28.05.2023).

[KAU22] Kauffeld,Simone; Tartler, Darien; Gräfe,Hendrik; Ann-Kathrin, Windmann; Sauer, Nils (2022). What will mobile andvirtual work look like in the future?—Results of a Delphi-based studyWie siehtdie mobile und virtuelle Arbeit der Zukunft aus? – Ergebnisse einer Delphibasierten Studie. Gruppe. Interaktion.Organisation. Zeitschrift für Angewandte Organisationspsychologie (GIO). 53. 10.1007/s11612-022-00627-8.

[KER23] Kerler, Wolfgang (11.03.2023). Die Futuristin Amy Webb fürchtet, dass Künstliche Intelligenz zu einem schlechteren Internet führen könnte In: 1e9. Online: https://1e9.community/t/die-futuristin-amy-webb-fuerchtet-dass-kuenstliche-intelligenz-zu-einem-schlechteren-internet-fuehren-koennte/18894 (accessed on: 21.05.2023).

[MAN98] Mann, Steve (Nov. 1998). Humanistic Computing. Proceedings of the IEEE. 86 (11). Online (via WaybackMachine): http://www.eyetap.org/papers/docs/HumanisticComputing_Mann1998_ProcIEEE.pdf (accessed on30.11.2023).

[MAN02] Mann, Steve. (2002). Humanistic Intelligence as a Basis for Intelligent Image Processing. https://doi.org/10.1002/0471221635.ch1. (accessed on: 21.05.2023).

[MAN12] Mann, Steve (02.11.2012). Eye Am a Camera: Surveillance and Sousveillance in the Glassage. In: Time. Online: https://techland.time.com/2012/11/02/eye-am-a-camera-surveillance-and-sousveillance-in-the-glassage/ (accessed on: 21.05.2023).

[MAN13] Mann, Steve (01.03.2013). My „Augmediated": Life What I've learned from 35 years of wearing computerized eyewear. In: IEEE Spectrum. Online: https://spectrum.ieee.org/view-from-the-valley/consumer-electronics/portable-devices/steve-mann-the-man-who-invented-wearable-computing (accessed on: 21.05.2023).

[MSF0J] MSF (o. J.). The Metaverse Standards Forum. In: MSF. Online: https://metaverse-standards.org/# (accessed on: 28.05.2023).

[PAR21] Parisi, Tony (22.10.2021). The Seven Rules oft he Metaverse – A framework for the coming immersive reality. In: Medium. Online: https://medium.com/meta-verses/the-seven-rules-of-the-metaverse-7d4e06fa864c (accessed on: 22.5.2023).

[RAV22] Ravenscraft, Eric (03.07.2022). What, Exactly, Is the Metaverse Standards Forum Creating? In: Wired Story. Online: https://www.wired.com/story/metaverse-standards-forum-explained/ (accessed on: 28.05.2023).

[SCH23] Schukz, Yogi (04.01.2023). Where's the beef in the Metaverse? In: IT Worls Canada. Online: https://www.itworldcanada.com/blog/wheres-the-beef-in-the-metaverse/519980 (accessed on: 28.05.2023).

[WEB23] Webster, Andrew (23.03.2023). Tim Sweeney explains how the metaverse might actually work. Online: https://www.theverge.com/2023/3/23/23652928/tim-sweeney-interview-epic-games-fortnite-metaverse (accessed on: 21.05.2023).

[WEBoJa] Webb, Amy (o. J.). Amy Webb. In: Future Today Institute. Online: https://futuretodayinstitute.com/team/amy-webb/ (accessed on: 21.05.2023).

[WEBoJb] Webb, Amy (o. J.). Biography. In: NYU Stern. Online: https://www.stern.nyu.edu/faculty/bio/amy-webb (accessed on: 21.05.2023).

[WEFoJa] World Economic Forum (o. J.). Defining and Building the Metaverse. In: World Economic Forum. https://initiatives.weforum.org/defining-and-building-the-metaverse/home (accessed on: 21.05.2023).

[WEFoJb] World Economic Forum (o. J.). Agenda Articles, filtered by „The Metaverse“. In: World Economic Forum. https://www.weforum.org/agenda/the-metaverse/ (accessed on: 21.05.2023).

[W3CoJa] W3C. (o. J.). About W3C. In: W3C. Online: https://www.w3.org/Consortium/ (accessed on: 21.05.2023).

[W3CoJb] W3C. (o. J.). Web Standards. In: W3C. Online: https://www.w3.org/standards/ (accessed on: 21.05.2023).

[W3CoJc] W3C. (o. J.). Privacy and Security. In: W3C. Online: https://www.w3.org/Privacy/ (accessed on: 21.05.2023).

[W3CoJe] W3C. (2020). Immersive Web Working Group Charter. In: W3C. Online: https://www.w3.org/2020/05/immersive-web-wg-charter.html (accessed on: 21.05.2023).

[W3CoJf] W3C (2021). W3C Mission. In: W3C. Online: https://www.w3.org/Consortium/mission (accessed on: 21.05.2023).

[W3CoJg] W3C Web Accessibility Initiative (2021). Introduction to Web Accessibility. In: W3C. Online: https://www.w3.org/WAI/fundamentals/accessibility-intro/ (accessed on: 21.05.2023).

[W3CoJh] W3C Privacy Interest Group (2021). Privacy Interest Group (PING) Charter. In: W3C. Online: https://www.w3.org/2019/09/privacy-ig-charter.html (accessed on: 21.05.2023).

[W3C23a] W3C. (03.03.2023). WebXR Device API. In: W3C. Online: https://www.w3.org/TR/webxr/ (accessed on: 21.05.2023).

7 Now is the Time to Build!

"I am not saying that we will abolish physical labor, because we are still physical beings in a physical world, but I think the concept of work is expanding and gaming is a part of that future."
(Cathy Hackl)

In view of the rapid technological developments and the growing importance of the metaverse, it is crucial that the opportunities offered by these virtual worlds are recognized and utilized early on. [KAU87, LAW22] As Cathy Hackl says, now is the time to build, because the metaverse offers enormous potential for creative collaboration, education, and social interaction, just waiting to be tapped. [DED09]

Only through active participation in shaping the metaverse and focusing on its sustainable and inclusive development can each individual user contribute to creating a positive and future-proof environment. Promoting community projects that also focus on issues such as environmental protection, social justice, or education can help ensure that the metaverse becomes a place that not only serves entertainment but also offers real societal value. [BAI10]

Scientists, technology developers, artists, and educators are called upon to explore the diverse possibilities of the metaverse and actively work to shape and improve these virtual worlds. This can create a future in the metaverse that fosters creativity, enriches social interactions, and expands the boundaries of what is possible.

In this vision, creative freedom and collaboration are utilized to develop innovative solutions for pressing global challenges such as environmental protection, social justice, and education. [DED09] The metaverse can serve as a testing ground where new ideas and approaches are tried out before being implemented in the real world. [KAU22, LAW22]

To ensure a sustainable future in the metaverse, it is important that ethical and ecological aspects are considered from the outset. This includes the responsible use of

P. Hoffmann, *Next Generation Internet*, https://doi.org/10.1007/978-3-658-46424-0_7

resources and data as well as the promotion of inclusion and accessibility to ensure that all people have the opportunity to participate in and benefit from the metaverse. Creating a shared, creative, and sustainable future in the metaverse requires the collaboration of scientists, technology developers, artists, educators, and users from around the world. Through joint commitment and the willingness to transcend existing boundaries, we can harness the potential of the metaverse and create a better future for all.

In the metaverse, creativity will play a central role, enabling users to design their own environments and avatars. [WILoJ, WAL21] This individual freedom of design promotes artistic expressions and allows users to create virtual galleries where their artworks can be displayed. The possibilities are almost limitless in terms of the type and scope of artistic creations that can emerge in the metaverse.

In addition to individual design, the metaverse also offers opportunities for collaborative creation. Community projects and shared worlds allow users to work together and pool their creative forces to create unique and extensive virtual experiences. [BAI10] In this context, open-source platforms and shared resources gain importance, as they enable users to access existing content and further develop or modify it. This not only fosters creativity but also the exchange of ideas and collaboration among users.

The creative freedom and individual design possibilities in the metaverse significantly contribute to the attractiveness and diversity of these virtual environments. By promoting artistic expression and collaboration, the metaverse offers countless opportunities for users to express themselves, experiment, and learn new skills.

"I always say: in the metaverse, we are all world builders—and now is the time to build!" (Cathy Hackl)

References

[BAI10] Bainbridge, William Sims (2010). Online Worlds: Convergence of the Real and the Virtual. Human-Computer Interaction Series, Springer 2010, ISBN 978–1–84882–824–7.

[DED09] Dede, Chris. (2009). Immersive Interfaces for Engagement and Learning. Science (New York, N.Y.). 323. 66–9. https://doi.org/10.1126/science.1167311.

[JAB22] Jaber, Tanya Abdulsattar (2022). Security risks of the metaverse world. In: International Journal of Interactive Mobile Technologies, Vol. 16 No. 13, 2022. Online: https://online-journals.org/index.php/i-jim/article/view/33187 (accessed on: 28.05.2023).

[KAU22] Kauffeld, Simone; Tartler, Darien; Gräfe, Hendrik; Ann-Kathrin, Windmann; Sauer, Nils (2022). What will mobile and virtual work look like in the future?—Results of a Delphi-based studyWie sieht die mobile und virtuelle Arbeit der Zukunft aus? – Ergebnisse einer Delphi-basierten Studie. Gruppe. Interaktion. Organisation. Zeitschrift für Angewandte Organisationspsychologie (GIO). 53. https://doi.org/10.1007/s11612-022-00627-8.

[LAW22] Lawton, Geroge (18.11.2022). How will the metaverse affect the future of work? In: TechTarget. Online: https://www.techtarget.com/searchcio/tip/How-will-the-metaverse-affect-the-future-of-work (accessed on: 21.05.2023).

[WAL21] Walden, Stephanie (06.05.2021). Guide to Virtual Reality Art: What It Is and How to Make VR Art Yourself. In: Skillshare Blog. Online: https://www.skillshare.com/en/blog/guide-to-virtual-reality-art-what-it-is-and-how-to-make-vr-art-yourself/art (accessed on: 21.05.2023).

[WILoJ] Wilk, Elvia (o:j.). Will virtual reality conquer the artworld?. In: ArtBasel. Online: https://www.artbasel.com/stories/virtual-reality-technology-and-art (accessed on: 21.05.2023).

8 Addendum 1—Because of its Relevance: Artificial Intelligence in the Metaverse?

The preparations and fundamental research work for this book date back to the spring of 2022. At that time, there were three technology areas whose development was largely driven independently of each other. The first was the Web3 area, in which blockchain technology, cryptocurrencies, and non-fungible tokens played a central role in the implementation of new services. Secondly, there was the metaverse itself, which also partially built on blockchain and NFTs, thus having some overlap with Web3. Finally, there was the area of artificial intelligence, whose development seemed to be primarily driven by marketing factors. While these areas were being advanced in peaceful coexistence with varying degrees of overlap at seemingly steady speeds, this changed abruptly in October/November 2022. The trigger was the release of the AI-powered service ChatGPT by OpenAI, which impressively demonstrated the possibilities and capabilities that AI-based applications already possess. [DOU23] As a result, new use cases were presented and discussed almost daily, with applications for other media forms such as images and videos quickly being showcased. Consequently, the discussion about the development of autonomous chatbots based on such services emerged, leading to the next logical discussion point about the extent to which autonomous chatbots can be coupled with digital twins, i.e., avatars in the metaverse. [ISL23] Thus, the connection between AI and the metaverse complex was established. Since this connection has the potential to significantly influence the future development of the metaverse, this topic will be briefly discussed in this work.

First, a general overview of the intersection of AI and the metaverse will be provided, followed by an analysis and presentation of the current state of development as of November 2023.

Virtual assistants and chatbots are two frequently used AI technologies in the metaverse. [AHU23, ZHO23, THA23] These are "intelligent" programs designed to help users retrieve information, complete tasks, and manage their interactions in the

P. Hoffmann, *Next Generation Internet*, https://doi.org/10.1007/978-3-658-46424-0_8

metaverse. [PER22] They typically have natural language processing capabilities, machine learning, and connections to knowledge databases to efficiently and accurately respond to user inquiries. [CHE17] Chatbots, on the other hand, are AI-driven text or voice dialogue systems capable of communicating with users in the metaverse in natural language and socially interacting. [JAI18] They are often used in virtual environments to provide customer service, technical support, or entertainment. [LUG16] By using techniques such as deep learning and neural networks, chatbots can conduct increasingly complex and human-like conversations. [VIN15]

Although the idea of the metaverse is still relatively young, significant progress has been made in recent years in integrating virtual assistants and chatbots into the metaverse. Examples include the integration of Apple's Siri and Amazon's Alexa into virtual reality platforms or the development of AI-powered chatbots for virtual games and social platforms like Fortnite and VRChat. [MAL23]

The integration of AI in virtual worlds and games plays a significant role in the development of avatars and non-player characters (NPCs). [YAN18] The application of AI technologies such as machine learning and natural language processing (NLP) has made it possible to create AI-driven avatars and NPCs that can simulate human-like behaviors and interactions in real-time. [RIE14]

- An example of this is the use of deep learning techniques to transfer users' facial expressions and gestures to their avatars in real-time, thereby improving non-verbal communication in virtual environments. [THI16] Similarly, AI algorithms based on reinforcement learning enable NPCs to learn independently and adapt to users' actions and decisions, providing a more realistic and immersive gaming experience. [VIN19]
- Another example of the application of AI in this area is the generation of procedural content, where AI algorithms are used to automatically create not only new environments or objects but also new characters in the metaverse. [SHA16] This technique can help reduce development time and costs while promoting greater diversity and dynamism in virtual worlds. [HEN13]

However, the growing prevalence of AI-driven avatars and NPCs in the metaverse also raises ethical questions, particularly regarding the boundaries between real and artificial identities, the potential dehumanization of social interaction, and the responsibility of developers for the actions of their AI-driven characters. [MOU15]

Certainly, the advances in computer graphics and simulation in recent years have significantly contributed to the development and improvement of the metaverse. [THA21] In particular, the integration of AI into these areas has led to users increasingly experiencing realistic and immersive experiences in virtual environments. One such example of the use of AI in computer graphics is the use of Generative Adversarial Networks (GANs) to create realistic and high-resolution textures and 3D models. [KAR17] This technique makes it possible to generate detailed and diverse objects and environments in the metaverse, enhancing users' immersion in the virtual world. [GOO14]

In terms of simulation, the application of AI technologies such as machine learning and deep learning has enabled the development of advanced physics, particle, and fluid simulations that run in real-time. These improvements help users experience more realistic interactions with objects and environments in virtual worlds. [KAJ86]

Furthermore, AI-based techniques have also enabled the improvement of real-time rendering and the optimized calculation of lighting situations, leading to more realistic light and shadow effects in virtual environments. [RIT12] These developments are crucial for achieving higher visual quality and aesthetics in the metaverse.

The rapid advances in computer graphics and simulation, made possible by the use of AI, point to the enormous potential of these technologies to further change and improve the metaverse. Future developments are expected to further blur the boundaries between the real and virtual worlds and intensify users' immersion in the metaverse. [Iso17]

The integration of AI into the metaverse has the potential to significantly enhance the user experience by enabling more realistic, personalized, and thus immersive experiences. [MIK11] Advances in AI technologies such as machine learning (ML), natural language processing (NLP), and computer vision contribute to making users' interactions in virtual environments more human-like and seamless. One aspect in which AI improves the user experience in the metaverse is the adaptability of the environment, the objects contained within it, as well as autonomous or externally controlled avatars. By using ML, virtual worlds and systems can recognize and analyze users' preferences and behavior patterns to provide individually tailored content and recommendations. [FOR17] These personalized experiences foster a stronger bond between users and the metaverse and increase user satisfaction. [OST01]

Another important factor contributing to the improvement of the user experience is the ability of AI systems to support natural language and multimodal communication. [CAS00] By using NLP and deep learning, AI-driven avatars and NPCs can conduct fluid and human-like conversations in real-time, thereby improving social interaction and collaboration in the metaverse. Furthermore, advances in AI-based computer graphics and simulation enable users to experience more realistic and visually appealing environments and objects in the metaverse. [THA21] These improvements help increase users' immersion in the virtual world and create a stronger sense of presence.

The advancement of AI enables the creation of dynamic and adaptive content in the metaverse, tailored to the individual needs, preferences, and interactions of users. [YAN18] This then leads to increased immersion and user engagement, as virtual worlds can respond much more flexibly to users' actions and decisions than is currently the case. [DOR10] One approach to creating dynamic content is procedural generation, where AI algorithms are used to automatically create new game and environment elements. [SHA16] This method allows for an almost unlimited variety of content and enables virtual worlds to change and adapt in real-time based on users' interactions.

Another aspect of AI-supported adaptability is the use of machine learning and reinforcement learning to optimize the behavior of avatars and NPCs. [VIN19] By learning and adapting to users' actions, AI-driven characters can offer more realistic and human-like interactions tailored to users' individual needs. [RIE14] Furthermore, the application of technologies such as NLP and sentiment analysis enables the recognition and interpretation of users' emotions and moods in real-time. [CAM13] This allows virtual environments and characters to respond to users' emotional states and provide appropriately adjusted interactions and experiences.

The generation of dynamic and adaptive content and interactions through the use of AI technologies has the potential to fundamentally change the understanding of what the metaverse is or should be by offering individually tailored experiences that increase user engagement and satisfaction. The further exploration and integration of AI into the metaverse are expected to lead to more innovative and highly personalized virtual environments and experiences. [BAI07]

The integration of Generative Pre-trained Transformer (GPT) into the metaverse represents a novel opportunity for developing interfaces between artificial intelligence and virtual worlds. In light of rapid technological advancements, it is increasingly evident that the metaverse is not merely an abstract concept but rather a real manifestation in the physical world. With the emergence of more complex structures within the metaverse, the question now arises as to how other novel technologies, such as GPT, can be utilized to accelerate and optimize the creation and design of this virtual environment. GPT has the ability to generate natural-sounding text and can be used for numerous applications.

In the context of the metaverse, GPT offers a variety of potential advantages and applications. One such application is the creation of virtual assistants and chatbots that can assist users in navigating within the metaverse and fulfilling various tasks. This can include, for example, finding specific locations or networking with other participants. Additionally, GPT can be used to create content for the metaverse, such as guides, descriptions of virtual places, or even dialogues between different characters or avatars.

An additional application of GPT in the metaverse is to enable interactive experiences in virtual reality. In this context, GPT can be used to capture and generate responses based on user inputs. This allows for the development of virtual games, events, or movies where GPT can generate responses and storylines individually for each participant.

Besides the direct applications of GPT technology in the virtual context of the metaverse, several advantages arise that could contribute to promoting the idea of the metaverse. One of the key advantages is that GPT can help make this virtual environment more accessible and user-friendly for a global audience.

By using GPT to generate texts and content in a variety of languages, users from different linguistic backgrounds can gain easier access to the metaverse and enjoy it more comprehensively. Thus, communication between users from different cultural and linguistic backgrounds could be facilitated by AI-supported tools through automated real-time translation. [MET22] Furthermore, the use of GPT functions enables the creation of realistic, credible virtual characters or avatars and immersive experiences, making the development of a lifelike and advanced representation of the metaverse possible. GPT is also capable of creating content tailored to the individual interests and priorities of users. This can be used for personalized metaverse experiences, which could be particularly attractive to consumers seeking an optimal experience. The use of GPT also leads to improved accessibility, allowing users to accomplish tasks more effectively. Finally, GPT enables the creation of virtual assistants and other interactive characters, making the metaverse more accessible and understandable for users who may not have the necessary prior knowledge or skills, such as inexperienced consumers.

AI, especially driven by the rapid development of various GPT approaches and models, will foreseeably play a significant role in how and where the idea of the metaverse will develop in the future. Here, too, it seems that only the creativity of the developers will define the limits of what is possible.

References

[AHU23] Ahuja, Abhimanyu S.; Polascik, Bryce W.; Doddapaneni, Divyesh; Byrnes, Eamonn S.; Sridhar, Jayanth (2023). The digital metaverse: Applications in artificial intelligence, medical education, and integrative health. In: Integrative Medicine Research, Volume 12, Issue 1, 2023, 100917, ISSN 2213–4220, https://doi.org/10.1016/j.imr.2022.100917.

[BAI07] Bainbridge, William. (2007). The Scientific Research Potential of Virtual Worlds. Science (New York, N.Y.). 317. 472–6. https://doi.org/10.1126/science.1146930.

[CAM13] Cambria, Erik; Schuller, Björn; Xia, Yunqing; Havasi, Catherine (2013). New Avenues in Opinion Mining and Sentiment Analysis. Intelligent Systems, IEEE. 28. 15-21. https://doi.org/10.1109/MIS.2013.30.

[CAS00] Cassell, Justina; Sullivan, Joseph; Prevost, Scott; Churchill, Elizabeth F. (Eds.). (2000). Embodied conversational agents. In: MIT press.

[CHE17] Chen, Hongshen; Liu, Xiaorui; Yin, Dawei; Tang, Jiliang (21.11.2017). A Survey on Dialogue Systems: Recent Advances and New Frontiers. In: ACM SIGKDD Explorations NewsletterVolume 19Issue 221 November 2017pp 25–35https://doi.org/10.1145/3166054.3166058.

[DOR10] Dormans, Joris. (2010). Adventures in level design: Generating missions and spaces for action adventure games. https://doi.org/10.1145/1814256.1814257.

[DOU23] Douglas, Will (03.03.2023). The inside story of how ChatGPT was built from the people who made it. In: MIT Technology Review Artificial intelligence. Online: https://www.technologyreview.com/2023/03/03/1069311/inside-story-oral-history-how-chatgpt-built-openai/ (accessed on: 29.05.2023).

[FOR17] Forsyth, Carol; Graesser, Arthur; Foltz, Peter (2017). Assessing conversation quality, reasoning, and problem solving with computer agents. https://doi.org/10.1787/9789264273955-17-en. .

[GOO14] Goodfellow, Ian; Pouget-Abadie, Jean ;Mirza, Mehdi; Xu, Bing; Warde-Farley, David; Ozair, Sherjil; Courville, Aaron; Bengio, Y. (2014). Generative Adversarial Networks. Advances in Neural Information Processing Systems. 3. https://doi.org/10.1145/3422622.

[HEN13] Hendrikx, Mark; Meijer, Sebastiaan; Velden, Joeri; Iosup, Alexandru. (2013). Procedural Content Generation for Games: A Survey. ACM Transactions on Multimedia Computing, Communications, and Applications (TOMCCAP). 9. https://doi.org/10.1145/2422956.2422957.

[ISL23] Islam, Arham (21.03.2023). A History of Generative AI: From GAN to GPT-4. In: Marktechpost. Online: https://www.marktechpost.com/2023/03/21/a-history-of-generative-ai-from-gan-to-gpt-4/ (accessed on: 29.05.2023).

[ISO17] Isola, Phillip; Zhu, Jun-Yan; Zhou, Tinghui; Efros, Alexei (2017). Image-to-Image Translation with Conditional Adversarial Networks. 5967–5976. https://doi.org/10.1109/CVPR.2017.632.

[JAI18] Jain, Mohit; Kumar, Pratyush; Kota, Ramachandra; Patel, Shwetak (2018). Evaluating and Informing the Design of Chatbots. 895–906. https://doi.org/10.1145/3196709.3196735.

[KAR17] Karras, Tero; Aila, Timo; Laine, Samuli; Lehtinen, Jaakko (2017). Progressive Growing of GANs for Improved Quality, Stability, and Variation.

[KAJ86] Kajiya, J. T. (1986). The rendering equation. In: ACM SIGGRAPH Computer Graphics, 20(4), 143–150.

[LUG16] Luger, Ewa; Sellen, Abigail (2016). "Like having a really bad PA": The Gulf between User Expectation and Experience of Conversational Agents. In Proceedings of the 2016 CHI Conference on Human Factors in Computing Systems (pp. 5286–5297). ACM.

[MAL23] Malik, Aisha (27.02.2023). Snapchat launches an AI chatbot powered by OpenAI's GPT technology. In: TechCrunch. Online: https://techcrunch.com/2023/02/27/snapchat-launches-an-ai-chatbot-powered-by-openais-gpt-technology/ (accessed on: 21.05.2023).

[MET22] Meta (19.10.2022). Using AI to Translate Speech For a Primarily Oral Language. In: Meta Newsroom. Online: https://about.fb.com/news/2022/10/hokkien-ai-speech-translation/ (accessed on: 29.05.2023).

[MIK11] Mikropoulos, Tassos; Natsis, Antonis (2011). Educational virtual en-vironments: A ten-year review of empirical research (1999–2009). In: Computers & Education. 56. 769-780. https://doi.org/10.1016/j.compedu.2010.10.020.

[MOU15] Mouton, Francois; Malan, Mercia M.; Kimppa, Kai K.; Venter, H.s. (2015): Necessity for ethics in social engineering research. DOI:https://doi.org/10.1016/j.cose.2015.09.001

[OST01] Osterloh, Margit; Frey, Bruno; Frost, Jetta (2001). Managing Motivation, Organization and Governance. In: Journal of Management and Governance. 5. 231-239. https://doi.org/10.1023/A:1014084019816.

[PER22] Perri, Lori (10.08.2022). What's New in the 2022 Gartner Hype Cycle for Emerging Technologies. In: Gartner Insights. https://www.gartner.com/en/articles/what-s-new-in-the-2022-gartner-hype-cycle-for-emerging-technologies (accessed on: 17.05.2023).

[RIE14] Riedl, Mark; Young, Robert (2014). Narrative Planning: Balancing Plot and Character. J. Artif. Intell. Res. (JAIR). 39. https://doi.org/10.1613/jair.2989.

[RIT12] Ritschel, Tobias; Dachsbacher, Carsten; Grosch, Thorsten; Kautz, Jan (2012). The State of the Art in Interactive Global Illumination. In: Computer Graphics Forum. 31. 160 – 188. https://doi.org/10.1111/j.1467-8659.2012.02093.x.

[SHA16] Shaker, Noor; Togelius, Julian; Nelson, Mark J. (2016). Procedural content generation in games (Computational Synthesis and Creative Systems). In: Computational Synthesis and Creative Systems, Springer International.

[THA21] Thalmann, Nadia; Interrante, Victoria; Thalmann, Daniel; Papagiannakis, George; Sheng, Bin; Kim, Jinman; Gavrilova, Marina (2021). Advances in Computer Graphics 38th Computer Graphics International Conference, CGI 2021, Virtual Event, September 6–10, 2021, Proceedings: 38th Computer Graphics International Conference, CGI 2021, Virtual Event, September 6–10, 2021, Proceedings. https://doi.org/10.1007/978-3-030-89029-2.

[THA23] Thakur, S.S., Bandyopadhyay, S., Datta, D. (2023). Artificial Intelligence and the Metaverse: Present and Future Aspects. In: Hassanien, A.E., Darwish, A., Torky, M. (eds) The Future of Metaverse in the Virtual Era and Physical World. Studies in Big Data, vol 123. Springer, Cham. https://doi.org/10.1007/978-3-031-29132-6_10

[THI16] Thies, Justus; Zollhöfer, Michael; Stamminger, Marc; Theobalt, Christian; Nießner, Matthias (2016). Face2face: Reall-time Face Capture and Reenactment of RGB Videos. In: Proc. Computer Vision and Pattern Recognition (CVPR), 2016, IEEE.

[VIN15] Vinyals, Oriol; Le, Quoc (2015). A Neural Conversational Model. ICML Deep Learning Workshop, 2015. .

[VIN19] Vinyals, Oriol; Babuschkin, Igor; Czarnecki, Wojciech; Mathieu, Michaël; Dudzik, Andrew; Chung, Junyoung; Choi, David; Powell, Richard; Ewalds, Timo; Georgiev, Petko; Oh, Junhyuk; Horgan, Dan; Kroiss, Manuel; Danihelka, Ivo; Huang, Aja; Sifre, Laurent; Cai, Trevor; Agapiou, John; Jaderberg, Max; Silver, David (2019). Grandmaster level in StarCraft II using multi-agent reinforcement learning. Nature. 575. https://doi.org/10.1038/s41586-019-1724-z.

[YAN18] Yannakakis, Georgios N.; Togelius, Julian (2018): Artificial Intelligence and Games. In: Springer Link. Online: https://link.springer.com/book/https://doi.org/10.1007/978-3-319-63519-4 (accessed on: 21.05.2023).

[ZHO23] Zhou, Pengyuan (12.04.2023). Unleashing ChatGPT on the Metaverse: Savior or Destroyer? In: University of Science and Technology of China. Online: https://www.researchgate.net/publication/369387206_Unleashing_ChatGPT_on_the_Metaverse_Savior_or_Destroyer (accessed on: 21.05.2023).

9 Addendum 2—Almost Even More Relevant: Is the Hype Already Over?

The mere use of the term "metaverse" has recently attracted great attention both in the economy and in research. At the beginning of this year (2023), it seemed unthinkable that the virtual space could do without a metaverse. Numerous companies invested heavily in their presence in the metaverse, while countless start-ups emerged, and shares of companies like Roblox and Matterport, which were already engaged in the metaverse, gained significant value. Recently (as of mid-2023), however, a certain disillusionment seems to be setting in.

Rising interest rates due to the current stronger inflation have led many companies to reconsider their visionary ambitions in the metaverse due to financial constraints. A prominent example of this is Facebook, which was penalized with an almost 70% drop in stock price for its costly plans in and with the metaverse. The company's recovery only began when CEO Mark Zuckerberg significantly scaled back the plans for the metaverse and focused on cost efficiency and revenue in the current business. This was immediately followed by the question of whether the metaverse was already passé. [LIN23]

Interest in the metaverse has noticeably decreased compared to the peak of the discussion about a year ago, as can be seen, for example, from the global online search queries for the term "metaverse." Furthermore, the value of virtual real estate has also significantly decreased compared to physical real estate in the same period. Some decentralized virtual worlds have also recorded a decline in daily user numbers, which fell short of expectations. Critics argue that the metaverse was merely a bubble driven by hype and marketing that has now burst. [KEM23, PAL22]

Despite the seemingly burst hype around the metaverse, the concept should not be prematurely considered a failure. The potential of the metaverse as a new opportunity for hosting virtual events and creating unique, immersive experiences for participants remains, even if the hoped-for breakthrough has not yet occurred.

P. Hoffmann, *Next Generation Internet*, https://doi.org/10.1007/978-3-658-46424-0_9

The numerous different metaverse concepts were—and still are—hotly debated. However, the actual results have so far proven to be significantly less impressive than predicted. An example of this is the Decentraland Metaverse Fashion Week 2023, where visitor numbers significantly declined compared to the previous year. [SAN23, DRE23] As a result, interest is increasingly shifting towards artificial intelligence, with Chat-GPT currently serving as the most prominent example.

Despite the disappointing results regarding the metaverse, hybrid and online events continue to enjoy great popularity. However, the general public does not yet appreciate navigating virtual worlds to the extent originally anticipated. According to James Au, an analyst and journalist in the field of the metaverse, platforms in the metaverse are growing slowly but steadily and are adapting to the circumstances. In the first quarter of 2023, such platforms recorded an increase of 15 million users to a total of 520 million monthly active users, as shown in a report by the analyst firm Metaversed. The analysis covers 149 platforms that are either already live or in the development phase, with the majority being browser-based and some relying on the use of VR headsets. Au emphasizes that the study mainly targets prominent platforms with strong usage in the USA and Europe. Garena Free Fire [TWIoJ], a game primarily known and widespread in Southeast Asia and South America, which reaches about 10% of the world's population, is, for example, not part of this analysis. Despite layoffs in the tech sector overall, metaverse platforms continue to hire employees. According to Au, more than 800 job offers were recorded, despite the current trend that even IT technology companies are currently laying off employees in large numbers. [AU23, METoJa, METoJb, METoJc]

Additionally, a report by S&P Global Market Intelligence shows that about 120 companies are working on metaverse technologies, notably many around the area of data integration for digital twins and also in the context of the Internet of Things, avatars, and secure identity management. But not only the software sector, but also the hardware development sector remains an actively driven area, such as the (further) development of input/output technologies like haptics, holography, spatial audio, and of course augmented reality. Investments in technologies and applications around the metaverse exceeded $24 billion last year, with the largest investments according to S&P Capital IQ Pro coming from Meta Platforms, Epic Games, Infinite Reality, and Roblox Corp. [HUG23, JOH23]

Despite the apparent collapse of the bubble, several hundred million people currently use or visit "the metaverse," with the majority of users, however, using regular screens and only a minority relying on VR headsets. According to a report by 451 Research, a subsidiary of S&P Global Market Intelligence, the metaverse is designed as a "long-term vision for the next phase of the internet," which "encompasses a unified, shared, immersive, and persistent virtual 3D space where people interact with each other and with data, complementing rather than replacing the physical world." Ian Hughes, an analyst at 451 Research, predicts that the metaverse will become as popular as social media in the future. Nevertheless, this change will occur gradually, with Hughes comparing the acceptance of the metaverse to the mainstream implementation of video conferencing over the past three years. [HUG23, JOH23]

Interestingly, the use of the metaverse enjoys popularity across a wide age distribution, encompassing not only teenagers and young adults but also middle-aged individuals and even seniors. According to Au, seniors in particular are increasingly using Second Life, despite the technical challenges and requirements that this platform entails. The various age groups use the metaverse to explore different worlds with entirely different goals in different identities. [Au23]

Another issue that Au addresses concerns Meta's strategy. Meta not only invests massively in niche products like headsets but also ties its metaverse to Facebook profiles, which are linked to the users' real identities. However, this does not align with the primary interests of the majority of users. Rather, they flock to the metaverse in large numbers mainly to form their own communities, including anime fans, gamers, and furries. The popular platform VRChat, for example, hosts an extensive nightclub rave scene and numerous social games.

Recently, even Mark Zuckerberg has tempered the enthusiasm regarding the metaverse by stating that it will not constitute the main part of his company's activities in the near future, as was originally planned. The company is now focusing more on efficiency and is cutting 11,000 jobs, with possibly thousands more to follow. The Reality Labs division, responsible for producing the Meta Quest VR headsets, recorded a loss of $13.7 billion last year. In contrast, Apple has been announcing the introduction of its own augmented reality headset since 2015. However, its market launch has been postponed several times, currently to fall 2023. It is expected that this product, once it hits the market, will be a great success for Apple and will drive the metaverse sector forward in a similar way to how Apple revolutionized the smartphone. (In the meantime, Apple has indeed introduced this device under the product name "Apple Vision Pro." [APPoJ]) Despite the significant investments in headsets, Au notes that they are unlikely to become the primary mainstream technology of the metaverse in the foreseeable future. Even today, successful metaverse platforms like Roblox, Fortnite, and VRChat are mainly accessible via smartphones, tablets, gaming consoles, and PCs. Screen-based platforms are therefore expected to remain the dominant future of the metaverse, according to Au. On a smartphone or other display-based device, attention can quickly switch between the metaverse environment and the real world. Virtual reality, on the other hand, requires the user's full attention. Au emphasizes that VR headsets have disadvantages in terms of usage and quick perception of the environment because the user is separated from the real world by wearing them. Additionally, these devices are not only insecure regarding user data and socially stigmatized but also expensive. For example, Meta's latest Oculus headset costs about $1500 and has a short battery life. [AU23, BER23]

> "95 percent of global executives we surveyed last year said they believe the metaverse will have a positive impact on their industry within five to ten years,"

says McKinsey. [MCK22a, MCK22b]

The focus on the metaverse and its commercial and industrial applications currently seems to lie mainly with large companies and industrial corporations. For example, Microsoft is integrating features for incorporating the metaverse into its collaboration tool Teams by using its own Mesh platform on Azure. This technology was presented during the World Economic Forum in Davos in January 2023. This allowed many participants to gain their first experiences with the metaverse, as Hughes notes. Siemens and Nvidia are cooperating in the development of Nvidia's metaverse platform Omniverse to create a virtual factory where autonomous robots can be trained. Additionally, people can work in this virtual reality to examine the ergonomics and efficiency of a factory hall prototype. Companies will be able to combine these technologies with the Internet of Things and digital twins to track assets throughout their entire lifecycle. Accenture has also made significant consulting investments in the metaverse, including the purchase of thousands of headsets, as Hughes reports. [DUS23, NVIoJ]

Another example of the upcoming "industrial metaverses" can be seen in the BMW Group and NVIDIA, which aim to move the planning of highly complex manufacturing systems into the metaverse using the aforementioned Omniverse platform. The tool for virtual factory planning integrates different planning data and applications and enables real-time collaboration without compatibility boundaries. The platform brings together data from various design and planning tools and creates photorealistic real-time simulations in a collaborative environment. Employees at different locations and time zones can access the simulations and jointly plan or optimize processes or production facilities. Previous virtual factory planning tools had difficulties with data compatibility and timeliness. The Omniverse platform solves these problems by merging live data from relevant databases into a common simulation, making data re-import unnecessary. This allows planners and production specialists to plan more accurately and quickly without interface losses and compatibility issues. [GEY23, BMW21]

It seems as if the peak of the first hype cycle has been surpassed and a discrepancy between reality and expectations has emerged. Ultimately, however, this corresponds to the typical hype cycle according to Gartner. Additionally, the aforementioned 95% of surveyed global executives are unusually unanimous in the assumption that the metaverse will nevertheless have positive impacts on their respective industries within the next five to ten years. In fact, the number of implemented use cases is continuously increasing, which raises the hope that an established enterprise metaverse will also reach the consumer and end-customer market in the not too distant future.

References

[APPoJ] Apple (o.J.). Apple Vision Pro. Online: https://www.apple.com/apple-vision-pro/ (accessed on: 30.11.2023).

[AU23] Au, Wagner James (27. Juni 2023). Making a Metaverse That Matters: From Snow Crash & Second Life to A Virtual World Worth Fighting For. Wiley.

[BER23] Berger, Dennis (14.01.2023). VR-Brillen-Verkäufe: Zahlen und Hintergründe. In: Mixed. Online: https://mixed.de/vr-brillen-verkaeufe-uebersicht/ (accessed on: 20.05.2023)

[BMW21] BMW Broup (13.04.2021). BMW Group und NVIDIA heben virtuelle Fabrikplanung auf die nächste Ebene. In: Pressemeldung. Online: https://www.press.bmwgroup.com/deutschland/article/detail/T0329569DE/bmw-group-und-nvidia-heben-virtuelle-fabrikplanung-auf-die-naechste-ebene%3Flanguage%3Dde (accessed on: 20.05.2023)

[DRE23] Dredge, Stuart (06.04.2023). Only 26,000 people attended Decentraland's Metaverse Fashion Week. In: Music:ally. Online: https://musically.com/2023/04/06/only-26000-people-attended-decentralands-metaverse-fashion-week/ (accessed on: 21.05.2023).

[DUS23] Dusold, Julia (04.06.2022). Nächste Ebene der Digitalisierung: Metaverse für die Industrie: Siemens und Nvidia gehen es an. In: Produktion. Online: https://www.produktion.de/technik/zukunftstechnologien/metaverse-fuer-die-industrie-siemens-und-nvidia-gehen-es-an-308.html (accessed on: 20.05.2023)

[GEY23] Geyer, Mike (21.03.2023). BMW Group Starts Global Rollout of NVIDIA Omniverse. In: Nvidia Blog. Online: https://blogs.nvidia.com/blog/2023/03/21/bmw-group-nvidia-omniverse/ (accessed on: 20.05.2023)

[HUG23] Hughes, Ian; Barbour, Neil; Partridge, Brian; Paxton, Michael (24.01.2023). Metaverse primer: Examining the future of all digital interaction. In: S&P Global Market Intelligence. Online: https://www.spglobal.com/marketintelligence/en/news-insights/research/metaverse-primer-examining-the-future-of-all-digital-interaction (accessed on: 20.05.2023)

[JOH23] Johnston, Alex (01.03.2023). Blockchain and the metaverse, part 1: Opportunities In: S&P Global Market Intelligence. Online: https://www.spglobal.com/marketintelligence/en/news-insights/research/blockchain-and-the-metaverse-part-1-opportunities (accessed on: 20.05.2023)

[KEM23] Kemp, Simon (28.01.2023). Digital 2023 Deep-Dive: Is the Metaverse going in reverse? In: Datareportal. Online: https://datareportal.com/reports/digital-2023-deep-dive-metaverse-in-reverse (accessed on: 20.05.2023)

[LIN23] Lindner, Roland (27.04.2023). Meta wächst wieder. In: Frankfurter Allgemeine. Online: https://www.faz.net/aktuell/wirtschaft/unternehmen/meta-ist-wieder-auf-wachstumskurs-18851388.html (accessed on: 20.05.2023)

[MCK22a] McKinsey & Company (21.06.2022). Studie: Das Metaverse kann bis 2030 einen Wert von bis zu 5 Billionen Dollar erreichen. In: McKinsey Press Release. Online: https://www.mckinsey.com/de/news/presse/2022-06-21-metaverse (accessed on: 20.05.2023)

[MCK22b] McKinsey & Company (2022). Value creation in the metaverse. In: McKinsey Growth, Marketing & Sales. Online: https://www.mckinsey.com/capabilities/growth-marketing-and-sales/our-insights/value-creation-in-the-metaverse (accessed on: 20.05.2023)

[METoJa] Metaversed (o.J.). The Metaverse Reaches 400m Monthly Active Users. In: Metaversed. Online: https://www.metaversed.consulting/blog/the-metaverse-reaches-400m-active-users (accessed on: 20.05.2023)

[METoJb] Metaversed (o.J.). Introducing the Web3 Metaverse Index. In: Metaversed. Online: https://www.metaversed.consulting/blog/introducing-the-web3-metaverse-index (accessed on: 20.05.2023)

[METoJc] Metaversed (o.J.). The Web3 Metaverse Index: February 2023 update. Online: https://www.metaversed.consulting/blog/the-web3-metaverse-index-february-2023-update (accessed on: 20.05.2023)

[NVIoJ] Nvidia (o.J.) Siemens und Nvidia – Aufbau des industriellen Metaverse. In: Nvidia Omniverse. Online: https://www.nvidia.com/de-de/omniverse/digital-twins/siemens/ (accessed on: 20.05.2023)

[PAL22] Paleja, Ameya (06.04.2022). Could the metaverse become a big flop? Here's what Google Trends says. In: Interesting Engineering. Online: https://interestingengineering.com/culture/metaverse-flop-google-trends (accessed on: 20.05.2023)

[SAN23] Sander Lutz (08.04.2023). And the Winner of Metaverse Fashion Week 2023 Is… In: Decrypt. Online: https://decrypt.co/125737/winner-decentraland-metaverse-fashion-week-2023 (accessed on: 21.05.2023).

[TWIoJ] Twitch (o.J.). Garena Free Fire. Online: https://www.twitch.tv/directory/category/garena-free-fire (accessed on: 28.05.2023).

[ZIE22] Ziegener, Daniel (17. Oktober 2022). Niedrige Nutzerzahlen: Kaum jemand interessiert sich für Metas Metaversum. In: Golem. Online: https://www.golem.de/news/niedrige-nutzerzahlen-kaum-jemand-interessiert-sich-fuer-metas-metaversum-2210-168982.html (accessed on: 20.05.2023)

Glossary

Augmented Reality (AR) Augmented Reality (AR) means "enhanced reality." In this way, human perception of the real (actual) environment is enriched with digital information.

Initially, the idea of AR was based on enriching perception with location-specific and precisely inserted 3D objects. To reduce the technical effort, AR was downgraded during the course of development to the extent that currently, the insertion of 2D objects and/or text is also referred to as AR.

Augmented Virtuality (AV) Like AR, Augmented Virtuality (AV) also means a mixing or "enrichment" of human perception. While AR assumes that real-world components predominate in perception, in Augmented Virtuality, perception is dominated by digital/virtual objects. This occurs, for example, when the user is in an immersive world/VR world and a video chat with a real person is displayed in a window.

Brain Computing Interface (BCI) A Brain Computing Interface (BCI) is an interface between a user's brain and a computer system. It enables direct communication and interaction through the capture and interpretation of brain signals. These signals can be used to perform actions, control devices. The transmission of information to the user is also a focus of research. The goal of BCI is, among other things, to help people with physical disabilities so that they can also interact with computers/applications as easily and seamlessly as possible.

CAVE CAVE stands for "Cave Automatic Virtual Environment" and refers to an immersive VR environment. In this setup, projections are generated on multiple sides of a room. The user stands in this room and thus in the middle of the projected VR world and can move within this world through integrated tracking technology in the room.

CAVEs are used, among other things, in medicine, architecture, and design for the visualization of complex scenarios, for example, in the form of realistic simulations.

Digital Twin/Digital Clone The term "digital twin" describes a virtual representation of a physical object, system, or process. It is created or kept up-to-date through continuous data collection and analysis in real-time. The digital twin enables the precise modeling and simulation of the state, behavior, and performance of the real object. This allows for predictions to be made, problems to be identified, and solutions to be developed. The digital twin is used in various fields such as industry, medicine, and

P. Hoffmann, *Next Generation Internet*, https://doi.org/10.1007/978-3-658-46424-0

urban planning. In the context of the metaverse, user avatars are intended to become digital twins that can also act autonomously in the virtual environment.

Direct Interaction Through the use of hand controllers, gesture recognition, or other input methods, users can grab, manipulate, and interact with objects as if they were physically present. This type of interaction enables a more immersive and realistic VR experience, where users can actively engage in the virtual world.

Emotes Emotes are short animated or static images that represent emotions or gestures and are used in online chats and social media. Unlike emojis, which are pre-made symbols, emotes are often created by users or selected from a library. They are a popular means of communication to express emotions or add humor. While emojis are universally understood, emotes often have a specific meaning within certain online communities and their particular cultures.

Extended Reality (XR) The discussion about whether the two extremes "100% Reality" and "100% Virtuality" of the reality-virtuality continuum also count as Extended Reality is concluded by Bellalouna et al. by defining Extended Reality as the sum of AR, AV, and VR.

Graphical User Interface (GUI) The term "Graphical User Interface" (GUI) refers to visual user interfaces that allow users to interact with a computer or an application. Instead of text-based commands, GUIs use icons, menus, and graphical elements such as buttons and windows to make operation more user-friendly. Through the GUI, users can perform actions by simply clicking, dragging, and dropping, which facilitates operation and reduces the learning curve.

Head-Mounted Display (HMD) A "Head-Mounted Display" (HMD) refers to wearable devices that the user wears on the head and which are intended to provide the user with immersive access to applications or information. It consists of glasses or a helmet in which one or more displays are integrated. By wearing the HMD, virtual content is displayed directly in front of the user's eyes, allowing them to immerse themselves in a virtual reality (VR) or augmented reality (AR).

Immersivity/Immersion Immersion refers to the state of being immersed, while immersivity describes the quality of how strong and convincing this immersion is. Both concepts play an important role in the design for entertainment and educational/learning systems or even for medical-therapeutic applications.

Immersive Environment/Immersive World By combining graphics, interactive elements, and immersive sound, the senses of the users are activated to enable a nearly realistic experience. Immersive worlds open up new possibilities for entertainment, learning, and exploration.

Interaction paradigm An interaction paradigm describes the fundamental way in which people interact with technology. It encompasses the design of user interfaces, interaction patterns, and conventions.

The chosen interaction paradigm influences how users perceive information, perform actions, and communicate with systems. Examples of interaction para-

digms include the graphical user interface, voice control, and gesture control. An effective interaction paradigm enables intuitive and efficient interaction between humans and technology.

Internet The Internet is a global network of computers that enables the exchange of information and resources worldwide. It connects millions of devices and is based on the TCP/IP protocol. It encompasses various services such as email, file sharing, video streaming, and much more.

The Internet forms the basis for the World Wide Web (WWW).

Internet-of-Things (IoT) The term "Internet-of-Things" (IoT) refers to the networking of physical devices that communicate with each other via sensors and the network connections of the Internet. This allows them to collect, exchange, and perform actions to improve the efficiency and functionality of everyday life. From smart home to industrial automation, the IoT aims to enable the seamless integration of technology into the environment and also to facilitate and optimize the automation of processes.

Lost in Hyperspace "Lost in Hyperspace" is a term from information design that refers to the feeling of being lost in an overwhelminginformation space. It describes the state when users cannot find their way due to poor navigation or unclear structuring of content. This can lead to frustration and disorientation. To avoid this problem, it is important to design clearly defined navigation paths and an intuitive user interface to help users avoid getting lost in the vastness of the information space.

Location Awareness Location awareness refers to the ability of a device or application to capture the location of a user and make it available for further use. By using GPS, Wi-Fi, or other technologies, location awareness can be utilized to provide personalized information, services, or recommendations based on the current location. This enables, for example, navigation, finding nearby stores, or adjusting settings based on the environment.

Media Disruption The term "media disruption" refers to the switch between different communication or information carriers, such as paper and digital media. This can lead to interruptions, loss of information, or friction losses. A media disruption occurs when data or content needs to be transferred from one medium to another. This can result in misunderstandings or inefficient processes. The goal is to minimize media disruptions to enable seamless interaction between different media.

Mixed Reality (MR) Mixed Reality is understood as the extension of AR and, to some extent, AV through the possibility of direct interaction with virtual objects. This interaction is not provided for in the classic AR paradigm.

Discussions arise from the question of whether the two extremes "100% Reality" and "100% Virtuality" of the reality-virtuality continuum also belong to Mixed Reality.

Mixed Reality is often synonymously referred to as "Extended Reality."

Modusage The term "Modusage" combines the ideas of prosumption according to Toffler and produsage according to Bruns to describe the characteristics of the cross-economy of the metaverse, which will form a new type of value creation across the boundary between the virtual and real worlds. Products and services from one world can be managed in their own, but also in the respective other world.

The merging of the physical and digital worlds opens up both the interpretation and integration of the classic value chain as well as that of the community-oriented value chain of the digital world.

Motion-Capturing Motion Capturing (MoCap) is a process for capturing the movement of people. In doing so, sensors are attached to the person's body to record their movements. The captured data is then transferred to digital characters or models to create realistic animations. Originally, Motion Capturing was developed for the film industry and video games. Nowadays, MoCap is also used in sports analysis and medicine to represent movements precisely and realistically.

In the context of the metaverse or virtual worlds, more realistic movements of avatars are intended to achieve higher immersion.

Multimedia Multimedia in the sense of a (media) informatics application means the individual or combined presentation of various media, which can be both time-dependent and time-independent.

This presentation can be a single medium as well as any possible combination at a singular point in time or a temporal sequence of such combinations in a context-related framework.

Multimedia can include the possibility for direct and indirect influence by a user on the combination or on the temporal sequence of the individual media.

Multimodality Multimodality refers to the ability of a system to capture and exchange information through multiple senses. It enables interaction by combining different modalities such as speech, gestures, gaze direction, and touch. By utilizing multiple channels, more diverse and effective communication is made possible. Multimodality is applied in human-machine interaction, for example, in voice assistants, virtual realities, and user interfaces, to create a more natural and intuitive interaction.

Natural User Interface (NUI) Natural User Interfaces (NUI) are user interfaces that aim to enable natural forms of interaction between humans and computers. Instead of conventional input devices like keyboard and mouse, NUIs use human actions such as gestures, speech, or touch to capture commands. This is intended to improve the user experience and reduce the barriers of technology interaction, allowing for seamless and user-friendly communication between humans and computers.

Proactivity Proactivity refers to the anticipatory action and the ability to recognize potential problems or needs early and take appropriate measures. Instead of waiting for reactive solutions, proactivity aims to take preventive measures to improve the efficiency, reliability, and security of IT systems.

Through proactive approaches, potential problems can be avoided or at least minimized, leading to a smoother and more effective use of technology.

Produsage Produsage is a term coined by Axel Bruns and describes the merging of production and usage in collaborative online communities. In this context, users are not just passive consumers but active co-creators of content. They produce, edit, and share information in an open, participatory manner.

Produsage enables the community to generate knowledge collectively and drive innovation. It is about cooperative creativity and communal engagement to achieve a dynamic and open form of collaboration.

Prosumption The term prosumption was coined by Alvin Toffler and describes the concept that individuals are not only consumers of products but also simultaneously producers. Through advancing digitalization and technology, people today can create, edit, and share content themselves in many areas. Prosumption combines the roles of producing and consuming in one person and represents a merging of traditional consumer and producer activities. This trend has impacts on the economy, culture, and society, as it changes the power relationship between companies and consumers.

Rendering Rendering refers to the process of generating images, animations, or videos from a 2D or 3D scene. In this process, two- and three-dimensional models, textures, and lighting information are converted into a displayable format. Through calculations, shadows, reflections, and other visual effects are added to achieve realistic or stylized results.

Reality-Virtuality Continuum (RVC) The Reality-Virtuality Continuum is a concept in computer science that describes the transition between real and virtualenvironments. It represents a spectrum on which various technologies and applications are located, fromthe real world on one side to the fully virtual world on the other side. The continuum includes, for example, Augmented Reality, Mixed Reality, and Virtual Reality, and offers increasing immersion and interactionfor the user.

Treadmill/VR-Treadmill A VR treadmill is a VR input/output technology that allows users to move in virtual environments by physically walking or running on a treadmill or a similar installation. By integrating sensors and motion capture technologies, VR treadmills can track the user's movements and transfer them into the virtual world, creating a more immersive VR experience. This allows users to move freely in the virtual environment.

User-generated Content (UGC) User-generated Content (UGC) refers to content created and shared online by users. This can include texts,images, videos, reviews, or comments. UGC enables users to actively participate in the exchange of information-and produce content, rather than just consuming it passively. Platforms such as social media, blogs, and forumsbenefit from the diversity and engagement of users who create UGC. This participatory approach promotes interaction, creativity, and the building of communities.

Virtual Reality (VR) The depiction of a scene as a computer-generated spatial representation with the goal of achieving the most complete immersion possible.

100% VR is, as virtuality, one of the two extreme cases of the reality-virtuality continuum according to Milgram and Kishino.

A characteristic of VR is the implementation of the paradigm of "direct interaction," which enables the user to interact with the objects in the depicted scene. This is the clear difference from, for example, 360° photos or 360° films, as interaction with the scene is not possible in them.

VR-Headset A VR headset is a device that is used to allow users to experience virtual worlds immersively. It typically consists of a special pair of glasses that is worn on the head and contains two displays that show stereoscopic graphics. The VR headset tracks the user's head movements and adjusts the virtual environment accordingly to create a sense of presence.

Wearable/Wearable Computing Wearable Computing refers to the technology in which computers and electronic devices are integrated into clothing or accessories and worn by the user. These devices enable interaction with digital information and applications in real-time. Examples of wearables include smartwatches, fitness trackers, and AR glasses. They offer convenient and practical solutions for communication, health monitoring, navigation, and much more. Through seamless integration into everyday life, wearables open up new possibilities for personal technology and digital interaction.

Wearable Computing is particularly an independent interaction paradigm, as the handling and use of wearable computers differ significantly from traditional computer systems.

WIMP WIMP is an abbreviation for "Windows, Icons, Menus, Pointer" and refers to a type of user interface for computers and applications and is considered a paradigm that facilitates the interaction between users and computers. "Windows" stands for the display of programs in their own windows, "Icons" represent files or programs, "Menus" allow access to functions, and "Pointer" is the mouse cursor for control.

WIMP interfaces are a form of GUI and are widespread because they enable simple and visual interaction with the computer.

World Wide Web (WWW) The WWW is a part of the Internet and specifically refers to the system of interconnected hypertext documents that are retrieved via the HTTP protocol. The WWW enables the display of web pages that are connected through hyperlinks. It is one of the most well-known and frequently used applications of the Internet, providing access to information, multimedia content, and interactive services.

The WWW is an important component of the Internet, but not the only one.

Printed in the United States
by Baker & Taylor Publisher Services